DOING BUSINESS INTERNATIONALLY

The Guide to
Cross-Cultural Success

DOING BUSINESS INTERNATIONALLY
The Guide to Cross-Cultural Success

Terence Brake

Danielle Medina Walker

Thomas (Tim) Walker

Boston, Massachusetts   Burr Ridge, Illinois
Dubuque, Iowa   Madison, Wisconsin   New York, New York
San Francisco, California   St. Louis, Missouri

McGraw-Hill

A Division of The McGraw·Hill Companies

Library of Congress Cataloging-in-Publication Data
Brake, Terence.
    Doing business internationally : the guide to cross-cultural
success / Terence Brake, Danielle Medina Walker, Thomas (Tim)
Walker.
        p.   cm.
    Includes bibliographical references and index.
    ISBN 0-7863-0117-1
1. Industrial management—Cross-cultural studies.
2. Intercultural communication. 3. Negotiation in business—Cross
cultural studies. 4. Success in business. I. Walker, Danielle
Medina. II. Walker, Thomas (Thomas D.) III. Title.
HD31.B7235 1995
658'.049—dc20

Printed in the United States of America

94–11217

10 11 12 13 14 15 16 17 18 19 BKM BKM 9 0 9 8 7 6 5 4 3 2 1

Foreword

Working in the field of executive education, I have experience in two of the world's business schools which claim to be international. They have multilingual faculty, and a student body of rich diversity.

At those schools, as in many of the corporations we have worked with, the challenge is to find creative ways of dealing with the diversity of cultures—ways that are both based on credible research and also useful to individual managers. This book makes a valuable contribution by drawing together the growing literature in the area. The authors have worked hard to translate their findings into practical tools for all who travel the world and work with cultural diversity almost every day.

This book has dug deep into the work of acknowledged experts like Trompenaars, Adler, Hofstede, Hampden-Turner and many others. So its conclusions are well founded in research. What makes it useful is its practicality. I have found the value orientations approach particularly valuable as a framework to start working with. It is easy to focus on only one or two aspects of cultural difference, but this analysis forces us to consider ten ways in which people of different cultures approach life, work, and relationships from differing standpoints. By using the value framework as a continuous thread of analysis, the authors enable us to grasp the different topics of regional understanding, communication, negotiation, and success in a way that we can act upon. Acknowledging that this level of analysis can lead to oversimplification, the authors have provided extensive further resource and reading lists for the discriminating reader who recognizes the need to go deeper into this complex subject.

That globalization is here to stay, and that many corporations are still quite unprepared for it, is a truism. I hope that this book will find its way into many of them, as it will surely into business schools and other training centers. As we have all learned, success will only come to those who continue to learn how to collaborate most effectively with our colleagues and customers from around the world.

Jerome Foster
Associate Dean
Director of Executive Education
London Business School

Preface

The objective of *Doing Business Internationally: A Guide to Cross-Cultural Success* is to provide executives and managers with the basic knowledge and skills needed to work and compete successfully in the new multicultural business environment.

It is clear that we can no longer do business as usual. The world is changing more rapidly than at any other time in history. Today's business environment is complex, chaotic, and very competitive. Even more important, it is global. Companies around the world are redefining themselves and their people as they seek to optimize their strategies and resources across borders. The intensity and speed of changes in world markets means that organizations and their managers must have the flexibility, confidence, and skills needed to overcome increased competitive pressures, pursue expanded opportunities, and grow market share. All of these challenges must be met in the context of profound cultural differences.

Our central focus is on exposing business leaders to a general framework for understanding culture, along with offering practical techniques and skills with which to achieve greater cross-cultural effectiveness.

Our book offers profitable insights into the impact of culture on business activities. Meeting today's and tomorrow's challenges in the global business arena requires a broadened and heightened awareness of cultural diversity. Managing cultural differences is now a key factor in building and sustaining maximum competitive advantage. ICI (Imperial Chemical Industries), Procter & Gamble, Ikea, Siemens, Toyota, and Toshiba are just a few of the companies that have learned that culture makes a difference. In order to benefit from these varied cultural orientations, we need to understand ourselves as well as others. We need to *unlearn* our cultural habits and recognize and value alternative ways of seeing, doing, and being.

In order to accomplish our objective, we have organized the book around concepts and methods of working with and managing people in global organizations. Each chapter offers practical tools and tips for developing a solid grounding in cross-cultural competence.

Chapter 1: Success in the New Global Environment sets the stage by describing the distinctive features of the international business environment in the 1990s and how the current models of business practice underline the importance of cross-cultural factors in conducting successful business.

Chapter 2: Success in Understanding Culture demonstrates the importance of having a framework for organizing cross-cultural experiences, and identifying and working with key cultural differences. While cultures can be distinguished from one another in many ways, we focus attention on their orientations to ten key variables: environment, time, action, communication, space, power, individualism, competitiveness, structure, and thinking. Grasping the differences between the primary value orientations to these variables allows a manager to develop cultural self-awareness as well as an ability to determine the cultural profiles of others.

Chapter 3: Success in Crossing Cultures takes the reader on a journey and presents an overview of six cultural regions in the world—Africa, Asia, Latin America, Europe, the Middle East, and North America—and offers practical suggestions on how to cope with working across cultures.

Chapter 4: Success in Communicating across Cultures looks at one of the most fundamental skills for doing business across cultural borders: communication. Unless we can connect and share meanings with others from different cultures, we cannot successfully do business. Sharing a common language does not guarantee communication. We speak and interpret through different cultural frames, and we must learn to overcome the destructive barriers that can undermine the fragile cross-cultural communication process.

Chapter 5: Success in Negotiating across Cultures follows up on the previous chapter by examining the most important cross-cultural communication skill: negotiation. No matter how well prepared a manager is to do business across cultures, conflict is inevitable. Every successful global manager understands that there are different cultural responses to conflict and is able to translate conflict into an opportunity for surfacing critical issues, facilitating creativity and learning, and developing respect, trust, and mutual understanding.

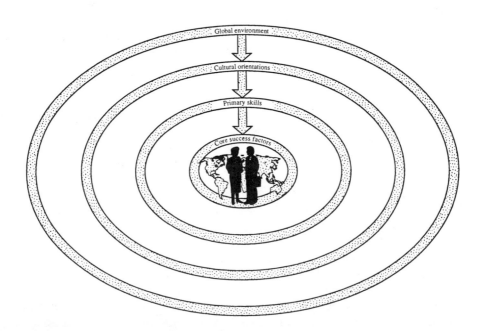

Chapter 6: Success in Global Management identifies the dynamics and scope of today's global workforce. The pressures of re-engineering the company impact at the global level, and culture is a thread that impacts the process. In the globalization of companies, international human resources management is a key strategic tool to support global competitiveness. A detailed summation of the key competencies needed by executives and managers to be top performers in the demanding global marketplace is provided. New business realities require new business competencies. Traditional, domestically oriented mindsets and skills cannot cope with the multidimensional and uncertain terrain of the new economic landscape. Every manager must be able to leverage culture and shape it into a competitive advantage. It is not an easy task, but it is one of the most exciting and rewarding areas in management today.

Another way to look at the contents of the book is as follows:

Chapter 1 introduces the major driving forces behind globalization.

Chapters 2 and 3 provide an overview of the dominant orientations in the major cultural regions of the world.

Chapters 4 and 5 explore the two primary skills executives and managers need to navigate their way through cultural differences: communication and negotiation.

Chapter 6 identifies the dynamics and scope of today's global work force and defines the core success factors for managing effectively in the global environment.

The information presented in this book represents a rich composite of research, interviews, and experience in international business management, training, and development gathered over 25 years in the global arena.

The intended audience is broad based, with the primary emphasis on executives, managers, and high-level trainers with—or likely to have—international responsibilities.

Doing Business Internationally: The Guide to Cross-Cultural Success is a challenge for those who want to work, learn, and grow in the fascinating and constantly changing world of international business. It challenges individuals to learn more about multicultural interactions while stepping back introspectively and defining their own cultural heritage, regardless of nationality. The journey, like any other, will have its twists and turns, and the traveler will change and grow along the route. We trust that by accepting the challenges of the multicultural business world, the reader will discover new areas of personal and professional development, areas that stimulate creativity, productivity, and enhanced human understanding and collaboration.

Acknowledgments

This book and its approach have been developed and tested over many years of consulting, designing, and delivering seminars on international business to managers and executives from many countries. The reader can therefore be certain that the cross-cultural concepts and skills discussed in the following chapters are *essential* to developing effective international business relationships and operating within complex global networks.

Developing a guide with practical examples and insights reflects the behind-the-scene contributions of numerous individuals from around the world, too many, unfortunately, to acknowledge individually. Their knowledge, influence, and support have helped form our understanding and appreciation of the diversity and potential synergy within and across cultures. Through their encouragement and advice, this book has come to fruition.

We are most grateful to and would like to thank the following people and companies, all of whom directly or indirectly contributed to the contents of this book.

- Our close friends at Training Management Corporation (TMC): Jane Silverman, president of TMC, for her insightful comments, editorial reviews, and continuous encouragement whenever it was needed; Kim Sullivan for creatively implementing and validating our cross-cultural framework within TMC's global management series; Louise Forman for her painstaking research of publications and help with the bibliography, glossary, and permissions; Rose Palma for her assistance with client interviews; Dr. Richard Punzo, TMC Vice-President of International Learning Systems; Peter Beckshi, TMC Vice-President of Global Training and Development; Serge Organovitch and George Buzaglo, TMC Senior Consultants for their work on the validation of the TMC Cultural Orientations Instrument; Kirsten Sharett, our summer intern, for her patient review of early drafts. Finally a special thanks to the excellent office support of Linda Conniff, Lynn Ludwig, Carol Palmquist, Laurie Quinn, and Li Kung.

- We are particularly appreciative of the insightful comments provided by participating managers in TMC global management training seminars at American Express, AMOCO, ARCO International, AT&T, Avon, Baxter Healthcare International, Bristol-Myers Squibb Company, Chase Manhattan Bank, Colgate-Palmolive Company, the Ford Foundation, Mead Nutritional, MCI, Merck, NCR, Sprint, Westinghouse, and many others, who gave us the opportunity to test and validate our cross-cultural models and framework.

- Colleagues who contributed to this project and deserve particular mention include: Peggy Pusch, Intercultural Press; Stephen Rhinesmith, Rhinesmith Associates; Cheri Oliver, Doris Palkovitch, Dick Lambert, Roberta Miller, Sam Sonnett, Walter Murphy, Dan Black, Winnie Tice, Joan Scaccia, Pat Walker, and Richard Bahner at American Telephone & Telegraph (AT&T); Ben Dowell, Alice Wright, Dave Long, Peter Brooker, and Joe Forish at Bristol-Myers

Squibb; Jerome Foster and Robert Davies, London Business School; Eric Campbell, Michael Michl, and Tom Pisano at Avon Products; Walt Winkler, ARCO; Anne Hill, Baxter Healthcare International; Phil Hoch and Michel Lauriol, Chase Manhattan Bank; Ora Fant, Colgate-Palmolive Company; Fred Almeida, Sikorsky Aircraft; Jackie Bohm, Bruce Willey, and Daniel Myerson at MCI; Kathleen Sarli, Merck; Rick Swaak, National Foreign Trade Council; Janice Hawley, Sprint University of Excellence; Melissa Pankove, American Re-Insurance Company; Anup Mody, GTE; Ben Blair, Bellcore; Jim O'Hern, Marriott; Jerry Untiedt; Georgia Staples; Jo Cole; Loretta Glover of Sprint University; Dick Contes, Ogden Services; John Kinney, GE Aircraft; Jean-Claude Goldenstein; Diane Simpson; Marlene Rossman; Tuula Piispanen-Krabbe; Paul Wilson; Anita and Robert Swallow; Elaine and Jerry Levine; and Lisa Holzkenner, among many others.

Finally, special thanks goes to our families and children. Terence Brake owes a special thanks to his wife, Dianne Brake, for her constant love and support, and to his sons—Morgan, Sam, and Ben—for the intense training they provided him in their teenage years on how—and how not to—manage differences (cultural and otherwise). Love and thanks also to his father, Ronald Brake, in Shrewsbury, England.

Danielle and Tim Walker want to give special thanks to Patrick, Caroline, Elan, Robin, Gregory, Rick, and Paul, whose patience, understanding, and encouragement were especially appreciated in the final stages of completing this manuscript. They also wish to express their thanks to their parents, Joe and Ruth Walker, and the Medina family in Paris, Jerusalem, and Chicago for their astute sense of global business and cultural understanding.

Contents

Chapter One

Success in the New Global Environment

In today's business environment, the traditional sources of competitive advantage cannot provide a sustainable edge.

Vladimir Pucik,
Globalizing Management

Diversity . . . will be the engine that drives . . . the corporation of the 21st century. Successful global managers will be . . . able to manage this diversity for the innovative and competitive edge of their corporations.

Stephen H. Rhinesmith
A Manager's Guide to Globalization

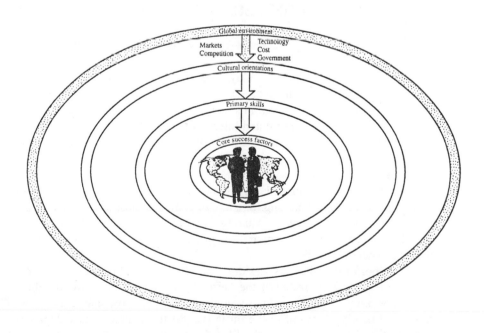

INTRODUCTION

In today's business environment, the world economy is undergoing a fundamental transformation as the result of globalization, a process not limited to the richer nations of the world. This movement is now so extensive that investment and patterns of trade are being decisively shaped by companies operating on a global scale and with global vision.

Responding to the challenge of maintaining global competitiveness, international business must address rapid, sudden, and complex changes in the world economic environment. Assumptions and frameworks about organizational structure, control mechanisms, and resources have changed and continue to change.

Business's ability to respond to the new challenges of globalization requires clarity of vision and understanding about the behavioral role of management and organizations in this constantly changing new world. The increasing importance of developing managers capable of working across cultures and competent in international business is the main challenge to global organizations. Given the expansion of world trade over the past 25 years, organizational competitiveness driven by a *diverse, fully competent, and skilled workforce* will be the force to determine the new global business environment of the 21st century.

THE CHANGING BUSINESS ENVIRONMENT

We are in an era of global business—a one-world market. The traditional orientation of companies working just within national boundaries is declining worldwide. Multinational firms play a key role in this growth and evolution process. Their commitment to direct foreign investment overseas denotes the trend for the developing global business network well into the 21st century. Distinctions between domestic and international markets are crumbling fast in virtually every part of the world. Many domestic businesses, their markets infiltrated by overseas competitors, are directly experiencing the impact of internationalization.

Since 1985, the trend in the level of foreign direct investments has grown over 15 percent annually, accounting for a rate of growth almost three times as fast as the growth in goods and services and two-and-a-half times as fast in real output. The dominant role exercised by multinational corporations in this growth phenomenon is undisputable.

Growth prior to 1985 was less dramatic due to the acute worldwide recession of 1980–1982, impacted by the Third World debt crisis. Currently, there is a slowdown, although direct investment continues to grow markedly—a positive trend firmly anchored in the initiatives of the United States, Japan, and countries in the European Union (EU). Corporations in these major markets possess all the critical elements required to assure competitiveness in the global market: well-established domestic markets capable of producing appropriate economies of scale and innovative manufacturing processes; familiarity with and efficiency in dealing with distribution and service issues characteristic of aggressively growing consumer markets; extensive experience in the management of complex organizations; and the financial resourcefulness required of collaborative agreements, such as joint ventures, strategic alliances, and so forth.

Growth projections for the next five years reveal aggressive global expansion plans by the key international firms, headquartered primarily in the United States, England, Japan, Germany, and France. This concentration is clearly changing as multinationals emerge from the Asia-Pacific and Latin American regions, particularly from countries such as Korea, Taiwan, Turkey, Mexico, and Brazil. These countries will exercise a more prominent role in international trade during the 1990s.

Commenting on global business trends, Robert B. Reich, in *The Work of Nations* (1991), aptly states:

> We are living through a transformation that will rearrange the politics and economics of the coming century. There will be no national products or technologies, no national corporations, no national industries. There will no longer be national economies, at least as we have come to understand that concept . . . all that will remain rooted within national borders are the people who comprise a nation. "American" corporations and "American" industries are ceasing to exist in any form that can meaningfully be distinguished from the rest of the global economy.[1]

Economic forecasters, especially the Organization for Economic Cooperation and Development (OECD), and the International Institute of Management Development (IMD), maintain that American competitiveness is making a modest recovery, stressing that there is little choice regarding whether one does or does not take a global view toward business. A global perspective is mandatory, even if one's business is domestic in focus.

There has been true and significant modification of the commercial landscape during the 1980s, with dominance in global industrial leadership shifting from West to East. Since the conclusion of World War II, the United States had held a distinct intellectual and market leadership position in a broad range of industries. This position decidedly changed around 1975, and today American industry finds itself challenged as it has never been before in a highly charged and competitive world order. In fact from 1990–1992, the American, European, and Japanese economies have suffered from a leveling off of the rise of fixed investment, a flattening of the annual growth rate of the per capita gross domestic product/gross national product (GDP/GNP), unemployment, exchange rate fluctuations, and falling interest rates, among other major factors impacting individual countries' ability to compete in global markets. The sustained diffusion of economic strength, reflected by the emerging economies in Asia and Central and South America, can be accounted for by the continued growth of a global economy.

Even so, by the year 2000, a high percentage of new investments will continue to flow from the mature economies with companies headquartered in Europe, the United States, and Japan—still the richest consumer markets. Nevertheless, a growing share of the world's capital is flowing into the emerging economies of Asia: Taiwan, Hong Kong, Singapore, and South Korea. Furthermore, China's economic expansion—provided the government supports the continued growth of economic freedoms—could cost both mature and emerging economies much in competitive position. What is striking in investment trends is the diversity of capital investment, which is reflective of the opportunistic nature of multinational business operations today. Owning a share of the world's funds will continue to drive the investment patterns, which remain concentrated in a limited group of nations. International activities tend to become more focused along rational patterns of business investment and expansion; for example, firms in the chemical, financial services, pharmaceutical, retailing, food, and beverage sectors are investing internationally within their own focus. This approach means seeing the world as a natural expansion of their existing domestic markets looking to sell similar products by differentiating them to wider markets globally.[2]

A recent annual evaluation of the world's top 50 industrial corporations revealed that 36 have their headquarters outside of the United States. In the top 500 listing of corporations, 161 are in the United States, 128 in Japan, 40 in Britain, 32 in West Germany, and 30 in France. In all, 16 countries are represented in the top 500. By contrast, in an industry that has already been highly globalized—the commercial banking sector—Japan heads the list of 50 largest commercial banks with 20; the United States has only 4; Germany has 8, and France has 6.[3]

TABLE 1–1
Distribution of Top Industrial Service Corporations on a Global Basis

	# Companies in Top 50		# Companies in Global 500	
Country	Industrial	Service	Industrial	Service
USA	14	12	161	135
JAPAN	13	22	128	128
BRITAIN	1	2	40	42
GERMANY	7	5	32	45
FRANCE	5	2	30	33

Source: Adapted from *Fortune,* "Guide to the Global Industrial 500," July 26, 1993, pp. 188–226; "Guide to the Global Service 500," August 23, 1993, pp. 159–196.

THE U.S. PERSPECTIVE

A number of world economic trends are exerting tremendous pressures on the United States, Europe, Asia, and emerging countries, especially in the sphere of global competition. The 1980s was a difficult decade for American business, characterized by strong competitiveness both at the domestic and international level. Of the 1,928 American corporations registered by The Conference Board in 1979, almost 1,200 firms disappeared by 1990, while about 750 new firms emerged. The tone and direction of events in the 1980s was measured by finance-related initiatives, such as mergers, acquisitions, and divestitures, as well as technological and increased international competition.

The trend of increasing U.S. business presence overseas, as a response to growing international competition, was a strong characteristic of developments in the 1980s. The multinational corporation found that its survival and profitability grew as the result of a strong commitment to an overseas presence. Many U.S. organizations have placed greater focus and energy on the international scene as their vision underscores the fact that success—and profitability—is inextricably linked to the global economy. The extent to which American companies have restored their competitiveness is explained by a variety of reasons:

- Financial strength of the dollar and narrowing of interest rate differentials along with intensified foreign competition led to a more equitable balance of exports and imports.
- Increased staying power from investment overseas resulted from the hedge against exchange rate fluctuation.
- Presence abroad put companies in direct contact with customers with leverage in the marketplace by having a voice in market developments.
- Economies of scale derived from presence in global markets.
- Higher profitability led to intensification in research and development, using brain power available overseas.
- Support for product diversification distinguished the 1980s for many companies.[4]

In addition to increased international presence, the rate of success for companies in the 1980s is reflective of the regrouping of efforts into "niche markets" resulting from the competitive pressures of the marketplace. For example, the strategy of low-technology-driven companies was based on exiting congested industrial sectors or buying competitors. Conversely, the high-tech companies developed proprietary products and technologies while targeting niche markets or newly created original markets. Overall, the 1980s was one of concentration for manufacturers.

The new environment of the 1990s underscores the dominance of foreign competition, rapid technological advances, and increasingly complex requirements of manufacturing. This is the tip of the iceberg, as the 1990s will continue to be a dynamic and uncertain environment, featuring trade and investment imbalances in conjunction with a developing "new order" in politics and economics. In many instances, succeeding as a global company is conditional upon GATT (General Agreement on Tariffs and Trade) and the evolution of the European, North American, and Asian-Pacific trading blocs.

American success in the 1990s depends on corporate and government response to shifts and changes in the market paradigm, which is rapidly evolving. Under an old paradigm, competitiveness meant sales of goods and services by companies to broad, ill-defined markets and their customers. Suggesting a new paradigm, a report by The Conference Board outlines a market comprised of two networks, reaching around the world, one superimposed above the other: above, an information network, permitting knowledge managers to monitor, control, and change manufacturing processes responding to market conditions; below, a network of goods moving between production and distribution platforms and consumption nodes. Much of the innovation resulting from the information network will originate at the point where company and customers meet, and from the resulting discussion, decision, and strategic planning to meet supplier and customer problems and demands—people meeting and dealing with people.

Companies in the global environment of the 1990s will need to use all the resources available to them on a worldwide basis: management strategies, organizational structure, corporate vision supported by R&D (research and development) expertise, management talent, global home office management teams that are value-added driven, and the attainment of performance objectives being ruthlessly pursued.[5] Corporations will need to be capable of adapting quickly and creatively to a unique set of forces. These forces create the contexts in which truly successful global businesses will emerge and continue to grow. Failure to acknowledge the influence of these driving forces, which cross national, cultural, and geographical boundaries, will hinder or impede an organization's achievement of global status.

DRIVING FORCES IN GLOBAL BUSINESS

As the mid-point of the 90s approaches, momentum toward globalization among businesses gathers speed driven by factors that reflect new business and management developments. Although the term *global* is used with greater frequency, companies tend to remain strongly national in their outlook, perspective, and strategies. Before considering the stages of development in globalizing, it is important to consider changes in perspective and its impact on the distinguishing characteristics that underlie the opportunities and challenges of the international marketplace.

Responding to change in a global context is no longer a progressive or incremental process—vertical and hierarchical; rather, it is punctuated by rapid and

TABLE 1–2
Basic Assumptions Driving the Business Environment[6]

1980s and Before	*1990s and After*
Continuity	Change
Planning	Coping with the unexpected
Adjustment	Transformation
Diversification	Focus and segmentation
Management	Facilitation
Instruction	Learning
Individuals	Project groups and teams
Knowledge	Competence
Scale and security	Flexibility, responsiveness, and speed
Uninformed customers	Demanding customers
National borders	Freedom of movement

dramatic fluctuation in conditions. The basic environmental conditions surrounding business have dramatically changed, as shown in Table 1–2.

The market and business forces driving companies to globalize as well as the impact of culture on the globalization process will be discussed. Change, change, and more change is the common thread in every area and market. In many cases, firms have no choice and must move toward being more global in their thinking and policies. The key reasons driving company expansion into the global marketplace can be grouped into five forces or categories. See Figure 1–1.

Global managers today are faced with a new set of demands: management tasks ever increasingly more complex as the competitive landscape has changed dramatically from the 1980s. The 1980s were defined by the requirement to meet new standards for quality, cost, cycle time, responsiveness to customers, and flexibility. In addition, the 1980s brought the need to provide global products to a global marketplace with the dual requirements of integrated global company presence and local responsiveness. The challenges of managing in the environment of the 1980s were met with varying degrees of success by both small and large firms. The new market environment of the 1990s has replaced the static, hierarchical, and vertical organization structure in all markets. Companies must cope with a new set of dynamic issues as they consider the international market. The new environment is highly fluid, marked by the participative exchange of people, ideas, intellectual property, processes, money, and expertise. Among the key issues that have to be taken into account for companies involved in the global market are:

- Easier and more open access to markets.
- Demanding customers.

FIGURE 1–1

Forces Driving Change in International Business[7]

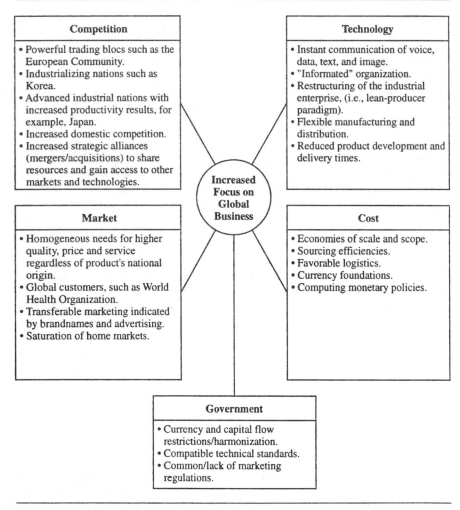

Competition
- Powerful trading blocs such as the European Community.
- Industrializing nations such as Korea.
- Advanced industrial nations with increased productivity results, for example, Japan.
- Increased domestic competition.
- Increased strategic alliances (mergers/acquisitions) to share resources and gain access to other markets and technologies.

Technology
- Instant communication of voice, data, text, and image.
- "Informated" organization.
- Restructuring of the industrial enterprise, (i.e., lean-producer paradigm).
- Flexible manufacturing and distribution.
- Reduced product development and delivery times.

Increased Focus on Global Business

Market
- Homogeneous needs for higher quality, price and service regardless of product's national origin.
- Global customers, such as World Health Organization.
- Transferable marketing indicated by brandnames and advertising.
- Saturation of home markets.

Cost
- Economies of scale and scope.
- Sourcing efficiencies.
- Favorable logistics.
- Currency foundations.
- Computing monetary policies.

Government
- Currency and capital flow restrictions/harmonization.
- Compatible technical standards.
- Common/lack of marketing regulations.

Source: Adapted from Terence Brake, Kim Sullivan, and Danielle Walker, *Doing Business Internationally: The Cross-Cultural Challenges* [Princeton, NJ: Princeton Training Press, A Division of Training Management Corporation (TMC), 1992].

- Continuing improvement in performance.
- The commodities product equation.
- Requirement for rapid and flexible response.
- Technological innovation and rapid replication.
- Growing importance of relationship management.

- Tolerance for diversity.
- Difficulty of "going it alone."[8]

Regrouping these issues into five major categories enables us to examine the consequences of these interrelated forces and the extent of their impact on the international scene:

- Market.
- Competition.
- Technology.
- Cost.
- Government.

Market Drivers

Customers in the international marketplace reflect homogeneous needs through demands for higher quality, price, and service at world-class standards regardless of the product's national origin. In many countries, markets are saturated with local products, and there is strong pressure to find export markets internationally. In the service industries area, for example, many firms are reaching maturity and product saturation in existing markets.

In short, globalization of markets depends upon the orientation of customers and the ability of companies to distribute goods to markets via appropriate distribution channels. The key elements driving markets in this context are homogeneous customer needs; global customers, such as international or national agencies; common geographic distribution sites; and global brand recognition and promotion.

Examples of these market drivers are global customers such as national defense ministries/agencies worldwide; the World Health Organization; brand names and advertising campaigns for products by Coca-Cola, Gucci, and Chanel; Goldstar, a member of the Korean-based Lucky-Goldstar Group, whose vision is to build brand image by strengthening its marketing efforts via adopting local circumstances in developing markets by "customizing" R&D, design, production, and sales to suit local economic, cultural, and consumer characteristics; Seiko Epson, the Japanese manufacturer of personal computers, office machines, and watches, which will expand design and R&D outside of Japan to drive product planning based on feedback of local customers and distributors leading to new products from those markets.

Competitive Drivers

The competitive environment has changed dramatically during the 1980s and 1990s, and the United States no longer dominates the international marketplace simply by virtue of being American. Foreign companies have invaded markets

and made major investments within the United States. Direct investments by for
eign companies in the United States reflect high percentage increases. Overall,
the total world pool of funds represented by foreign direct investment is estimated to have risen tenfold from 1967 to 1989, an increase from approximately
$105 billion to $1,236 billion, with the U.S. share rising 6.7 times, from $59 bil-
lion to $370 billion. At the same time, foreign direct investment in the United
States increased measurably: England rose to $90 billion, Japan to $60 billion,
and Germany to $22 billion. These growth rates are representative of the explo-
sive expansion of U.S. and foreign multinational firms. Key competitive drivers
include open trading systems, regional groups, and collaborative structures.

Open trading systems.   Foreign competition is shown in the recent
Uruguay round of the GATT talks where easier access for foreign agriculture and
service industries into domestic markets is being negotiated. Foreign competition
will likely rise in industries such as banking, insurance, retailing, airlines, and
telecommunications, among others, where foreign companies can bring capital,
experience and knowledge, and organizational capability to foreign domestic
markets.

Regional groups.   The shifting patterns of trade and funds flow across
the regions of the world. The "disappearance" of nation states has caused managers to factor in the emergence of economic trading blocs, i.e., the North American Free Trade Agreement (NAFTA), encompassing the U.S., Canada, and
Mexico; the European Union (EU), including all of Northern and Western Europe, potentially the Eastern European community as well; the Asia-Pacific region, dominated by Japan.
    In any of these regions, national goals and aspirations may be incorporated in
bloc goals. The resulting impact on company planning and market objectives will
be undeniable. These trading groups represent the growing interdependence of
countries in the marketplace. Conversely, within domestic markets there is increased foreign penetration and competition for products and market segments
that were protected in the past. *Competitors are investing to build scale in world
markets,* as shown in Table 1–3.
    Companies are positioning themselves to address the market potential of these
new regions in a manner that uses local resources to help them fully understand
and penetrate the regional market. For example, Baxter International, a major U.S.
producer of health care products and services, established a Euro-board, com-
posed of the heads of the operating group in Europe and the head of European operations, to position and promote pan-European initiatives, optimize operations in
Europe, and increase active communication among Baxter's Euro-businesses.

Collaborative structures.   Global structuring is a major issue in the
competition for emerging and mature industries, as witnessed by the high rate of

TABLE 1–3
Foreign Direct Investment Inflows

Markets	Billions of U.S. dollars (1991)
Developed	
Britain	21.1
France	15.2
United States	11.5
Germany	6.6
Other European countries	30.4
Non-European countries	9.2
Emerging	
Mexico	4.8
Singapore	3.6
Malaysia	3.5
Other Asian countries	4.6

Source: Adapted from *Fortune,* July 26, 1993, p. 91.

mergers, leveraged buyouts, acquisitions, and joint/strategic alliances during the period 1985–1993.

Restructurization or reengineering of corporations is based on many reasons, including deregulation, growth of market share, aggressive national competition, emerging industries, new product niche markets, and so on, with the bottom-line impact being significant change in the competitive environment.

Strategic alliances or joint ventures are frequently seen in industries where competition is strong, such as automotive, high technology, telecommunications, computing and pharmaceuticals, and generic and bio-tech drugs. Such partnering arrangements are often made prior to a product being launched on the market during the highly competitive struggle to gain market position; for example, through establishment of an industry standard or creation of new products. These alliances need to be created out of an in-depth understanding and knowledge of prospective markets and should be based on an understanding of the customer's future needs, to allow for positioning oneself to take advantage of the opportunities.

The following are examples of such arrangements:

The French telecommunications giant Alcatel established a core opportunity focus as shown by its acquisition of Rockwell International (U.S.) and a merger with Telettra, a subsidiary of Fiat (Italy).

The Netherlands retail chain Royal Ahold joined with Argyll (UK) and Casino (Italy) to form a European retailing alliance.

Bristol-Myers (U.S.) acquired E. R. Squibb to form a major diversified pharmaceutical-nutritional-consumer goods company to address health care issues on a worldwide basis.

Microwave Communications, Inc. (MCI), the second largest U.S. long-distance telecommunications carrier and the fifth largest carrier of international traffic in the world acquired Western Union International (1982) and RCA Global Communications, Inc. (1988) and directed a partnering strategy through alliances and acquisitions, such as with British Telecom (BT).

The success level of collaborative arrangements does not parallel the consensus existing between partners at the outset of the arrangement. Questions raised about these arrangements are well known and bring under scrutiny the basis of competition in general where two companies may cooperate in a specific area or product, requiring sharing of various resources, yet stay competitive in broader areas.

Technology Drivers

As corporations adopt global market structures, the fundamental technological revolution in computers, information/data, and telecommunications resources "are rapidly moving us to the position of having a magic genie capable of satisfying almost any logically feasible information need."[9] The continuous change in technologies will dramatically affect the way we do business, both our structural business organization and our office work environment.

Information technology tools represent both the organizational glue to integrate business activities and the lubricant to keep the flow of business on target. In the Institute for the Future's 1993 Ten-Year Forecast report, the term *glubricant* is used to identify this essential element of organizing business in the 1990s. Technology will serve as the principal tool for coordinating global production and distribution, exercising operational control, and driving policy formulation and implementation. Companies lacking the full capability for putting in place efficient communication networks supported by adequate computing capabilities will be unable to maintain a global presence in the international marketplace.[10]

There will be a sustained growth in new applications and hardware as shown in Table 1–4.

The fundamental business drivers of these profound changes can be consolidated into a few basic ones:

- The restructuring of the industrial enterprise has been referred to in several ways: business reengineering, the lean production paradigm, and the total quality company.

TABLE 1–4
Technology Implications for the 1990s [11]

Technology is a major force in the globalization of business. Its impact on the management processes of global organizations will be inestimable. Principal technology-driven factors that will influence business in the 1990s include those listed below.

Technology

Cost performance will improve by two orders of magnitude.

The billion bit network will become the international highway of business communication.

Services

Electronic mail will become ubiquitous, integrating graphics, voice, and text with extensive support capabilities.

Economics

Major investments in increasingly cheaper technology will be made and the accompanying competitive advantages will go to those who apply it well.

Applications

Applications will be designed and built to accommodate the larger and more complex needs of high-level business models.

Change Management

Change management skills will be fundamental to the success of global organizations and will need to be built into the information technology organization and its end users within the company.

- The globalization of business and the emergence of a global market society, which is already reflective of the financial, automotive, and telecommunications markets.

- The changing global labor market where the supply of labor and skills will force organizations to design better business processes and systems to make use of expert systems, databases, relying on the "informated" organization, enabling all levels of the hierarchy to have accessibility of information for control and decision making, which will conflict with traditional management processes and structures.

- The increasing volatility of business environments.

- Protecting intellectual property, the ideas and concepts of individuals, is an issue of competitive advantage; for example, the chemical composition of an active ingredient in a drug or the architectural design of a new and more powerful microchip as distinguished from capital and intellectual investment in a design for a new automated manufacturing plant. Loss of individuals or groups of people and/or their ideas is highly relevant in a world where technology encourages the flow of information at an astounding rate with a greater risk to security.

- The blending of hardware and software.

- Intellectual transformation of major industries where basic paradigms and the disciplines behind certain industries are changing rapidly. For example, ethical drug production using active chemical ingredients protected by fixed-term patents is increasingly under pressure from producers of generic products where research and development requirements are not so time-consuming or costly. Further, the emergence of biotechnology companies is leading to a whole host of new opportunities, potentially transforming an entire industry based on new skills and technical processes. Among the companies in the telecommunication industry, AT&T is an example where simple telephone equipment and support has given way to a broad gamut of telecommunications products such as computers, video games, fax machines, mobile phones, and so on. These transformations demand educating the organization, marketing approach, customers, suppliers, and distributors.[12]

Cost Drivers

Leveraging large capital and development investments to reduce units costs is required in many industries on a global scale, such as semi-conductors, pharmaceuticals, and telecommunications. The resulting economies of scale represented by major differences in country labor/skills and manufacturing costs are fundamental considerations. Despite currency fluctuations and competing monetary policies in some markets, the favorable logistics costs encourage multiple market development. The following are examples of effective cost factor management:

Thomson, a French electronics firm, acquired RCA TV from General Electric (GE) (scale & scope economies).

Volkswagen (Germany) shifted production to Spain (differences in country cost/skills).

Ford Motor Company "Centers of Excellence" program prevents "reinventing the wheel" by leveraging Ford specialists worldwide (product development costs).

Governmental Drivers

Favorable trade policies and falling trade barriers affect globalization through their impact on important tariffs and quotas, nontariff barriers, export subsidies, local content requirements, currency and capital flow restrictions, and requirements on technology transfer. Protectionist policies affect the compatibility of technical standards, whereas differences are often imposed as protectionist actions. Common marketing regulations are frequently restricted due to individual country requirements. The following are good examples:

- The harmonization of EU regulations for banking and finance services permits the free flow of capital among member countries (favorable trade policies).
- Motorola found electronics products excluded from the Japanese market because of different frequencies (technical standards).
- France has more liberal attitudes about sex in advertising than the United States or Britain.
- Dismantling of the command economies of Eastern Europe and the former Soviet Union creates open market opportunities.
- Sweden reversed its long-standing "collectivist model" in 1991 in favor of a deregulated free-market economy.
- South Korea opened its market in the same year to permit foreign companies to invest in domestic companies.[13]

Given these five factors—market competition, technology, cost, and government—it is clear that in order for companies to be competitive in the global marketplace there must be a clear agenda that directs companies to provide products or services in an integrated fashion, as recapped in Figure 1–2.

STAGES OF GLOBAL BUSINESS DEVELOPMENT

International markets beckon corporations to become global organizations, a transformation based upon building competitive advantage and market leadership in a series of stages. A universally accepted definition of *globalization* does not exist, which contributes to much of the confusion about what constitutes a "global" organization; however, the expression "think globally, act locally" captures the essence of a global company: an organization managing operations around the world through functionally integrated, standardized operations, while being responsive to national market differences, where necessary. The definition is less important than the forces that shape and direct companies toward a certain level of involvement on the international scene. As such, it is appropriate to consider attainment of global status reflective of a series of developmental steps.

Today, the dominant stage appears to be the multinational or diversified multinational corporation (MNC/DMNC). The time required to evolve from a purely domestic to a truly global or transnational organization varies considerably, entirely dependent upon each company and its pressures of structural, organizational, and human resources issues.

Briefly, the sequence of steps represented in Figure 1–3 diagrams the typical path of evolution from the domestic to global and transnational stages in international company organization development.

FIGURE 1–2
The Competitive Agenda for Global Business[14]

To be competitive in today's business environment, companies must provide:

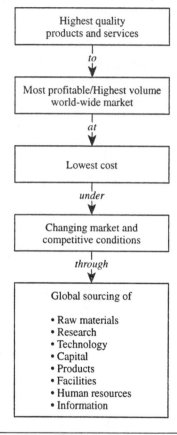

Source: Adapted from Stephen H. Rhinesxmith, *A Manager's Guide to Globalization: Six Keys to Success in a Changing World* (Homewood, IL: Business One Irwin, 1993); and Training Management Corporation (TMC), *The Effective Global Manager Seminar and Coursebook* (Princeton, NJ, 1993).

Stage 1: Domestic

A domestic company is defined primarily according to where it sells its products, its use of domestic suppliers, and the marketing of its services to customers at home. A domestic company can be characterized further as:

- Collecting and using information only on domestic market trends, resources, and environmental conditions.

FIGURE 1–3
Evolution of International Business[15]

A business goes through the following five distinct and progressively complex stages as it evolves from a successful domestic organization to a transnational corporation.

Source: Adapted from Terence Brake, Kim Sullivan, and Danielle Walker, *Doing Business Internationally: The Cross-Cultural Challenges* [Princeton, NJ: Princeton Training Press, A Division of Training Management Corporation (TMC), 1992].

- Having competitive strategies, plans, and tactics that operate inside a domestic marketplace.
- Organizing and reorganizing resources, technologies, marketing/distribution systems, networks, operating systems, and so on in response to local competitive and market changes.
- Creating, organizing, and managing cross-functional teams as its central operating mode.
- Protecting itself against unpredictable change by being highly flexible.
- Requiring its managers to understand themselves and their associates.

Increasingly, domestically focused companies are finding themselves losing market share to foreign competitors. Traditional markets are being broken up, and the distinction between "domestic" and "international" is becoming increasingly irrelevant.

Stage 2: Export/International

An export company is a successful national business that sells or markets its products and services in foreign countries but operates primarily from its sense of domestic competitiveness and advantage. An export company sells or markets its products and services abroad through export agents or foreign distributors. Growth in exporting may lead to the establishment of an export department co-equal with the domestic sales department.

Very often, an export/international business is organized through an international division(s), whose sales and distribution of products or services may be supplemented with localized manufacturing. This may result in staffing by host country nationals (HCNs) if country-specific factors (market, language, local needs, government policies, and so on) are deemed important. Foreign operations are usually treated as appendages of home country headquarters with greater emphasis placed on control mechanisms and staffing by headquarters personnel.

Export/international companies are further distinguished by the following characteristics:

- Collecting and using information on offshore market trends and conditions as well as domestic strategic resources.
- Extending competitive strategies, plans, and tactics to include offshore markets.
- Organizing and reorganizing resources, technologies, marketing/distribution systems, networks, operating systems, and so on in response to emerging foreign market opportunities.
- Creating, organizing, and managing cross-cultural distribution linkages as a central operating mode.
- Adapting to destabilizing changes by being flexible in entering or withdrawing from foreign markets.
- Requiring managers to understand cross-cultural needs.

Stage 3: Multinational Corporation (MNC)

A multinational company is one whose national or regional operations act independently of one another, causing problems of communication and efficiency of operation. Pioneered in Europe by Philips and ICI, the MNC was seen as the final stage of organization development in the 1980s. Within the MNC, tensions begin to emerge from the need for national responsiveness at the subsidiary level as opposed to the need for more centralized integration from headquarters at a truly global level of operation. Strategic planning is completed at the headquarters level. The multinational corporation is further defined by the following characteristics:

- Collecting and using information on multidomestic trends, environmental conditions, and strategic resources.
- Adapting successful domestic market models to cultural contexts.
- Adapting systems and processes to international competitive conditions.
- Developing multinational alliances and ventures, managing cross-cultural work teams.
- Responding and adapting to destabilizing change by being flexible in real-locating resources across national markets.
- Requiring managers to work effectively in cross-cultural situations.

Stage 4: Global

A global company shares resources on a global basis in order to access the best market with the highest quality product at the lowest cost. The global MNC pushes for tighter integration at headquarters level, while host country operations emphasize local responsiveness. In the matrix structure response, authority is shared jointly between headquarters/international division and production entity in the host country. In this more complex business environment, the global MNC faces worldwide competition, pressures for strategy integration, and control. In the latter, the issue of decentralization versus centralization and related control mechanisms become a key factor in responding structurally to the need to coordinate global activities. The decision process usually sees strategic issues centralized and operational matter decentralized, although there is frequently a mix of approaches.

The most common characteristics of global companies are:

- Integrating holistic competitive strategies.
- Creating global strategic partnerships—inter- and intra-organizational linkages.
- Creating destabilized conditions in order to be proactive in the marketplace and gain advantages.
- Requiring that managers be able to manage and transcend cultural differences effectively.

Stage 5: Transnational

A transnational organization is characterized by an integration of resources and responsibilities across all business units regardless of national boundaries, yet with an anchoring to a strong corporate identity. A key problem facing the

FIGURE 1–4
Organizational Form and the Importance of Culture[16]

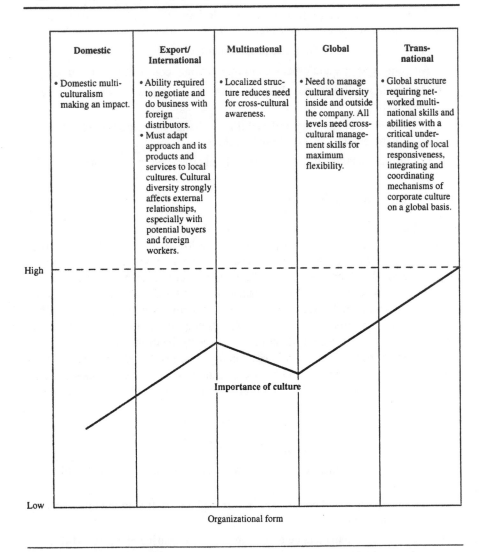

Source: © Training Management Corporation (TMC), *The Effective Global Manager,* Seminar
Coursebook and Seminar (Princeton, NJ, 1992).

transnational company is the complexity of decision making and efficiency resulting from the flexible linking of local operations in order to leverage local and
headquarters' capabilities.[17] The complexity embedded in a formal matrix structure of coordination and control, typical of the transnational company, often creates pressures to adopt a more informal matrix concept.

C. A. Bartlett and S. Ghoshal, proponents of this new form of global entity, describe the transnational company in their work, *Managing Across Borders* (1992), as having surpassed the multinational and global companies by developing the capability of managing across national frontiers, retaining and leveraging local/central headquarters capabilities in a manner that achieves global integration, maintaining a strong corporate identity, and communicating a clear worldwide management perspective. Key features of the transnational company include:

- An integrated network that shares decision making and whose components, products, resources, information, and people flow freely between its interdependent units. Every part of the organization has to collaborate, share information, solve problems, and collectively implement strategy.

- Decision making is often limited by narrow perspectives and parochial interests, leading to substandard decision making. In particularly complex, multitiered organizations, this problem is exacerbated by conflicting interests and overlapping responsibilities. This often leads to complex matrix structures. Transnationals use "co-option" to develop consensus; each individual must understand, share, and internalize the company's purpose, values, and key strategies.

- Control through a single method is insufficient. Highly formal and institutionalized control mechanisms and centralized decision making are necessary in combination with socialization and co-option as the most effective means of coordination.

Instead of encouraging local innovations or imposing ideas from the center, the transnational allocates worldwide product responsibilities to different national subsidiaries according to their relative skills and strengths. The transnational's greatest strength is its ability to facilitate organizational learning by fostering a flow of intelligence, ideas, and knowledge around the organization.

Not all companies must evolve toward a particular stage of development. It is premature to predict that one form will be *the* type of organization of the future. Many stages are being explored with a varied picture of strategic evolution. Each company is grappling with the evolution process within a different context and host of challenges—each perceiving itself to be only at the starting point of its own definition of internationalization.

As companies move through these stages, the role and importance of culture shifts as shown in Figure 1–4.

A NEW GLOBAL MANAGEMENT PARADIGM

To be successful in the global business environment, organizations must constantly adjust their focus to changing realities. Emerging global business policies and practices will test and change existing paradigms of global business. Key managers must lead the process, fostering new patterns of thinking to position the organization in a world without traditional boundaries and shaped by local environments.

To gain a competitive edge, Dr. Stephen H. Rhinesmith, in *A Manager's Guide to Globalization,* emphasizes a wholly new paradigm regarding the management of global companies where, for example, the traditional American or European values of competitiveness and marketplace success are no longer appropriate. André Laurent of INSEAD (Institut Européen d'Administration des Affairress) further reinforces the belief that it will no longer be "business as usual" in his analysis of reasons impacting the need for change in strategy based on the diverse, multicultural approach to managing a multinational corporation. Laurent singles out several primary observations governing our ability to implement strategy and structure uniformly on a global basis:

1. Multinational companies do not and cannot submerge the individuality of different cultures.
2. Contact with other nationalities can promote the determination to remain different.
3. It is useless to present new kinds of management theory and practice to individuals who are culturally unable or unwilling to accept it.

The globalization guide offered by Rhinesmith and his new paradigm of management development address in an integrated manner three levels of alignment for an organization that is determined to achieve competitive success as a global company: 1) strategy and structure, 2) corporate culture, and 3) people.

Strategy and structure defines the mix of centralization-decentralization and geographical-functional-business-product structure to be used to attain the most competitive advantage.

Corporate culture represents the values, norms of behavior, systems, policies, and procedures through which the organization adapts to the complexity of the global arena. Research indicates that the composition of a company's culture model stresses five essential elements: 1) a clear and simple mission statement, 2) a clear vision communicated by the CEO (Chief Executive Officer), 3) company-controlled management education, 4) project-oriented management training programs, and 5) an emphasis on the processes of global corporate culture.

People emphasizes the continuous development of the corporation's human resources to manage teams, uncertainty, and personal and organizational learning. This enables the company to be a true learning organization, able to adapt and grow in the face of the constant change and disruption characteristic of emerging global markets.

Of these three elements, people constitute the most critical factor in a company's drive to progress, stage by stage, toward attainment of global or even transnational status. Global managers are ultimately the key players in attaining a global company's global scale of efficiency and competitiveness. They are the strategists, architects, and coordinators of this effort, requiring the insight to recognize opportunity and risk across national and regional boundaries, while exercising the skills and abilities necessary to make timely and accurate decisions about opportunities and risks, to coordinate actions, and to manage the capabilities of the organization around the world.[18]

In this world of challenges, the global manager must possess certain competencies linked to a mindset of what working in the international marketplace entails.

GLOBALIZATION CHALLENGES IN PEOPLE MANAGEMENT

The complexity of effective management of business in each of these stages of international development, represented by the monitoring of global market conditions, strategic planning, managing local operations, and so on, emphasizes the demand for a skilled and competent cadre of global managers able to monitor global markets, respond to global opportunities and threats, and formulate and execute business strategies in a global context. Preparing managers to possess the necessary "global mindset" and attain the competencies and skills represents a key strategic objective for multinational companies today.

Going global in the rapidly evolving environment of the 1990s calls for a renewed approach by management, which focuses on issues of global integration, local differentiation, creativity and innovation on a worldwide basis, and the computer networked organization. These compelling reasons drive not only management development on an individual basis, but the organization's collective capability and commitment to using all strategies to build the competitive edge.

Concerning management development, today's companies need to focus on a critical number of issues to tactically ensure competitiveness. To build an integrated human resources management process, the following tasks are critical:

- Identifying and retaining highly qualified people.
- Ensuring sufficient quality and quantity of management.
- Sustaining and improving performance at all levels in all areas of the business.
- Increasing the depth of talent in the organization.
- Ensuring that people have the technical and managerial skills to compete.
- Making the management competencies and culture that are required sufficiently clear to people.
- Emphasizing total quality management and changing people's attitudes to quality.
- Establishing training as part of the management culture.

- Gaining top management and line management interest in human resource development.
- Linking human resource management to strategic business objectives.

It appears that management and organizational development require integration to build on the requisite parts of the company. A principal task is to create an effective learning organization that recognizes the flow of information and shared experiences and pushes development, formally and informally, to a worldwide scale to enable dialogue between the diverse elements and cultures within the organization.

International competitive position and international learning are highly interrelated; yet, developing managerial talent within the organization is complicated by the multitude of issues, principal of which is the ability of the organization to determine the best fit and integration between international strategic business intent and objectives, structural considerations, and human resource (development) policies.

Development must contribute to the creation of a corporate culture dedicated to global competitiveness, as well as to individual managerial mind-sets, competencies, and skills—all of which encourage cooperation and exchange throughout the organization on a global basis. Thus, individual competencies linked to the universal competence of the organization have to be collectively addressed.

The critical issues in this approach to development are certainly 1) top management's involvement and commitment, often achieved by human resource and management development specialists who convince senior management of the vitality of such a concept; and 2) development of dialogue and participation by counterparts throughout the organization on a worldwide basis. In implementing a well-conceived approach to international management development, senior management and human resources staff need to be cognizant of three principal foci: creating an international spirit, establishing critical success factors for the effective global manager, and communicating a global human resource policy.

Every organization needs to define its own profile of the effective global manager and identify the attributes critical to implementing a company's strategic objectives and intent. Research on the key characteristics needed by international managers in their organization indicates that functional skills are rated as less critical than human skills involved in managing people from different countries and cultures coupled with the manager's ability to handle ambiguity. For example, a study by the Economist Intelligence Unit in cooperation with the Ashridge Management Research Group in England indicates that the top five characteristics of an effective global manager are strategic awareness, adaptability in new situations, sensitivity to different cultures, ability to work in international teams, and language skills.

Many leaders and managers involved in international business activities do not have sufficient intercultural skills to be successful. Managers are often sent abroad with little, if any, training. Too often, management appears confident that an individual's understanding and knowledge of business will easily compensate for the lack of cultural understanding.

Companies' strategic agendas, including that of managing its human resources, must be focused around the process of organizational learning. The capability of reaching greater levels of competitive advantage must involve a carefully planned and executed learning strategy.

Rosabeth Moss Kanter identifies the search for a new business mind-set as one of the most important changes happening today. She points to the "triumph of process over structure" as a key indication of this change. "What is important is not how responsibilities are divided but how people can pull together to pursue new opportunities."[19] The real challenge is developing the ability of management from different countries and cultures to think and work together—a primary factor for the success of global organizations.

SUMMARY INSIGHTS

Trade, high technology advances, cheap labor, and so on have inexorably pushed the process of globalization to the forefront for major multinationals. The increased presence of foreign nationals in corporate headquarters, the increased numbers of foreign assignments, and the renewed commitment to training and development of personnel (as one of the key elements in the competitive equation) have underlined the continuous interaction, task force, and team concepts of conducting business efficiently at the global level. In addition, leveraging resources and plant investments on a worldwide basis, which draws the best from an integrated and highly networked capital investment process, places emphasis on people at the focal point of the strategic planning and implementation process. People from different cultures with different cultural values and beliefs stress the importance of understanding both the basic definitions and the areas of cultural impact where management practice and process are critically affected and success and attainment of performance objectives are critically influenced by the most subtle, invisible, yet ingrained elements of the human character. Culture is a key, domineering spirit of the human condition to which today's manager, working in a highly competitive, ever-changing global context, must be sensitive and observant.

DISCUSSION QUESTIONS
A CHECKLIST OF GLOBAL COMPANY SUCCESS[20]

- To what extent does your company measure up to these common attributes of successful global enterprises?

Yes	_No_	_Attribute_
____	____	1. Participates directly in local economies.
____	____	2. Exhibits local responsiveness.
____	____	3. Demonstrates effective communication.
____	____	4. Assures blending of corporate cultures between headquarters and local subsidiaries, or with joint venture or strategic alliance partners.
____	____	5. Globalizes human resources activities.
____	____	6. Fosters cooperation between business units, subsidiaries, and management teams to support each other's and overall company goals.
____	____	7. Balances central control and local autonomy (without losing the advantages of worldwide coordination and product strength).

- What forces are driving your company to be a global player?
- Where would you place your company in the globalization process (Domestic, Export/International, etc.)?
- What do you see as the major challenges to your company in going global?

NOTES

1. Robert B. Reich, *The Work of Nations: Preparing Ourselves for 21st Century Capitalism* (New York: Alfred Knopf, 1991), pp 3 and 77.
2. *1993 Ten-Year Forecast* (Menlo Park, CA: Institute for the Future, 1993), pp 9–14.
3. *Fortune,* "Guide to the Global 500," July 26, 1993, pp 188–226; "Guide to the Global Service 500," August 23, 1993, pp 159–196.
4. Charles R. Taylor, "Prospering in the 90s," *Across the Board,* January/February 1992, pp 43–46.
5. Conference Board Report, "The Changing Global Role of the Human Resource Function," Report #77 (New York: Conference Board, 1994).
6. Colin Coulson-Thomas, *Creating the Global Company: Successful Internationalization* (New York: McGraw Hill, 1992), pp 2–3.
7. Terence Brake, Kim Sullivan, and Danielle Walker, *Doing Business Internationally: The Cross-Cultural Challenges* [Princeton, NJ: Princeton Training Press, A Division of Training Management Corporation (TMC), 1992].
8. Coulson-Thomas, *Creating the Global Company,* pp 12– 13.
9. James Emery, "Editor's Comments," *MIS Quarterly,* December 1991, pp xxi–xxiii.
10. *1993 Ten-Year Forecast,* pp 93–98.

11. Benjamin E. Benjamin and Jon Blunt, "Critical IT Issues: The Next Ten Years," *Sloan Management Review,* Summer 1992, pp 7–19; chart—p 9.

12. C. K. Prahalad, "Globalization: The Intellectual and Managerial Challenges," *Human Resource Management* 29, no. 1, pp 27–38.

13. George S. Yip, "Global Strategy . . . In a World of Nations," *Sloan Management Review,* Fall 1989, pp 29–41.

14. Stephen H. Rhinesmith, *A Manager's Guide to Globalization: Six Keys to Success in a Changing World* (Homewood, IL: ASTD and Business One Irwin), 1993, p 49.

15. Brake, Sullivan, and Walker, *Doing Business Internationally.*

16. Training Management Corporation (TMC), *The Effective Global Manager,* Seminar Coursebook and Seminar (Princeton, NJ TMC, 1992).

17. Christopher Bartlett and Sumantra Ghoshal, *Managing Across Borders: The Transnational Solution* (Cambridge, MA: Harvard Business School Press, 1989).

18. Stephen H. Rhinesmith, *A Manager's Guide to Globalization* (Homewood, IL: ASTD and Business One Irwin, 1991), pp 4–39.

19. Rosabeth Moss Kanter, *When Giants Learn to Dance* (New York: Simon and Schuster, 1989), pp. 12–13.

20. *Organizing the New Global Competitor* (New York: The Economist Intelligence Unit, 1993), pp 12–13.

Chapter Two

Success in Understanding Culture

*The influence of a nation's history, infrastructure, and culture perme-
ates all aspects of life within the country, including the norms, values,
and behaviors of managers in its national companies.*

Christopher A. Bartlett and Sumantra Ghoshal
Managing Across Borders: The Transnational Solution

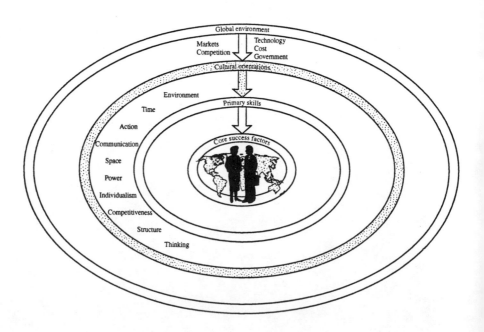

INTRODUCTION

Thomas Jefferson once said, "The merchant has no country."[1] Jefferson, like many others of his and our time, made the erroneous assumption that business is business wherever it is conducted. Commerce in this view is perceived to be a universal superculture into which men and women can step at will without carrying in the very heavy cultural baggage of their own society. This assumption rests on three dubious premises:

- The culture of money and profit transcends national or regional boundaries.
- The language of bottom-line profitability is recognized across the globe.
- A good deal is a good deal from New York to Beijing to Bonn.

On a superficial level, all three premises have some credence. But as we expand trade across new borders, form strategic alliances and joint ventures with foreign partners, and develop new relationships with overseas suppliers and distributors, we are learning—although still very slowly—that *culture matters,* that business is not an activity that cuts across cultural boundaries easily. If Jefferson resided in the White House today and made the same remark, he would undoubtedly receive telephone calls, faxes, and cables from CEOs, executives, and managers from around the globe saying, "Think again, President Jefferson!"

CULTURAL COMPETENCE AND COMPETITIVE ADVANTAGE

Many international companies are learning to integrate cultural competence into their competitive strategies. Take, for example, Procter & Gamble (P&G). They first entered the Japanese market in 1973 and had lost $200 million by 1987. Entering the market with their American goods and American-style advertising just didn't work. P&G then turned Japan into its second biggest market after Germany with over $1 billion in sales for the year ending June 30, 1990. The company sells over twenty products in Japan, including the number one brand in seven categories: disposable diapers, liquid laundry detergent, fine fabric detergent, acne treatment, adult incontinence diapers, feminine hygiene products, and laxatives.[2] P&G built their success on five principles:[3]

- Knowing the customer's habits, biases, and attitudes.
- Tailoring products to the market.
- Being sensitive to Japanese cultural differences.
- Penetrating the multitiered Japanese distribution system.
- Selling the company as well as the brands.

While many Western companies have shied away from entering the Japanese market, P&G decided to *unlearn* their primarily American and European business practices and to explore doing business from a different viewpoint. P&G came to understand that advertising that knocks the competition is offensive to the Japanese, who value harmony and avoid direct conflict. They found that product performance is a top priority for Japanese customers, who place a lower premium on price than do customers in the United States. They also discovered how to adapt their products to the space constraints of Japanese homes. And they quickly realized that the Japanese are also very company conscious and are quick to relate a product to the image and reputation of the company. Paying close attention to the Japanese culture and market transformed P&G's performance.

The company continues to focus on learning how to do business internationally. Its 1993 restructuring announcement was not only aimed at reducing the levels of management and simplifying the business, but was also directed at increasing the company's ability to further tap into overseas markets such as China and Eastern Europe.[4] In fact, the restructuring plan was titled "Strengthening Global Effectiveness."

In an excellent report written for The Economist Intelligence Unit, Lisa Adent Hoecklin describes several other cross-cultural business success stories:[5]

- The British Imperial Chemical Industries (ICI) has been working since the early 1980s to instill a more global perspective into the organization. This has involved introducing more cultural diversity onto the board of directors and finding ways to create cultural synergy at all levels. Hoecklin describes an exercise called "Project Management in a Multi-cultural Environment," in which British and Italian managers worked with consultants to reveal their different cultural approaches and identify the strength and appropriateness of each one in the context of what needed to be done. Both the British and Italians felt that the exercise helped them to understand and apply each other's strengths and to create competitive advantage. The participants met again a year after to celebrate their success in completing an important phase of a collaborative project.

- When Toshiba gained ownership of Rank in the United Kingdom (UK), a lengthy and involved process of cultural analysis was put into effect. Business objectives were established, and then the British and Japanese managers discussed their different approaches to meeting the objectives. The outcomes combined the English managers' understanding of appropriate communication methodologies, motivational factors, and information requirements with Japanese manufacturing practices. George Williams, managing director, said, "We try to blend the best of both cultures . . . If you can say, 'We bring this, this, and this—you bring that; help us understand it,' that's ideal."

- Motorola and Toshiba have been conducting a successful joint venture since mid-1987. The aim was to reap benefits from combining Toshiba's memory and process technology with Motorola's microprocessor technology. Two major cultural differences have arisen in the venture. First, decisions made in the United States tend to be made in a more top-down fashion. Secondly, Japanese and American employees tend to have different conceptions of company loyalty. Other differences were noted in how meetings were conducted, the levels of detail required in negotiations, and human resource practices (for example, seniority played a much larger role in promotion at Toshiba than at Motorola). Strategies to achieve success in the joint venture included establishment of a common management philosophy and the formation of task forces and project teams to determine best approaches to meet common objectives.

As we have seen, focusing attention on culture can dramatically improve effectiveness. How? By enhancing creativity and innovation, productivity, problem solving, communication, customer responsiveness, planning, organizing, and so on.

If ignored, culture may have the opposite effect and inhibit competitiveness by alienating customers, destroying workforce cohesiveness, and degrading efficiency and effectiveness. Hoecklin identifies a number of situations in which companies have suffered setbacks because of a misreading of or ignorance about the impact of culture. For example, an insurance company from the United Kingdom took ownership of a 50 percent stake in three Italian companies in 1989. The policies of these three companies were altered to create standardization throughout the enterprise. The venture suffered a pretax loss of approximately $90 million in just over a year.

No company can afford to neglect the cultural context of doing business, and no manager has the luxury of ignoring cultural differences. The challenge is to build synergy from what sets us apart. As Edward T. Hall said about the human race in general, but which can also be applied to business specifically, "The future of the human race lies in maintaining its diversity and turning that diversity to its advantage."[6]

In response to the increasing internationalization of business activity, and the growing awareness of the power of the cultural factor, many companies are developing initiatives to train managers in intercultural competence and global management:[7]

- American Express Co.'s Travel Related Services unit assigns American business-school students summer jobs abroad for as long as 10 weeks. It also moves lower-level managers with at least two years experience to other countries.

- Colgate-Palmolive trains about 15 college graduates each year for 15 to 24 months prior to their undertaking a range of overseas assignments.

- General Electric Co.'s aircraft engine unit trains midlevel engineers and managers in foreign languages and cross-cultural understanding.

- Honda of America Manufacturing, Inc., has transferred about 42 U.S. supervisors and managers to the parent company in Tokyo for up to three years. Prior to the transfer, they are prepared with six months of Japanese language lessons, cultural training, and life-style orientation.
- PepsiCo Inc.'s international beverage division brings about 25 young foreign managers a year to the United States for one-year assignments in bottling plants.
- Raychem Corp. transfers relatively inexperienced Asian employees (from clerks through middle managers) to the United States for six months to two years.
- Motorola Inc. has opened a special center for cultural training at its headquarters in Schaumburg, Illinois. Mr. Rs. Moorthy, a Malaysian who runs the center says, "It is imperative that we understand all national cultures and respect all cultures—and use it as a competitive advantage." The company's goal is to make Motorola's managers "transculturally competent."[8]

Business schools in the United States and Europe are increasingly focusing MBA (Master of Business Administration) programs on the international marketplace. Schools like the Institut Européen d'Administration des Affaires (INSEAD) near Paris, the London Business School (LBS), and the International Institute for Management Development (IMD) in Lausanne, Switzerland, are among the elite business schools attracting students with eyes on the global economy. One recent project at LBS involved a team of students assigned to Burger King's London headquarters. Burger King wanted to expand its European operations, and the students were assigned to develop a business plan to "spread the Whopper from Piccadilly to Prague." Harvard is just finishing a review of its MBA curriculum. "The whole internationalization thrust is becoming a very dominant theme in our review," says Harvard professor Christopher A. Bartlett. The University of Pennsylvania's Wharton School and Columbia Business School have already reworked their programs to reflect the challenges faced by managers in the global market.[9]

As companies seek to recruit and develop professionals who can transfer their skills across cultural boundaries and relate to customers, suppliers, and distributors with different conceptions of *how the world works,* we need to bring the issue of cross-cultural competence to the top of the competitive agenda. Cultural competence is no longer a nice skill to have; it is an economic necessity. We have been successful in developing the hardware of increased globalization; for example, computer and communications technologies, transportation methods, and flexible manufacturing systems. Our weakness has been in developing individuals with the flexibility and knowledge needed to maximize the value of the cultural capital available to the organization.

The cultural competence needed by managers in our business organizations is constructed on the four interrelated levels presented in Figure 2–1.

FIGURE 2–1:
Four Levels of Cultural Competence

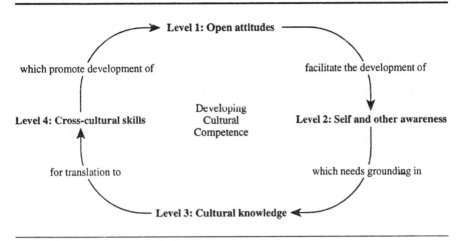

Source:© Training Management Corporation (TMC), *Doing Business Internationally: The Cross-Cultural Challenges*, Seminar and Coursebook (Princeton, NJ, 1992).

*Level 1: Open Attitudes©**

Objective: Develop receptivity to cross-cultural learning.

- Am I open to recognizing cultural differences by not assuming that "we are all the same"?

- Am I open to examining my own cultural orientations in an honest and objective fashion and unlearning cultural habits that might be counterproductive?

- Am I open to receiving information about other cultures (information that may conflict with my existing thoughts and feelings about what is real, efficient, effective, appropriate, proper, etc.)?

- Am I open to experiencing other cultures without rushing into evaluations, becoming trapped in stereotypes, or falling into ethnocentric behaviors?

- Am I able to empathize and see from different viewpoints while still being secure in myself, resilient, and able to act?

---

*© Training Management Corporation (TMC), *Doing Business Internationally: The Cross-Cultural Challenges,* Seminar and Coursebook (Princeton, NJ, 1992).

Level 2: Self and Other Awareness©*

Objective: Recognize key differences and similarities between self and others.

Self-Awareness

- What are my primary cultural orientations? How do they affect how I do business?
- How do I differ from my mainstream culture and mainstream business culture?
- How adaptable am I? How can I increase my capacity for intercultural learning?

Other-Awareness

- What are their primary cultural orientations? How do these orientations affect the way they do business?
- What is their mainstream culture and their business culture? What are the significant variations among their cultures?
- How adaptable are they? How willing are they to learn more about me and my style of working?
- What common ground exists? How can we build on our shared understandings?

Level 3: Cultural Knowledge©*

Objective: Ground awareness in a solid base of cultural knowledge.

- What do I need to know about all cultures? Specific cultures?
- What resources will help me find the knowledge I need, when I need it?
- How can I continue to build a practical knowledge base of cultural information that will serve me over the long term?

Level 4: Cross-Cultural Skills©*

Objective: Develop behaviors that maximize cross-cultural effectiveness.

- How do I translate my awareness and knowledge into functional skills?
- What skills will help me minimize cross-cultural conflict and maximize productivity and effectiveness?
- How can I continue to refine my skills and develop my level of cultural competence and adaptability?

---

*© Training Management Corporation (TMC), *Doing Business Internationally: The Cross-Cultural Challenges,* Seminar Coursebook (Princeton, NJ, 1992).

- How can I use my cross-cultural skills to further enhance my openness to cross-cultural learning?

Open, receptive attitudes built on curiosity and a willingness to undertake continuous learning are the foundation for developing cultural competence. In turn, these attitudes facilitate the development of self and other awareness. To become useful, however, awareness needs to be grounded in a knowledge of culture (general and specific), and that knowledge needs to be translated into skills for working across cultures. By developing on all four levels, a manager builds the confidence and ability to integrate cultural differences into new and more rewarding ways of doing business.

But what is culture? And why is it so powerful?

FINDING OUR FEET: CULTURE EXPLORED

Clifford Geertz, in *The Interpretation of Cultures,* uses a quotation from the philosopher Ludwig Wittgenstein that can also serve as a frame for our discussion of culture:[10]

> We . . . say of some people that they are transparent to us. It is, however, important as regards this observation that one human being can be a complete enigma to another. We learn this when we come into a strange country with entirely strange traditions; and what is more, even given a mastery of the country's language. We do not *understand* the people. (And not because of not knowing what they are saying to themselves.) We cannot find our feet with them.

An inability to *find our feet* is an apt description for the feeling of intense disorientation that can accompany contact with a new culture.

The simple question that drives our consulting work is, "What will help us find our feet in other cultures so that we can do business effectively?" A traditional—and popular—approach to teaching cultural awareness and sensitivity has been to offer courses in "Dos and Don'ts around the World: A Guide to Business Etiquette" or "Doing Business in . . ." programs for those about to work with or within a specific country or region. This approach has great value. It provides the participant with critical insights into the repertoire of behaviors and beliefs typical of a culture or cultures. Every employee being relocated abroad should receive country or regional training. In our increasingly global marketplace, however, employees are finding themselves moving to wherever they can add value quickly and efficiently. An engineer from the United States may find herself working on a multicultural project team in Poland during April, troubleshooting problems in South Korea in May, and not returning home until she has delivered a training program to engineers in India, Egypt, and Sweden. Is it likely that she will have received training in each culture before her trip? It's possible, but unlikely. It simply isn't cost-effective for the company to offer such training at short notice to a small number of people. Our engineer needs a mental model for understanding the fundamentals of all cultures so that she can accumulate and organize the rich data presented by different cultures, including her own. This will allow her to build a personal database of cultural know-how that will serve her across the world.

When you hear the term "culture," what springs to mind? Types of music, art, and literature? Laws, customs, rituals, gestures, ways of dressing, food and drink and methods of greeting, and saying good-bye? These are all part of culture, but they are just the tip of the cultural iceberg (see Figure 2–2).

The most powerful elements of culture are those that lie beneath the surface of everyday interaction; we call these value orientations. Value orientations are preferences for certain outcomes over others; for example, private space over public space, or deductive thinking over inductive thinking. Our patterns of value orientations are manifested in our behaviors, beliefs, attitudes, and patterns of thinking, which are key components in our individual and national identities. Culture guides our actions, our decisions, our methodologies, our feelings, and our thoughts, and shapes our experience of ourselves, others, our institutions, and the world around us. It defines our fundamental beliefs in how the world works and gives form and substance to our ways of dealing with such fundamental aspects of being alive as relationships, time, space, and communication. These powerful, underlying (or implicit) elements are the relatively static patterns of value that we learn as we grow and develop in our social groups. Even though we may dress similarly to the other person, and perhaps speak the same language, we may notice that the other person never shows up to meetings on time, that when meetings do begin they seem to be chaotic with people coming in and out and interrupting the flow of the session, and that the people in the meetings seem to be reluctant to identify sources of conflict and deal with them directly.

Every society has a distinctive set of value orientations. These orientations define what it means to be an American or a Chinese. While each of these societies will contain significant variations on the mainstream culture, a dominant set of values prevails at any one time. As Florence Kluckhohn and Fred Strodtbeck point out, these cultural phenomena have been variously defined as "systems of meanings," "unconscious canons of choice," "integrative themes," "ethos," or "configurations."[11] We prefer the term "value orientation" as used by Kluckhohn and Strodtbeck, although, when discussing a specific culture we may also use the term *value cluster* or *configuration of values.*

Kluckhohn and Strodtbeck define a value orientation in very broad terms as "a generalized and organized principle concerning basic human problems which pervasively and profoundly influences man's behavior." These principles "give order and direction to the ever-flowing stream of human acts and thoughts as these relate to the solution of 'common human problems.'" Underlying Kluckhohn and Strodtbeck's work is the following set of assumptions:

- There is a limited number of common human problems for which all people at all times must find workable solutions.

FIGURE 2–2
The Iceberg Model of Culture

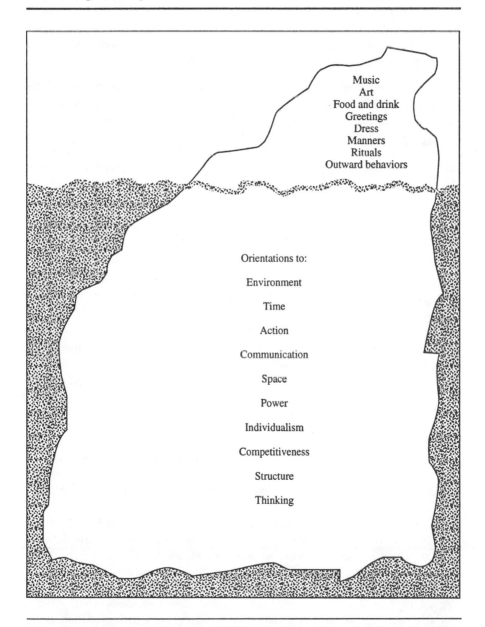

Source: Training Management Corporation (TMC), *Doing Business Internationally: The Cross-Cultural Challenges,* Seminar Coursebook (Princeton, NJ, 1992).

- While variations in these workable solutions certainly exist, they are neither limitless nor random, but are instead variations within a limited range of possible solutions;
- All variants of recurring solutions are present in all cultures at all times but receive, from one society to another or one subculture to another, varying degrees of emphasis.

This universalistic approach to the study of culture was described earlier by Clyde Kluckhohn.[12] In his view, human biology and the human situation in general (including needs for food, shelter, and sex, differences in age and capabilities, and the dependency of the young) generate universal circumstances that must be met by every society. Every society, therefore, develops a "pattern for living" that is internally approved and sanctioned. The common human problems and their associated orientations were identified by Kluckhohn and Strodtbeck as follows:

- Human beings' relation to their own nature (human nature orientation with the possible designations of good, good-and-evil, neutral, and evil).

- Human beings' relation to nature and supernature (human-nature orientation with the possible designations of humans' mastery-over-nature, subjugation-to-nature, and the harmony-with-nature positions.

- Human beings' place in the flow of time (time orientation with the possible designations of past, present, and future).

- Human beings' characteristic orientation to activity (activity orientation with the possible designations of being, being-in-becoming, and doing).

- Human beings' relationships to other human beings (relational orientation with the possible designations of lineality, individualism, and collaterality).

In this view, culture is seen as an interlocking network of dominant (most preferred) value orientations and variant value orientations. While the theoretical notions of "common human problems" and "value orientations" are not without controversy in academia, we find that they give us a very useful platform on which to build a practical and very business-oriented approach to thinking about culture.

Additional insights into the value orientations of cultures have been provided by numerous researchers, including Talcott Parsons and Edward Shils; Edward T. Hall; Geert Hofstede; Edward Stewart and Milton Bennett; Stephen Rhinesmith; and Charles Hampden-Turner and Alfons Trompenaars. Talcott Parsons and Edward Shils, for example, demarcated five "pattern variables," which they argued are key to understanding human action across societies. These pattern variables are basic dilemmas that face human actors in any social situation. A society, therefore, can be defined by the dominant choices made in relation to these dilemmas.[13]

- **Affectivity** (we stress feeling, emotion, and gratification) versus **affective neutrality** (we stress practical or moral considerations).

- **Self-orientation** (we stress self interests) versus **collectivity-orientation** (we stress group goals and interests).

- **Universalism** (we use common evaluative standards across situations and groups) versus **particularism** (we use different evaluative standards across situations and groups).

- **Ascription** (we stress who you are) versus **achievement** (we stress what you do or have done).

- **Specificity** (we stress interaction for specific purposes) versus **diffuseness** (we stress interaction across a wide range of activities).

While individuals in specific situations may give preference to both sides of each dilemma over time, overall a society will tend to favor one side over another. How does mainstream American (Anglo-American male) culture relate to the pattern variables? In general, it stresses the following:

- Affective Neutrality. Most social interactions are based on practical, instrumental concerns rather than feelings and emotions.

- Self-orientation. Self-interests tend to predominate over broad social interests.

- Universalism. Standards embedded in such documents as the Constitution and the Bill of Rights are meant to be applied across different situations and groups.

- Achievement. While America is not a classless society, stress is placed on merit rather than group membership.

- Specificity. Obligations to others tend to be narrow and restricted, and well defined in role expectations; for example, doctor, mechanic, salesperson.

Edward T. Hall has spent much of his career determining the implicit messages of different cultural orientations to time, space, material possessions, friendship, and agreements. Differences in these matters present us with unspoken cultural languages that affect relationships. For example, differences in relation to agreements can be quite profound; as Hall says:

Few Americans will conduct any business nowadays without some written agreement or contract . . . Americans consider that negotiations have more or less ceased when the contract is signed. With the Greeks, on the other hand, the contract is seen as a sort of a way station on the route to negotiation that will cease only when the work is completed. The contract is nothing more than a charter for serious negotiations. In the Arab world, once a man's word is given in a particular kind of way, it is just as binding, if not more so, than most of our written contracts. The written contract, therefore, violates the Moslem's sensitivities and reflects on his honor.[14]

Also, in Latin America many things get done because of relationships rather than because of formal agreements or laws. While friendships are not developed so quickly in many other cultures, the friendships do tend to be much deeper and less casual than in the United States and carry more extensive obligations.

Hall found that the languages of space and time are also meaningful. In terms of space, Americans like to be at least an arm's distance from others (as opposed to the 12–18 inches typical in Latin America), and they also demarcate space in terms of status and privilege. To an American, a corner office on a top floor with a window is high status. The French or Japanese supervisor, on the other hand, may well be seated in the middle of his or her employees. For an Arab, the location or size of an office bears little relation to the importance of the person occupying it. Additionally, the American time system is not universal. Americans tend to perceive time as a phenomenon to be sliced into discrete bits—seconds, minutes, hours, and so on—and controlled through the use of detailed and precise schedules and plans. Americans also focus on the immediate present and short-term future rather than the past or long-term future. As Akio Morita, chairman of Sony Corporation, said, "America looks 10 minutes ahead; Japan looks 10 years."[15] Americans also tend to focus on one thing at a time. The American system is alien to Arabic, Southern European, and Latin American cultures that integrate the past into current decisions, have a less precise definition of punctuality, formulate less detailed plans, and tend to focus on many things at once.

Additional research has also been presented by Geert Hofstede in *Culture's Consequences*.[16] Defining culture as "collective programming of the mind," Hofstede identified four major cultural dimensions (among the middle classes) across 66 countries between 1967 and 1973. The four cultural dimensions he identified are:

- **Power Distance.** The degree to which inequality is felt to be desirable or undesirable in a society, and of the levels of dependence and interdependence. In countries with high power distance (such as Malaysia) the holding of power needs less legitimation than in those with lower power distance (such as Austria).

- **Uncertainty Avoidance.** The degree to which uncertainty is perceived as a threat. It deals with the level of anxiety about the future and the protection of society through technology, rules, and rituals. In high uncertainty avoidance countries (such as Guatemala), there is a need for comprehensive rules and regulations, a belief in the power of experts, and a search for absolute truths and values, while in low uncertainty avoidance countries (such as Singapore), there is less emphasis on rules and procedures, a greater reliance on relativism and empiricism, and more of a belief in generalists and common sense.

- **Individualism.** The degree to which individual interests are given priority over the group. In countries with high individualism (such as the United States), the emphasis is upon the self and, at most, the nuclear family. Private life is valued, as is independence, individual initiative, and autonomy.

Countries with low individualism (such as Guatemala) value collectivity. Personal identity is based on membership in a group.

- **Masculinity.** The degree to which achievement and success are given priority over caring for others and the quality of life. Countries high in masculinity (such as Japan) value performance and growth very highly, try to excel, and value work as an end in itself. Countries low in masculinity (such as Norway) have a people rather than a results orientation, see work as a means rather than an end, and focus heavily on the quality of life rather than money and material objects.

Charles Hampden-Turner and Alfons Trompenaars investigated the seven major cultures of capitalism—the United States, Japan, Germany, France, Britain, Sweden, and the Netherlands—in relation to wealth creation. In line with our own view, they argue that "a deep structure of beliefs is the invisible hand that regulates economic activity."[17] Hampden-Turner and Trompenaars identify seven basic valuing processes which are critical to the existence of wealth-creating organizations. For each valuing process they also identify two complementary values which exist in tension in each process (see Table 2–1).

According to Hampden-Turner and Trompenaars, the economic success of a culture will depend on an ability to balance these values in tension. They also

TABLE 2–1
Capitalistic Cultures and Values in Tension

Process	Values in Tension
1. Making rules and discovering exceptions	Need to reconcile universalism (rules of wide generality) with particularism (special exceptions).
2. Constructing and deconstructing	Need to alternate mental and physical process of analysis (breaking down) and integration (putting together).
3. Managing communities of individuals	Need to reconcile individualism of employees, shareholders, and customers with the communitarianism of the larger system.
4. Internalizing the outside world	Need to reconcile inner-direction (those things invented here) with outer-direction (most things not invented here).
5. Synchronizing fast processes	Need to reconcile speed of processes (sequential time) with coordination of processes (synchronized time).
6. Choosing among achievers	Need to balance achieved status (based on performance and results) with ascribed status (based on, for example, age/seniority).
7. Sponsoring equal opportunities to excel	Need to balance equality (of input) with hierarchy (the structure for evaluating the input).

Source: From *The Seven Cultures of Capitalism* by Charles Hampden-Turner and Alfons Trompenaars. Copyright © 1993 by Charles Hampden-Turner. Used by permission of Doubleday, a division of Bantam Doubleday Dell Publishing Group, Inc.

show how different cultures emphasize one value over another. For example, they argue that the United States is being held back in developing a long-term approach to its economic difficulties by the following dominant cultural biases: universalism, analysis, individualism, inner-directedness, achieved status, time-as-sequential, and equality. It is not that the form these values take is wrong. It is just that they have consequences we need to pay attention to and, if necessary, rethink.

Although they were not the first to do so, Hampden-Turner and Trompenaars help us focus our attention on value preferences in patterns of thinking. They refer to Americans as "Analyzers Extraordinary" who spend "more energy deconstructing than constructing." More integrative cultures, such as Japan, France, Germany, and China, may now have the edge as complex systems (those not reducible simply to parts) become increasingly important in establishing and maintaining a competitive advantage.

Stewart and Bennett draw distinctions between American and other patterns of thinking by linking the different styles to a continuum.[18] At the one end of the continuum, the focus is on the sensory aspect of perception, which favors thinking based on concrete description. At the other end, stress is placed on symbolic systems that favor theoretical thinking (see Figure 2–3).

How do such differences manifest themselves? Stewart and Bennett give two examples:[19]

- Production figures in Japan are counts of actual units produced.

- Quality control in Japan is based on the inspection of each item.

Both demonstrate the emphasis placed on concrete description in Japan.

FIGURE 2–3
Some Variations in Thinking Style

Perception-based		*Symbol-based*
Japanese	*American*	*European*
• Direct perception	• Action orientation	• Thought and action
• Concrete description and intuition	• Probability research (general principles)	• Theoretical reasoning
• Meaning attached to immediately perceived events	• Inductive thinking (operation)	• Deductive inquiry (concept development rules-of-thumb)

Source: Adapted from Edward C. Stewart and Milton J. Bennett, *American Cultural Patterns: A Cross-Cultural Perspective,* rev. ed. (Yarmouth, Maine: Intercultural Press, 1991), pp. 28–30.

In contrast, Americans, and to some extent Europeans, will rely more on sampling and the gathering of data to perform risk analyses and probability studies. In an interesting introductory brochure produced by the London Business School, a Japanese student discusses how his experience at the school enabled him to understand differences between how the Japanese, Europeans, and Americans develop strategies for action. He points to how American and European companies will invest a great deal of money in market research and product surveys. In contrast, a Japanese company is more likely to launch a new product (based on informed intuition) and then make product improvements and positioning enhancements based on actual consumer responses. For the Japanese, numbers are a commitment, not a measure of probability.

The American style of inductive thinking is based on analysis: the breaking down of problems into small chunks that can be organized into linear cause-and-effect relations and developed into general principles of action. In juxtaposition to this thinking preference, other cultures—notably in Europe—demonstrate an affinity for deductive thought. Deductive thought places the emphasis on logically deriving principles from theoretical constructs rather than from raw data.

In addition to the contrasting thought patterns described above, Stewart and Bennett and Hampden-Turner and Trompenaars, as well as Stephen Rhinesmith,[20] draw attention to what is known as holistic, big picture, integrative, synthetic, or systems thinking (we will refer to it as systemic thinking). Cultures that value systemic thinking, such as Japan, Singapore, France, and Germany, pay attention to integrated wholes, not just the parts. In such a view, the system has characteristics that cannot be reduced to the parts. Systemic thinking places value on the context, not just the data; without understanding the context we have no real understanding of what the data means. Hampden-Turner and Trompenaars give the following powerful example:[21]

> [A] steep rise in profits may be an "unshakable fact," but it could be most unwise to rely on this as an unambiguous sign of virtue. Depending on the context, this could mean the company has switched to larger, gas-guzzling cars with higher margins, that less value is being given to consumers as compared with shareholders, that the volume auto business is being ceded to Japanese imports, and that the whole industry is headed for a precipice.

What can we learn from the above? The work of all the authors mentioned in this section provides us with insights into the different value orientations held by cultures across the globe. However, unlike Hampden-Turner and Trompenaars (and other cultural commentators like Lawrence Harrison in *Who Prospers*[22] or Joel Kotkin in *Tribes*[23]), we are not trying to demonstrate how cultural values relate to economic success. Our task is to provide managers with a framework, a vocabulary, for understanding and working with cultural differences, not evaluating their economic utility. We are attempting to pull this work together into a mental model that will empower managers to find their feet in unfamiliar cultural environments, and help them transfer their understanding of *culture* across cultures.

As mentioned earlier, cultural competence is about more than understanding the intricacies of bowing in Japan or the inappropriateness of accepting food with the left hand in Saudi Arabia. Cultural competence is the ability to recognize the primary cultural orientations of ourselves and others and to be conscious of the potential impact of these differences on working relationships. It involves going beyond the explicit components of a culture, and working with the implicit value orientations that shape and motivate behavior. We now turn to a conceptual model that presents an organizational framework for understanding the key components of culture. It also provides executives and managers with a tool for analyzing their cross-cultural encounters and for determining appropriate strategies for effective cross-cultural exchange.

A MODEL OF KEY CULTURAL ORIENTATIONS

Anyone who has travelled abroad understands the feeling of disorientation that can be induced when coming into contact with cultural differences. Usually referred to as "culture shock," this phenomenon may cause feelings of depression, aggressiveness, resentment, superiority, inferiority, curiosity, excitement, loneliness, fear, frustration, and so on. We have talked about being unable to find our feet in another culture. Another way to look at this is to think of being in an unfamiliar culture as being in the middle of an ocean. To navigate through this ocean, you need to be able to get your bearings by relating yourself to specific features in the environment, for example, the sun, moon, stars, and the horizon. When trying to get our bearings in a new culture, we can also pay attention to a number of key features—the dominant value orientations of the culture.

A key question is value orientations toward what? Given the findings of the anthropologists, psychologists, communication experts, and business consultants listed in the previous section, as well as our own experiences in teaching cross-cultural seminars to thousands of executives and managers throughout the world, we have chosen 10 variables (and 36 relevant orientations to those variables—see Figure 2–4 and Table 2–2) that have been of practical value to international businesspeople in distinguishing between cultures and guiding key decisions.

CULTURAL ORIENTATIONS AND
BUSINESS PRACTICES

Now that you have an overall picture of the framework, it is time to consider each piece separately. As you read through the descriptions of the different cultural orientations, it is important to keep the following distinction in mind. Generalizations are an important starting point for any kind of study; it is difficult to think of any field of inquiry that does not depend on generalizations. But in the field of

FIGURE 2–4
A Cultural Orientations Framework

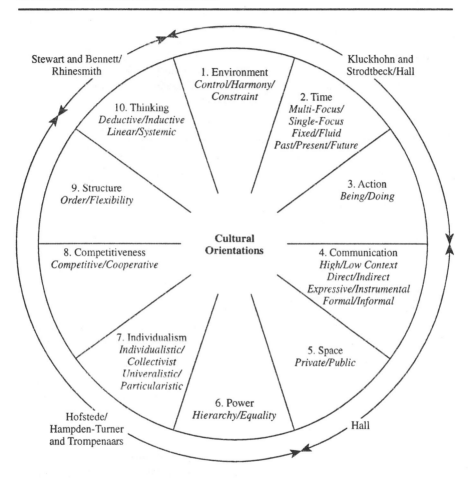

The variables are listed in the circle as: 1. Environment; 2. Time; and so on. The key cultural orientations are in italics beneath each variable. See Table 2–2 for a brief description of each orientation.

Source: © Training Management Corp. (TMC), *Doing Business Internationally: The Cross-Cultural Challenges*, Seminar and Coursebook (Princeton, NJ, 1992).

cross-cultural studies, generalizations become destructive when they degenerate into stereotypes. Generalizations are open to review and change; stereotypes are closed systems of belief. No matter what new information is presented, the stereotype channels it into the pre-existing categories (either positive or negative). Although we generalize about Asian, European, Latin American, and

TABLE 2–2
Cultural Orientations: A Summary

Variable	Description of Different Value Orientations toward Variable	
Environment	*Control:*	People can dominate their environment; it can be changed to fit human needs.
	Harmony:	People should live in harmony with the world around them.
	Constraint:	People are constrained by the world around them. Fate, luck, and change play a significant role.
Time	*Single-Focus:*	Concentration on one task at a time; high commitment to schedules.
	Multi-Focus:	Emphasis on multiple tasks and relationships rather than deadlines.
	Fixed:	Punctuality defined precisely.
	Fluid:	Punctuality defined somewhat loosely.
	Past:	High value placed on continuance of traditions.
	Present:	Short-term orientation aimed at quick results.
	Future:	Willingness to trade short-term gain for long-term results.
Action	*Doing:*	Task centered. Stress placed on productive activity in goal accomplishment and achievement.
	Being:	Relationship-centered. Stress placed on working for the moment, experience rather than accomplishment.
Communication	*High context:*	Shared experience makes certain things understood without them needing to be stated explicitly. Rules for speaking and behaving are implicit in the context.
	Low context:	Exchange of facts and information is stressed. Information is given primarily in words, and meaning is expressed explicitly.
	Direct:	Preference for explicit one- or two-way communication, including identification, diagnosis, and management of conflict.
	Indirect:	Preference for implicit communication and conflict avoidance.
	Expressive:	Emotive and personal communication style with high degree of subjectivity. Stress on relationships.
	Instrumental:	Unemotional and impersonal communication style with high degree of objectivity. Stress on task achievement.
	Formal:	High emphasis on following protocol and social customs.

TABLE 2–2 (continued)

Variable		Description of Different Value Orientations toward Variable
	Informal:	Stress on dispensing with ceremony and rigid protocol.
Space	*Private:*	Individual orientation to the use of physical space. Preference for distance between individuals.
	Public:	Group orientation to the use of physical space. Preference for close proximity.
Power	*Hierarchy:*	Value placed on power differences between individuals and groups.
	Equality:	Value placed on the minimization of levels of power.
Individualism	*Individualistic:*	The "I" predominates over the "we." Independence is highly valued.
	Collectivist:	Individual interests are subordinate to group interests. Identity is based on the social network. Loyalty is highly valued.
	Universalistic:	Focus is placed on abstract rules before relationships. What is true, correct, and appropriate can be identified and applied to everyone. Societal obligations are emphasized.
	Particularistic:	Focus is placed on relationships before abstract rules. Weight is given to changing circumstances and personal obligations.
Competitiveness	*Competitive:*	Achievement, assertiveness, and material success are reinforced.
	Cooperative:	Stress is placed on the quality of life, interdependence, and relationships.
Structure	*Order:*	High need for predictability and rules, written and unwritten. Conflict is threatening.
	Flexibility:	Tolerance of unpredictable situations and ambiguity. Dissent is acceptable.
Thinking	*Inductive:*	Reasoning based on experience and experimentation.
	Deductive:	Reasoning based on theory and logic.
	Linear:	Preference for analytical thinking, which breaks problems into small chunks.
	Systematic:	Preference for holistic thinking, which focuses on the big picture and the interrelationships between components.

Source: Training Management Corp. (TMC), *Doing Business Internationally: The Cross-Cultural Challenges,* Seminar and Coursebook (Princeton, NJ, 1992).

Middle Eastern cultures in this book, don't lock yourself into the information given here. Always be open to new information that can offer you new insights and a richer and deeper understanding of inter- and intra-cultural nuances. Every culture contains each one of the orientations; the key difference among cultures is in emphasis.

Environment

Sue and Sue draw attention to the fact that groups operate with dissimilar orientations as to the locus of control in the world.[24] Internal control defines a people's belief that individuals and groups can shape their own destiny, control their own environment. External control defines the belief that events are determined by chance, luck, or a supernatural force.

Control orientation.   Control cultures say things like: "Go for it," "Life is what you make of it," "Don't let anything stand in your way," "Hard work and perseverance pay off," "You got a problem, fix it." In this view, the environment, including other people, can be molded to fit human needs. The future can be planned for, and organization structures and systems can be put in place and controlled in order to achieve goals and objectives. Plans tend to be very detailed, precise, task centered, and aimed at producing results that are measurable and reproducible. Risk analysis is routine and is based upon a forecast of the forces to be overcome. Organizational thinking tends to be very analytic and linear, with problems broken down into small manageable components and processes charted in sophisticated critical paths and project maps. It is assumed that individual leaders can take charge and push through changes and that staff will be evaluated on their ability to implement appropriate actions, impact bottom-line performance, and add value to the organization.

Western societies tend to be highly control oriented; problems are opportunities just waiting for solutions. One saying among the volunteers working to stem the 1993 Mississippi flood was, "Problems are opportunities dressed in work clothes." Certainly, most Americans believe that people can master their environment. Problems should be attacked head-on, and any conflict arising from the effort should be dealt with in the same direct manner. High value is also placed on systematic organizing, monitoring, and control systems.

Sociologist Max Weber, in *The Protestant Ethic and the Spirit of Capitalism,* demonstrated a relationship between systems of religious and ethical belief and economic outcomes. He showed how such cultural *control* phenomena as saving, investment, and entrepreneurship have been nurtured by Protestant Calvinism with its asceticism and doctrines of calling and election. Lawrence Harrison describes these doctrines and Weber's contribution as follows:[25]

> Calling requires an individual to discharge the personal and social responsibilities of his or own station in life; election is the doctrine that God has blessed a chosen few

whose state of grace is apparent from their prosperity . . . he [Weber] believed that the Roman Catholic emphasis on the afterlife and what he perceived as a more flexible ethical system put Catholics at a disadvantage to Protestants and Jews in this life: "The God of Calvinism demanded of his believers not single good works, but a life of good works combined into a unified system. There was no place for the very human Catholic cycle of sin, repentance, atonement, release, followed by renewed sin."

While religion is only one factor nurturing a *control* orientation, it has undoubtedly been, and will continue to be, a powerful shaping force.

Harmony orientation.   Harmony cultures say things like: "Don't make waves," "Don't rock the boat," "Go with the flow." In this view, people are an integral part of nature, and their actions and thoughts should facilitate harmonious relations with the world and with others. Cultures that emphasize harmony believe that plans should set challenging goals but have flexibility built in to allow for environmental changes. Risk forecasting is part of the planning process, but it is understood that not all risks can be controlled. Decision making may take longer in such a culture because of the need to involve many different parties and build consensus. Organizational thinking will tend to be holistic (big picture) and cross-functional rather than strictly analytical and narrowly focused. Leaders will need to facilitate harmonious relationships and provide staff with stability.

Asian cultures with such embedded belief systems as Confucianism, Taoism, and Buddhism stress harmonious relations with the world. As the *Tao Te Ching* written in China in the sixth century B.C. says:[26]

Attain the highest openness;
Maintain the deepest harmony.
Become a part of all things;
In this way I perceive the cycles.

External harmony is related to harmony within. Decision making in such a culture is aimed at facilitating harmonious relations with nature and with others. For example, a Japanese friend recently told us that the Walkman players sold in Japan have in-built volume limitation; they are audible to users, but inaudible to someone standing next to the user. Here is one small example of how culture affects decision making and product design. At a recent multicultural sales training program we conducted in New York, we were interested to hear from our Chinese participants on how difficult it can be to sell a house to the Chinese. Several stories were told of Chinese buyers refusing to buy houses in cul-de-sacs or on land with large trees. The realtor was told that a cul-de-sac is a road that goes nowhere and, therefore, living on such a street could harm the occupant's career. Big trees could also potentially block a person's career. These decisions are rooted in the Chinese concept of *feng shui,* which is that earth forces affect success or failure.

Constraint orientation.   Constraint cultures say things like: "It's a matter of luck," "It's fate," "Insh'allah" (Allah willing), "You take what life gives you," "If God wishes it to be so." From this perspective, it is presumptuous to claim direct control over a business—or any other—environment. This orientation can be seen in societies that stress the influence of external forces, the cycles of time, and resource limitations rather than the impact of personal actions.

Latin American and Middle Eastern cultures display a constraint orientation. In the past, we worked with a Venezuelan consultant on a training project for a major telecommunications company. We called the consultant to arrange a meeting with her in New York. The consultant replied, "I will be there unless, of course, it rains and there is a problem with the train." We were a little surprised by her response (being Americans with a control orientation) and took her answer to mean she had reservations about the meeting. Being polite, we asked if she would like to switch the meeting, or rethink her involvement in the project. Offended, she said, "No, of course I don't. I'll be there. But you know how things are. A storm is expected, and I hope my daughter doesn't get sick." The emphasis on external forces continued to shock us, and we seriously doubted if we could work with this consultant. But as we grew to understand her constraint orientation, our relationship strengthened and we found a workable approach to functioning together.

Planning in constraint cultures will tend to be at the strategic rather than the detailed level. Things get done through relationships rather than an emphasis on monitoring and control systems.

A poignant example of the constraint orientation in the United States is highlighted by the sociologist Charles Lemert in a discussion of Alex Kotlowitz's book *There Are No Children Here*.[27] In this book, Kotlowitz tells the story of two boys living in a dangerous Chicago public housing project. In a telling moment, Lafeyette—a ten year old—says, "If I grow up, I want to be a bus driver." The use of *if* carries a world of cultural meaning that abstract theories cannot convey.

Time

As Edward T. Hall says, "Time talks. It speaks more plainly than words."[28] Our use of time, therefore, conveys powerful messages about how we relate to each other and the world around us.

Single-Focus.   Single-Focus cultures demonstrate a high commitment to doing one task at a time and meeting set deadlines. Such cultures say things like, "Let's get down to business" or "Let's get down to the job at hand." The focus is on the task rather than the relationships through which the task will get done. Plans and schedules tend to be detailed, followed quite strictly, and changed infrequently. Step-by-step performance of tasks is the model for organizing work flow. Meetings will tend to be highly focused, with a set agenda and a time frame for each item.

In general, Americans and those of Northern European heritage are single-focus individuals. Asian cultures that have fully industrialized (such as Taiwan, Japan, Singapore, Hong Kong, and South Korea) have generally adopted a single-focus approach to time, although the emphasis on relationship-building is still very strong.

Multi-Focus. In multi-Focused cultures, greater emphasis is placed on doing simultaneous tasks with a high commitment to relationship building rather than just task completion or meeting arbitrary deadlines. Tasks will be completed through the strength of the relationships rather than complicated plans. Hall describes a friend of his—of Spanish heritage—who might have up to fifteen people in his office at any one time.[29] It is not unusual to be in a business meeting in Southern Europe or Latin America and suddenly find yourself in several meetings at once. Cultures in the Middle East also tend to be multifocused. It can be very frustrating for a manager from a single-focus culture to find himself or herself being continually interrupted. To a single-focus person, this kind of approach is considered rude. To a multifocus person, not attending to an important task or relationship at once—even while in the middle of another meeting—would be rude.

Fixed. Cultures with a fixed time orientation say things like "Time is money," "Get it done yesterday," and "Every second counts," and they define punctuality precisely. Meetings are expected to begin on time, and deadlines and schedules are taken seriously. Edward T. Hall comments,[30] "People of the Western world, particularly Americans, tend to think of time as something fixed in nature, something around us from which we cannot escape." Time is sliced into fixed categories, such as seconds, minutes, and hours, and is scheduled and managed in great detail. To be perceived as "wasting time" is unethical. American, German, and Swiss cultures are particularly time conscious. Speed is of the essence, and time management is perceived as critical at work and at home. "Soon" to an American usually means in the next few minutes, hours, or days. "Soon" to someone from an Asian culture may mean three months, six months, a year, or simply "When we're ready."

Fluid. Cultures with a fluid time orientation define punctuality in looser terms. Some delays are expected, and deadlines and other commitments are not written in stone. Rather than being divided into fixed categories, time is perceived to be an organic, flowing process more related to the prolonged agricultural seasons than to industrial seconds, minutes, and hours. Nancy Adler tells the story of an American engineer working in Bahrain. The American engineer was profusely apologetic when explaining that the opening of the plant under construction would be delayed by six months. To the American's surprise, the Bahrainian's response was: "We have lived for thousands of years without this plant; we can easily wait another six months or a year. This is no problem."[31] When sending a package to an island in the Caribbean, we were warned several times to take account of "island time." The package might arrive at the island the day after we mailed it, but then it might take a week or so to arrive at its final destination.

Past/Present/Future.   Past-oriented cultures say things like, "Keep up the tradition" or "It doesn't fit with who we are," and place a high value on the maintenance of historical sensibilities. Ancestor worship and strong family traditions relate to this preference. The prevalent view in historical China was that nothing new ever happened in the present or would happen in the future. Everything had happened before in the distant past. Kluckhohn and Strodtbeck tell the story of a proud American who thought he was showing some Chinese a steamboat for the first time. The Chinese remarked, "Our ancestors had such a boat two thousand years ago."[32] In this orientation, plans need to *fit* with what has happened previously, and they tend to have long time frames if they introduce relatively significant change. Precedents guide decision making, organizing, and controlling, including the hiring of staff who should fit well-established criteria and demonstrate loyalty and adherence to accepted norms, policies, and procedures. In such a culture, the leader is expected to carry the vision of the past into the future, for change is not valued for its own sake. The past is always the context for evaluating the present.

Present-oriented cultures aim for quick results and stress the "here and now." This orientation can be seen in proverbs like "Take care of today, and tomorrow will take care of itself" or "Don't look back." Organizations in such cultures will formulate short-term plans, divide and coordinate resources based on present demands, and select and train employees to meet current goals.

Future-oriented cultures demonstrate a willingness to trade short-term gains for long-term results. Organizations in such cultures will divide and coordinate work and resources to meet longer-range goals and projections of the future. Recruitment and professional development will be directed at future needs, not just those in the present.

American culture displays a short-term and near-future orientation. In the United States, an annual report will focus on the activity of the past year and the goals of the company for perhaps the next five years. This does not mean, however, that Americans are content with the present; they focus on change within pragmatic and defined boundaries. East Asian cultures, in general, are both past and future oriented; they emphasize the goals and traditions of the past as well as long-term plans for the future. Japanese annual reports explore both the history and philosophy of the company as well as lay out business plans that may stretch 100 or 250 years into the future. It is also not uncommon in Japan to have multigenerational (i.e., 100 year long) mortgages for houses. Middle Eastern cultures tend to be strongly rooted in the traditions and customs of the past. Latin American societies honor past traditions, are present oriented, and display a future orientation in that business relationships are forged for the long term. European cultures honor tradition, but they also display a future orientation. In general, European business plans are longer term than those of the United States, but shorter than those of Asia.

Action

The action orientation focuses on a person's relationship to activities. Both doing and being cultures are active; a being culture should not be thought of as passive. The difference tends to lie in whether the primary mode of activity is task driven or relationship driven.

Doing.   In doing cultures, emphasis is placed on achieving external, measurable accomplishments, achieving goals, and improving standards of living. Doing cultures say things like "God helps those who help themselves" or "If at first you don't succeed, try, try, again." Motivation is achievement based; performance objectives are given, performance is measured against set standards, and rewards such as bonuses, recognition, promotions, and so on, are given on the basis of goal achievement.

Dr. Stephen Rhinesmith, author of *A Manager's Guide to Globalization: Six Keys to Success in a Changing World,* once told us the story of the time he stayed with a host family in Germany as part of an exchange program. One day his German "brother" announced they were going to visit his friend Hans. "Great," Steve said, "What are we going to do when we get there?" Puzzled, his "brother" repeated the information, "We are going to visit Hans." Thinking his "brother" had not heard him, Steve repeated the question: "Yes, but what are we going to *do* when we visit with Hans?" Steve, coming from a high doing culture, could not comprehend a visit that did not revolve around "doing something" like bowling or some other activity.

One of the authors was very surprised on arriving in the United States from England at always being asked, "What do you do?" He not only found the question rude and intrusive, but also constraining. He didn't like the feeling of being defined by what he did for a living, rather than who he was as a person. In cross-cultural training seminars, we will often ask the participants, "Who are you?" not just once, but several times. Invariably, Americans will answer with their job titles, and only later with family information or personal interests. Latin Americans, Africans, and those from the Middle East will tend to answer with an affiliation-type answer, such as family, clan, or tribe name. Europeans, in their first three answers, will often answer with a brief description of their humanistic or philosophical outlook.

Being.   While members of doing cultures stress tasks and achievements, those in Being cultures stress their affiliations, character, and personal qualities. Emphasis is placed on quality of life, on nurturing, caring, and relationships. Job satisfaction has value over task accomplishments, and motivation is based less on the promise of future rewards and more on factors related to the quality of organizational life, such as relationships with superiors and peers, the work environment, and challenging, interesting work. In strong being cultures, business is awarded not simply on prior accomplishments and technical merit, but on personal compatibility, trust, affiliations, and personal and organizational considerations.

A strong being orientation is demonstrated in the Middle East, Latin America, and many Southeast Asian countries. One night in September 1992, one of the authors was driving home from the office and listening to National Public Radio. The story being broadcast related to Syria lifting travel restrictions on Jews living in that country. A Jewish businessman in Damascus was talking about his friends who now wanted to go to America but were worried about the culture they would find there. To paraphrase what he said: There's no time in New York. Here you can sit with a cup of coffee and develop a relationship. You visit a friend's business in New York, and they don't even have a chair for you to sit down. East Asian cultures, such as Japan, tend to display both doing and being orientations in business in that there is an emphasis on task achievement and relationship building.

Communication

A culture's orientation to communication is often very subtle. Differences in communication preference cause a multitude of problems in sales, negotiation, performance appraisals, teamwork, and so on.

High context.   High-context cultures are also relationship centered. In such cultures, a great deal of contextual information is needed about an individual or a company before business can be transacted. Business is personal and trust is critical to the relationship; little gets done without it. A significant amount of time may be spent on what Americans might consider to be small talk, such as family issues, food and drink, the weather. As a Japanese business man said to one of the authors, "Every business relationship should begin with a sake party." In addition, the communication of meaning is transmitted not just in words, but relies heavily on group understandings of voice tone, body language, facial expressions, eye contact, speech patterns, use of silence, past interactions, status, and common friends. Meaning tends to be implicit rather than direct, and less literal. For example, in various Asian cultures, a "yes" may mean "yes," "maybe," "I don't know," "If you say so," or "I hope I have said this unenthusiastically enough for you to understand that I mean no." The precise meaning depends on the context, not just the words. Greeting rituals—as in business card exchange in Japan—may be elaborate. Also, information may not be communicated in a linear form—moving directly to a conclusion through a series of logical step⁵. It is more important for the high-context speaker to establish the broad context in which the conclusion makes sense. The order in which this contextual information is presented is secondary to the formation of the contextual whole. In such cultures, as Stewart and Bennett point out, "Conclusions are often not stated explicitly; it is up to the listener to divine the conclusion implied by the context."[33]

Shared experience in group-oriented societies makes certain things understood without them needing to be stated explicitly. Silence, therefore, plays an important role in high-context cultures. Silence in Asian cultures is active, not passive. An American dealing with, for example, a Japanese, may become anxious to fill silences. Silence in Asia designates thought, not disengagement. Rushing in to fill a silence may be considered pushy or impulsive, or even emotional. Silence can also be a strategy for helping others to save face, to take advantage of another's impatience, or to leave options open. We can see this latter strategy at work in the following extract from a short story by the Japanese writer, Yuko Tsushima called "The Silent Traders":[34]

> I don't know when there will be another opportunity for the children to see the man. They may never meet him again, or they may have a chance two or three years from now. I do know that the man and I will probably never be completely indifferent to each other. He's still on my mind in some obscure way. Yet there's no point in confirming this feeling in words. Silence is essential. As long as we maintain silence, and thus avoid trespassing, we leave open the possibility of resuming negotiations at any time.

Most cultures outside of the Anglo-American, Swiss, and German cultures are middle to high context. In conducting business in a high-context culture, therefore, it is not only important to communicate your own and the company's expertise, it also becomes important to provide your own and your company's contextual frame—education, work background, family, political and social connections, philosophical beliefs, affiliations, and experience. The primary purpose of communication in high-context cultures is to form and develop relationships rather than exchange facts and information. In relationship forming, communication often becomes an art form rather than a utilitarian activity; you may often see this stress on communication as art in Latin American cultures where eloquence is highly valued. The emphasis on relationships also places a high value on the concept of "saving face." Plans in high-context cultures tend to be implicit rather than explicit, depending more on relationships for implementation than detailed instructions. Contracts also tend to be fairly short and general in scope, placing faith in the spirit of the agreement rather than numerous written clauses. One of our clients wanted to open a second office in Saudi Arabia. The company brought a number of lawyers to the contract meetings, wanted many contingency plans, and loaded the contract with details. The negotiations went on for months with little progress. The Saudis refused to sign the contract, saying that it was too specific.

Low context.   Low-context cultures are primarily task centered. Business tends to be impersonal. Relatively little information is needed about an individual or a company before business can be transacted. Trust and compatibility are not primary considerations when doing business. Meaning is communicated directly and explicitly, and the words used are the most important carriers of meaning. The primary function of communication in low-context cultures is to exchange information, facts, and opinions. Low-context cultures say things like, "Let's get to the point," or "Just give me the bottom line," "Let's get down to business," or "Lay it on the line." The low-context individual is impatient with details, digressions, and the lengthy establishment of context. The low-context American is likely to say "So what!" to much contextual information.

In a low-context culture, job descriptions, authority relationships, monitoring and control procedures, and task and responsibility guidelines are communicated through detailed oral or, most likely, written instructions. Good relationships between the parties involved are not considered to be critical for tasks to be accomplished. In addition, the criteria and methods for recruitment, selection, compensation, and firing will be stated explicitly. Performance appraisals will be impersonal and direct. Plans tend to be very explicit and detailed.

A high-context person will often find a low-context person's directness uncomfortable and rude. A low-context person will often find a high-context person shifty, hard-to-read, and unclear.

Direct.   Direct cultures meet conflict head on. They say things like "Let's deal with this, right now!" or "Give it to me straight." Communication in such a society tends to be either one-way or two-way. In one-way communication, information flows down the system in the form of orders and directives. Conflict is dealt with from the top by means of power and force. With the emphasis on following orders and instructions, there is little, if any, participative management or teamwork. In two-way communication, information flows up and down the system. Conflict is handled on an interpersonal basis by negotiation, and employees will feel free to discuss issues with their superiors. There is often a high level of participation and teamwork, and time is taken to build consensus.

Americans can find indirect communication frustrating. It doesn't sit with their "Let's get down to business," "Say what you mean, mean what you say," and "Fight for what you want" mentality. For the indirect communicator, such bluntness is perceived as aggressive and ill-mannered. Even continued direct eye contact in Japan is considered to be rude. The direct manager working in an indirect culture must develop a high tolerance for ambiguity; he or she cannot interpret everything at face value. Richard Mead clearly summarizes the direct/indirect trade-off when he says, "There is a trade-off between directness, which gets your purpose across but can create resentment and hence be less persuasive, and indirectness, which maintains a cordial relationship but at the risk of misunderstanding."[35]

Indirect. Indirect cultures use a mix of conflict avoidance and third parties to handle conflict. Much indirectness in communication is the desire to save "face," protect honor, and avoid shame. Such indirectness is maintained by a number of strategies (see Table 2–3).

As Stephen Rhinesmith points out in his monograph *Cultural Organizational Analysis*,[36] friends in Latin America may be asked to act as an intermediary between boss and subordinates. In India, the tradition of parents acting as intermediaries in arranged marriages reflects and reinforces the indirect patterns of communication and decision making found in organizations.

The Japanese tend to be very indirect in handling conflict and negative thoughts. Such communication tends to be highly ritualized and understated.

Americans are direct in both one-way and two-way modes. The one-way orientation is still found in many business organizations, but there has been a tendency in recent years to seek to leverage input from all levels within organizations by opening up a two-way flow.

Directness should not be confused with aggressiveness (although it can be interpreted as such). Maintaining a membrane of civility and politeness is evident in the United States and in other direct cultures in the west. The American style of communication (including direct eye contact) can be perceived as highly competitive, adversarial, and impersonal to those used to an indirect style. It is easy

TABLE 2–3
Indirect Communication Strategies

Strategy	Description
Mediation	A third person is used as a go-between.
Refraction	Statements intended for person A are made to person B while person A is present.
Covert revelation	A person portrays himself or herself as a messenger for another in order to state own opinions, or a person allows some kind of self-communication, such as notes or a diary, to fall into the hands of another party.
Correspondence	Allows communication to occur without the parties being actually present.
Anticipation	Understatement and unobtrusive behavior based on empathy allow accommodation to the unspoken needs of the other person.
Ritual	Rituals help maintain control of uncertain situations.

Source: Adapted from Edward C. Stewart and Milton J. Bennett, *American Cultural Patterns: A Cross-Cultural Perspective,* rev. ed. (Yarmouth, Maine: Intercultural Press, 1991), pp. 97–98.

for an American to come across as pushy and insincere. This can be a distinct disadvantage in, for example, sales and marketing.

Expressive.   Expressive cultures are not shy when it comes to displaying emotions. Such cultures are less concerned with the precision of communication than with the establishment and maintenance of personal and social
connections. Those who hide their emotions may be perceived as "cold fish" or
even deceitful.

Emotions in the expressive workplace may run high. Voices may be raised in
anger, joy, or another intense emotion. Body language is likely to be demonstra-
tive, and touching or hugging may be considered an acceptable form of behavior
among acquaintances.

Expression may be raised to the level of an art form, and eloquence and sub-
tlety may be highly valued. Latin American, Middle Eastern, and Southern and
Eastern European cultures can be highly expressive.

Instrumental.   Instrumental communication is problem centered,
pragmatic, impersonal, and goal oriented. *What* is said is placed above *how*
something is said. Stress is placed on the accuracy of the communication rather
than its appropriateness or style. The primary objective is to reach a factual, objective, unemotional conclusion that leads to action. Displays of emotion are perceived as lacking in professionalism or rationality.

Being "out of control" is frowned upon and causes embarrassment. The ideal
in such cultures is to keep emotions hidden as much as possible, even under
stress. The English refer to this as "keeping a stiff upper lip." The Japanese also
shy away from being overly expressive, especially in the workplace. Outside of
work, and among friends, they are likely to display a more expressive orientation.
Americans tend toward the instrumental end of the spectrum, but are more expressive than, for example, the Japanese and the English.

The meeting of expressive and instrumental people in business situations can
have mixed results. Individuals with instrumental orientations may interpret expressive individuals as difficult, embarrassing, or irrational. As Hoecklin points
out, there is no reason to believe that emotions held in check will be less detrimental to reason than those expressed.[37] It is critical to suspend judgment and not
get defensive. On the other hand, instrumental individuals may find being in an
expressive environment invigorating and even liberating.

Formal.   Formal cultures say things like, "There's a proper way to do
things, and an improper way." Formal cultures place a high value on following
business protocol and social customs. Such cultures tend to have a strong sense
of history, national culture, and tradition. There also tends to be a stronger class
or hierarchy consciousness and a respect for rules and procedures. The businessperson shows sincerity and seriousness by observing appropriate customs
and rituals, such as dress, greetings, business card exchange, forms of address,

scheduling and conducting meetings, eating and drinking, entertaining, and gift giving. Relationships in formal cultures tend to build more slowly, but once developed are deeper and more permanent.

Plans in formal cultures are developed through the "proper channels," and appropriate procedures are followed. Organizations in such cultures tend to be hierarchical, and communication with superiors tends to be more indirect and guided by protocol. When hiring new personnel, a great deal of consideration is given to how the person will fit into, or adapt to, the system of rules and regulations. Managers establish trust by adhering to business and social customs and by leading from within the established norms of behavior.

Latin American, Arab, Asian and European cultures are all formal to varying degrees.

Informal.   Informal cultures say things like: "Let's get rid of the red tape" or "Let's just be ourselves." Such cultures tend to place a high value on change and give minimal significance to historical continuity. Progress is perceived as being of higher value than custom. Individuals from informal cultures tend to feel uncomfortable with social or power differences, want to be more direct and candid when communicating, and want to establish a friendly, relaxed atmosphere when doing business. They may also place more emphasis on the observance of schedules or deadlines rather than on the maintenance of image or status.

The United States and Australia are widely considered to be two of the most informal cultures in the world. In a recent global management seminar we ran for one of our health care clients, there was a sole Japanese participant among about 25 mainstream Americans. Asked to introduce himself, the Japanese participant used his first name. The instructor asked him if he felt uncomfortable using the American custom of calling each other by first name. He said he did not, and that it had been difficult for him to adjust to this practice since he had come to the States a few months earlier. He was asked how he would like to be addressed, to which he replied "Kawata-san" (Kawata being his last name and "san" being a polite form of address). For the remainder of the class, that is how everyone addressed him, and he felt much more comfortable participating in the group.

It is also worth taking note of the extent to which a culture's formal–informal orientation is embedded in its language. English is one of the few languages that does not differentiate between formal and informal forms of address (for example, tu/vous in French, tu/usted in Spanish, and du/sie in German). In many Asian languages, there are multiple forms of address with varying degrees of formality.

Space

Cultures can be categorized according to the distinctions they make between public and private spaces. This includes distances between individuals as well as the organization of work space. It is often useful to think about cultural space in terms of two questions: How much space do people want around them? and How is this space organized?

Public.   Public space cultures will contain private, personal spaces, but the primary orientation is toward open public space. In terms of office space, this will entail large, open rooms with few partitions, and managers may be sitting in the midst of their employees. A Japanese office may look like the drawing in Figure 2–5.

In this instance, the department manager sits at the head of the front of the room (furthest from the exit) with his back to the window. Status is not indicated by proximity to a window; in fact, it can indicate that you are good for very little, and can only stare out of the window. Smaller sections are grouped in such a way that individuals face each other. This facilitates group communication and control.

Public space cultures tend toward relationship-centered organizations, and location of office space is not necessarily an indicator of status, although in a

FIGURE 2–5
Typical Japanese Office Space

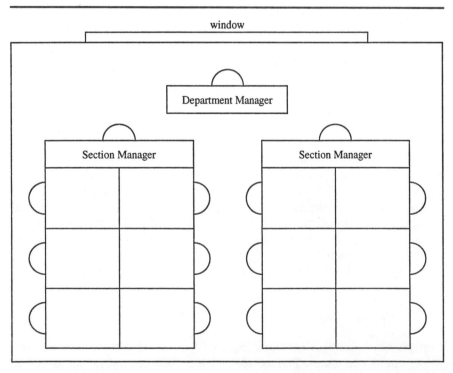

French office, the key person is the one in the middle, the one who "has his fingers on everything so that all runs smoothly."[38] On the one hand, public space allows more personal and informal interaction between managers and employees. On the other hand, it also facilitates centralized authority and more authoritarian monitoring and control systems. Such a use of space fits with the Japanese collective orientation summed up in the saying, "The nail that sticks out begs to be hit down," and with its need for high structure.

   Private.   Private space cultures work within individual offices or rooms divided by partitions or cubicles. There is an increased emphasis on closed-door meetings with minimal interruptions. Permission is also needed to enter a private space. In contrast with Japanese office space, an American office looks something like Figure 2–6.

   The highest-level manager is likely to have the largest corner office, and other managers have offices with windows. One or two rooms with windows may be reserved for conference rooms. Employees are located in private cubicles on the remainder of the floor. The manager is not overseeing the employees as such.

FIGURE 2–6
Typical American Office Space

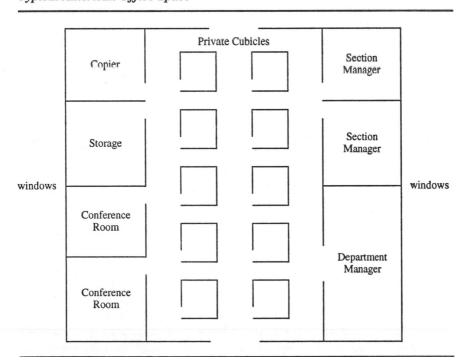

Each employee is an individual with assigned tasks that will be performed in a largely independent manner. Groups of employees may come together for short periods (in the conference room) and then return to their private work spaces to complete their assignments.

In terms of personal space, cultures can be differentiated by the distance considered to be acceptable for conducting business. In the West, people tend to stand farther apart and tend not to touch during conversation. A comfortable social distance for Latin Americans or Arabs is equivalent to a personal or intimate distance for most Americans, and touching is frequent.

Power

Hierarchy.   Hierarchical cultures say things like: "Know your place," "Don't go around the boss," "Respect your betters." Power and authority are centralized, and organizational structure—in terms of highly demarcated levels—is tightly controlled. Managers are expected to behave in ways that reinforce their standing. An informal American manager arriving in Mexico, for example, and bringing all levels of his or her staff together for a meeting to get their input might soon find that he or she has a credibility problem. The boss is the boss. Respect for position is seen as vital to the maintenance of company operations.

Knud Christensen, a Danish personnel manager with BP (British Petroleum) Oil Europe, explains that "the company promotes 'upward feedback' under which managers comment on their bosses' performance. That works well in Scandinavia, Britain, and the Netherlands, where managers tend not to be overly intimidated by their superiors. But it is more difficult in France, Turkey, and Greece, where tradition calls for showing more deference toward authorities. Managers in such countries might be less direct in providing their feedback."[39]

Planning in such cultures is autocratic and paternalistic. On the whole, managers make decisions without consulting with lower levels, work will not bypass the chain of command, employees expect managers to take the initiative for subordinate training and development, and plans will be implemented according to the manager's wishes. A great deal of political thinking may go into the planning, as appropriate relationships and connections may be the only way for the plan to be put into place. Anyone negotiating with a hierarchy culture needs to command respect by having an appropriate title and status.

Arab, most Latin American, and Asian cultures have a higher tolerance for hierarchy than Western cultures do. The Latin American exceptions include Argentina and Costa Rica, which have been heavily influenced by Anglo cultures in Europe. Within Europe itself, France, Belgium, Spain, and Turkey also demonstrate a high tolerance for hierarchy. A client of ours in a telecommunications company organized a conference for the Americas region. To introduce the conference, she planned a social event for all levels (from secretaries up to managing directors) in order to help foster a sense of teamwork. It backfired, however, when the Mexico office more or less boycotted the event. All levels were insulted; hierarchical levels were expected to be adhered to at work and in social gatherings.

Many American companies are now giving their international managers two sets of business cards: one to use in the United States and one to use overseas. This is in recognition of the fact that in many cultures it is not appropriate for high-ranking directors or vice presidents to negotiate or communicate with lower-ranking managers. An American supervisor of training may need to print director of training or senior vice president of training on his or her business card when traveling abroad.

Equality.   In equality cultures, inequality is thought to be an unsatisfactory condition, and attempts are made to minimize it through legal and political means. Organizations tend to be flatter, and power is decentralized; organizational structure aims to encourage individual autonomy and responsibility. In general, employees in equality cultures don't accept that a manager has an automatic right to more power and privileges; they must be earned—and to some extent shared. The manager is perceived as a consultant figure rather than as an authority figure. Many employees in an equality culture prefer the impersonal authority of mutually agreed upon goals and objectives rather than the arbitrary power of a superior. To get things done, work often bypasses organizational levels, and employees are given a significant amount of leeway in implementing plans and performing tasks. Delegation is an important means of not only getting things done, but of developing employees to reach their potential. Disagreeing with a manager is not uncommon, and employees are expected to take the initiative. Participation in decision making is often encouraged, as well as consultation between levels in the organization.

Cultures that value equality include the United States, and other Anglo countries such as the United Kingdom, Australia, and Canada.

Individualism

Most of the world identifies strongly with membership in a group: family, caste, clan, tribe, or class. The United States is fairly unusual in that American identity is based more on independent, individual attributes.

Individualistic.   Individualistic cultures say things like "It's everyone for themselves" and value the person (individual identity) over the group (shared identity). In general, people in individualistic cultures place a high value on independence; the obligations between people are few (except for very close family); and the social bonds between people are relatively loose and flexible. Speaking one's mind is a sign of honesty and is respected. Social control is based on individual guilt and fear of losing self-respect. Motivation in individualistic cultures tends toward achievement and power, tasks are valued over relationships, and hiring and promotion is based largely on skill and achievements. The employer-employee relationship is based on mutual advantage.

Value is placed on individual decisions rather than those arrived at by committee or other groups. Individuals are expected to make their views known when plans are being developed and implemented, and it is usually the case that impersonal standards of performance measurement will be used to distinguish between individuals. It is not uncommon in such cultures for conflict to be perceived as an inevitable phenomenon, as something to be managed not avoided. It is the organization's responsibility to provide opportunities for individual accomplishment and recognition. Task assignments, resource allocation, and performance appraisals are focused on the individual, managers aspire to become leaders, and self-reliance is encouraged. Somewhat paradoxically, staffing policies and procedures in an individualistic society tend to be applied in a universal fashion, and compensation is based on a prescribed system.

Cultures that place a high value on individualism include most Northern and West European countries, Australia, Canada, and the United States. Finland and Germany, however, place a relatively low value on individualism compared to the other North European cultures.

Collectivist. Collective cultures subordinate individual interests to group interests. Cohesive groups protect their members in exchange for loyalty and obedience. Personal identity is grounded in the social network to which the individual belongs, and harmony rather than speaking one's mind is a key value. Social control is based upon fear of losing face and the possibility of shame. Publicly singling out and praising an individual's achievements in the midst of his or her work team might cause embarrassment. Likewise, putting co-workers in competition with one another to ascertain which one is best qualified for a promotion could be very detrimental to morale. Motivation in a collective culture tends toward affiliation and security, and relationships rather than tasks are of central concern. Hiring and promotions are not simply merit based, but take into account group membership and loyalty. Employees expect organizations to protect their interests in terms of retaining, developing, and compensating them, and people are generally not fired unless they step outside of the group's moral and political boundaries. Promotion is often based on seniority (or another ascriptive factor), and evaluations will take into account conformity to group norms and loyalty. Staffing policies and procedures may vary by individual, depending on his or her relationship to the decision makers. Compensation may be in the form of special bonuses or "perks" outside of any prescribed system. The employer-employee relationship aims at developing a "family relationship" rather than an impersonal relationship between capital and labor.

In a collectivist culture, group decisions take precedence over individual decisions. Not showing respect or patience for a businessperson's need to consult with others before making a decision—even if that process is fairly lengthy—is considered offensive and pushy. It is expected that plans will be developed based on the shared values of the group and will be implemented through the strength of relationships in the group rather than a simple assignment of tasks. Tasks and resources are likely to be allocated to groups of individuals; these groups may be evaluated rather than each individual in them. Individual accountability is diffused into group accountability; individual job descriptions may be vague or non-existent. Conformity to group standards, policies, and procedures is expected.

Cultures with a more collective orientation include most Asian, Arab, Latin American, and Southern European cultures. Italy, however, has a relatively high individualistic orientation.

Universalistic.   Universalistic cultures stress the consistent application of generalizations, rules, and procedures and the manufacture of universal products and services. From automobiles to fast food, the American orientation is toward items that can be mass-produced in identical batches and sold to a mass audience through mass marketing. Perhaps no other American product is more symbolic of this orientation than Coca-Cola.

Hampden-Turner and Trompenaars point to the universal codes established in America: the Declaration of Independence, the Constitution, and the Bill of Rights. These documents provide insiders and outsiders with a common frame of reference for understanding what it means to be an American. As they say, "One can be un-American, as we said during the McCarthy era, but not un-Dutch."[40] It is the leader's role in such cultures to embody and implement universal principles in decision making.

Reality in such cultures can be reduced to generalizable laws and widely applicable formulas and prescriptions. No field of human activity is immune from this approach, as the shelves of self-help books in our stores and libraries indicate. Each one offers the latest five- or six-step program for success or relief.

Behaviorism is an interesting product of American universalism, and its influence has been widely felt throughout the culture. The search for the underlying laws and principles governing human behavior has led (especially in the field of training and development) to the creation of some simple models to explain and predict behavioral outcomes. One of the authors remembers a time when he was teaching a multicultural group in New York. Using a well-known model of behavioral types, he attempted to show how different combinations of types in an interview situation may lead to very different results. The audience, many of whom were from outside of the United States, soon reacted strongly to the use of the model. It was described as "too simplistic," "too American," "too naive." While predominantly American audiences have found the model a useful tool, others have found it inappropriate to the reality they perceive, a reality that is more complicated, messy, and irreducible to simple models of universal intent.

Universalism is often expressed in detailed contracts that are impersonal and meant to be enforced regardless of subsequent situations. While there may be some flexibility, the contract is an expression of universal agreement.

Cultures tending to a universalistic orientation include the United States, Germany, Sweden, the United Kingdom, and Switzerland.

Particularistic.   In contrast, particularistic cultures emphasize difference, uniqueness, and exceptions. Rules (as embedded in contracts) are secondary to relationships, which are the most important factors in getting things done. The notion of universal principles, products, or services applicable in all situations, regardless of circumstances, is inappropriate.

Japan is strongly particularistic. The evidence for this, as Hampden-Turner and Trompenaars point out, "is seen in the extraordinary range of differences in its products, with its estimated 27,000 bookstores, 75 percent of its television presenting news and education, and dozens of products for every age group—for example, nine varieties of motor scooters for the female office worker between age eighteen and twenty-two. The image is expressed in art and gardening. A dynamic harmony is created from myriad differences, with no tree leaf, flower, or stone like any other."[41]

This orientation builds principles from the ground up rather than imposing them in an abstract, institutional form. In this view, contracts are not set in stone, but are guidelines that may be modified in the light of change. Extended family and friend obligations are likely to predominate over those of the society at large. Particularism and collectivism are, therefore, closely linked; the distinction between in-groups and out-groups is fundamental to decision making. Organizations may be smaller and formed as communities rather than entities based on contractual arrangements between owners and employees. Mobility may be reduced, and power may be concentrated in groups rather than distributed. As a consequence, policies and procedures may be developed and applied according to relationships, not common standards.

Countries tending to a particularistic orientation include Venezuela, China, Japan, Hong Kong, and the countries of the former Soviet Union.

Competitiveness

Competitive cultures stress that everyone is in business to get the most done, in the least amount of time, in order to make the most money. Cooperative cultures tend to value quality of life more than job and material success.

Competitive.   Competitive cultures are predominantly materialistic with an emphasis on assertiveness and the acquisition of money, property, goods, and so on. High value is placed on ambition, decisiveness, initiative, performance, speed, and size. Competitive cultures say things like "We're number one," "Let's kick butt," "We'll kick the pants off of them," "Winner takes all." The ethos is "We live to work." Material success, achievement, and performance are high motivators.

Competitive cultures tend to measure success in narrow terms, such as profits or task achievement. Plans are developed and implemented quickly, and, wherever possible, results are measured and compared. In general, competitive cultures structure work to permit and encourage individual achievement and satisfaction and to satisfy such motivational factors as high earnings, recognition, advancement, and challenge. People are hired and trained to take aggressive, independent action, to lead, to achieve, and drive for success. Leaders expect employees to fulfill or exceed their responsibilities and defend their own interests. The role of the leader is to track and reward achievement as well as model success and encourage a strong work ethic.

The United States, Great Britain, Australia, Japan, the Philippines, Hong Kong, Germany, Switzerland, Belgium, Greece, and Italy are competitive cultures. Some Latin American countries such as Venezuela, Mexico, Ecuador, Columbia, and Argentina are also competitive cultures. Japan is considered to be one of the most competitive cultures in the world. This can be seen in the long work weeks put in by many Japanese managers. The Japanese even have a word for early death caused by overwork, *karoshi*.

Cooperative. Cooperative cultures say things like "We're in this together." When cooperation is highly valued, stress is placed on the quality of life, sympathy, nurturing, and relationships. The ethos is "We work to live." Material success is less motivational, and there is a higher concern with job satisfaction, quality of life, and interdependence. Success, therefore, is measured in broader terms than monetary ones, for example, service. While task performance is important, it is only one factor to be considered in overall performance.

In cooperative cultures, stress is placed on consensual decision making. Work is structured to facilitate group integration and satisfy such motivational factors as security, a positive working environment, and schedules that allow for a full personal and family life. Employees are hired not only for their skills, but also for their ability to fit into the group, to promote its shared values, to facilitate communication, demonstrate loyalty, cooperation, and service, and to contribute to the welfare of the overall work environment. The leader's role is to encourage mutually beneficial relationships.

High-cooperative cultures include the Scandinavian countries of Northern Europe (as witnessed in Norway's role in bringing Israel and the PLO [Palestine Liberation Organization] together in peace talks). Requests for working after hours and on weekends in Northern Europe are perceived as invasive and are often rejected. Highly cooperative cultures such as Denmark, the Netherlands, Norway, and Sweden believe that personal time and time spent with the family is very valuable and that organizations should not interfere in one's private life. Countries in Latin America that place a fairly low value on competitiveness include Panama, Chile, Costa Rica, Guatemala, Peru, and Uruguay. Arab countries are midway between being competitive and cooperative, as are most Asian countries. Quality of life issues tend to be more central in Southeast Asian countries as opposed to the more industrialized East Asian countries of South Korea, China, Taiwan, and Singapore.

The effects of differences between competitiveness and cooperation are often felt in multicultural team situations. Highly competitive members may perceive cooperative members as lazy or uncommitted, while cooperative members may perceive their competitive co-workers as being invasive or disrespectful, or having no sense of priorities.

Structure

Structure tells us the extent to which the members of a culture experience threat or discomfort by ambiguity and uncertainty.

Order.   Cultures that value order seek to reduce ambiguity and uncertainty and make events predictable and interpretable. Conflict and change are perceived as threatening, and there is a perceived need for rules, regulations, and procedures—both written and unwritten. In such cultures, lifetime employment (or at least low job mobility) is often valued, there is a need for clear roles and responsibilities, and avoiding failure is stressed. Hierarchical structures are also respected.

High-order cultures often leave planning to specialists or have formally defined planning roles and responsibilities. They also display stress in the face of uncertainty, display emotional resistance to change, and are less willing to take risks. Job or task descriptions are likely to be detailed to avoid conflict or ambiguity. Loyalty is seen as a major criterion for promotion, and seniority can play a major part in decisions that are made. It is felt that work processes should be strictly prescribed and consistent.

Countries that place a high value on order include those in Latin America, the Middle East, Southern Europe, the German-speaking countries, and some Asian countries, including Japan, South Korea, Taiwan, and Thailand. A client of ours who works for a very large health care company was once told to oversee a business unit's activities in Japan; the unit was having some problems marketing and selling its product over there. He flew to Japan and asked to see samples of their marketing plans. The Japanese managers were not able to produce any. He told them that they knew better than he did about the marketing environment, and he empowered them to develop a marketing plan. He gave them general guidelines and a month to come up with a plan for his review. After a month, no plan was forthcoming. Frustrated, he developed the plan himself and sent it over. On his next trip to Japan, he discovered the reason why no plan had been produced. The Japanese managers did not feel comfortable being "empowered," and felt uncomfortable proceeding without detailed, clear instructions and development procedures. In the absence of such a structure, they were, in fact disempowered.

Flexibility.   Flexible cultures are more tolerant of unknown situations, people, and ideas. Tolerance of deviation from norms is higher, and conflict is natural rather than threatening. Such cultures say things like: "There's more than one way to skin a cat," "If it isn't broken, break it," "It's what works that counts." Job mobility in flexible cultures is higher, role and responsibility definitions are relatively loose, and there is a greater willingness to take calculated risks. Pragmatism is the dominant philosophy: What works in the given situation is what counts.

Flexible cultures show a preference for broad guidelines in planning rather than for specific methodologies; they tolerate conflict and dissent and continually search for alternative ways of getting things done. Job and task descriptions are likely to be broadly interpreted, leaving room for the individual to make his or her decisions. Formal relationships are less precisely defined, and organizational forms that accommodate conflict and competition are preferred. Loyalty to the employer is not considered to be a major factor in promotability, and managers select on merit rather than seniority. Achievement motivation is higher than in ordered cultures, and there is a greater reliance on individual ambition, leadership, and initiative for achieving results. The role of the leader in this type of culture is to provide the strategy and to let others determine how to carry it out.

Thinking

Deductive.   Deductive-oriented cultures emphasize abstract thinking and the reality of ideas, moral values, theories, and the principles that can be derived from them. Priority is given to the conceptual world and symbolic thinking rather than the amassing of facts; generalizations are derived from other concepts by means of logic, rather than from facts. High value is placed on the powers of thought *per se.*

The influence of the past and future is greater in this type of thinking process. Appeal is made to theories, principles, or examples that have produced results in the past or are expected to produce results in the future. Problems—in the main—are classified, and solutions discovered based on previous experiences and contextual circumstances.[42]

French and Latin American thinking tends to be highly deductive, focusing on the Why rather than the What and How. Negotiations between French and Americans can be very frustrating for both parties. Very often, the Americans want to begin with specific items for discussion, for example, price or distribution channels. The French, on the other hand, are likely to want to establish agreement on general principles to guide the negotiation.

Inductive.   Inductive-oriented cultures derive principles and theories from the analysis of data. Models and hypotheses are based on empirical observation and experimentation, and the goal is verification through empirical proof.

The amassing of facts and statistics is valued, and a good deal of faith is placed in methodologies and measurements.

Inductive decision making is guided less by the past or future than by the present. Surveys, one of the most popular methodologies, are usually set up to reflect a current condition, although results may be projected into the future. The focus tends to be on the costs and benefits associated with alternative courses of action—the operational impact. In this process, "facts" are given high priority and are assumed to be impersonal and reliable.

American thinking is very inductive.

Linear.   When faced with a problem, linear-oriented cultures will dissect it into small chunks that can be linked in chains of cause and effect. The emphasis tends to be on detail, precision, and pragmatic results. Peter Senge comments on the American thinking pattern as follows:[43]

> From a very early age, we are taught to break apart problems, to fragment the world. This apparently makes complex tasks and subjects more manageable, but we pay a hidden, enormous price. We can no longer see the consequences of our actions; we lose our intrinsic sense of connection to a larger whole.

Systemic.   When faced with a problem, systemic-oriented cultures stress an integrated approach, sometimes called "holistic" or synthetic. This integrated viewpoint focuses on relationships between parts and their connections. There is often a reliance on analogy, metaphor and simile for explanations.

In juxtaposition to American thought, many other cultures such as Japanese, Chinese, and Brazilian are more systemic than analytical in their thinking style.[44]

Some companies, Toshiba America Consumer Products, for example, are seeking to leverage differences in thinking patterns and enhance their competitive advantage.[45] Toshiba found that American engineers think analytically and follow a step-by-step approach to problem solving. Japanese engineers look at the whole and relationships. To take advantage of the differences, Toshiba may have American engineers work on relatively narrow focus—complicated parts—while the Japanese engineers work on the standardized parts and the whole design.

WHAT ELSE DO YOU NEED TO KNOW ABOUT CULTURE?

We have covered a lot of ground in this chapter, out before we end we need to make several more points:

• **Cultures are clusters of related values.**

The 10 variables and the associated cultural orientations have been treated as though they are separate and distinct from one another. This is not the case. Culture is fluid and immensely complex; analytical boundaries like control orientation and doing orientation are not as separate as portrayed in our model. They relate to each other quite closely; it is difficult to imagine the one orientation without the other (although it is always possible).

What do those relationships allow us to do? If we are visiting a foreign culture for the first time, and all we know about it is that it is highly collectivistic, what can we deduce that may help us to prepare ourselves? If we think through the other orientations in the model, we can say with some degree of certainty that the culture is also likely to have a harmony or constraint orientation to the environment, it may stress being over doing, and high context over low context. It may also value public over private space, and indirect/formal communication over direct communication.

An individualistic culture on the other hand is more likely to have a control orientation to the environment, a single-focus/fixed/present and future orientation toward time, a doing orientation to action, low-context/direct/instrumental/informal orientations to communication, and a stress on private space and equality.

Being a global manager is sometimes like playing detective. We always need to be searching for—and recognizing—clues establishing connections, and establishing meaning.

- **Cultural differences entail management differences.**

Being global managers also means selecting techniques that will be compatible with the cultures in which we are working. Take, for example, goal setting. Employee participation has been popular in management circles for some time, but will it be effective in every culture? A culture that places a high value on hierarchy is likely to reject it as inappropriate.[46] Cultures that place a high value on individualism may also find it difficult to implement, unless the individuals in the group feel that the process is contributing to their personal needs and wants.

Appropriate reward systems are also determined by cultural preferences. As Erez and Earley point out in *Culture, Self Identity, and Work,* reward systems tend to be based on one of three basic principles:[47]

Equity: To each according to his or her contribution. This principle encourages differentiation between people and is motivational within an individualistic culture.

Equality: Maintenance of group harmony. This principle is more conducive to collectivist cultures.

Need: Sensitivity to others' needs. This principle is influential in collectivist cultures, often where per capita income is low and needs are highly visible.

Whether we are trying to motivate, negotiate, communicate, or facilitate, we need to take into account the primary cultural orientations of those we are working with, ourselves, and our organization. From this base of understanding we can generate ways of moving forward consciously and productively.

- **Culture is complex.**

We have been talking at the level of regional and national culture. An individual's cultural profile, however, is influenced by many other factors, and so each individual is to some extent culturally unique. The factors that affect an individual's cultural profile include family, region, neighborhood, education, corporate culture, religion, profession, social class, gender, race, and generation (see Figure 2–7).

The importance of each one of these factors will vary depending on the characteristics of the national culture, the situation faced by the individual, and the individual's background. The individual may switch cultural orientations depending on whether he or she is at work, visiting family, attending a professional association meeting, or meeting with friends. It is very important, therefore, that we do not make too many assumptions about a person from another culture. We

FIGURE 2–7
Some Factors in Shaping an Individual's Cultural Profile

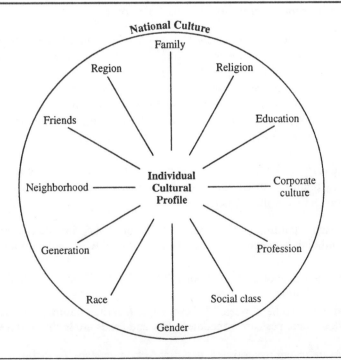

may understand the dominant value orientations of a national culture, but the individual we are interacting with may have significant differences. We need to pay attention, listen and observe, and have the flexibility to adapt. Certain business activities, such as legal and advertising, may require us to relate to the national culture as a whole. Many other business activities, however, such as delegation and negotiation, are performed at a more individual level and may require a high level of adaptability. Some cultures are more homogeneous than others; for example, Japan is far more homogeneous than the United States. But no culture is without internal variation.

- **Cultures are dynamically stable.**

Dynamic stability sounds like a contradiction, but it is perfectly descriptive of cultural change. Core value orientations change very slowly; behaviors that are acceptable and expected are passed on from generation to generation through such institutions as the family and schools. Culture satisfies a need for belonging, for membership in something beyond the isolated self. At the same time, the wider environment in which the culture exists is in a state of flux; economic, political, demographic, and social changes make their influence felt, and cultures may need to adapt to new conditions. New communication technologies bring multiple cultures to the young, and cultural isolation is less of an option.

It is also important to understand that the value orientations within a culture may exist somewhat in tension with one another. For example, within American culture, the values of individualism and equality are not totally compatible; individualism pulls apart while equality pulls together. It is because of such tensions that change can occur.

- **Cultural adaption is not cultural adoption.**

"Culture" is not an abstraction; it is a powerful human reality and is an integral part of what it means to be a human being in a specific place at a specific time. We cannot escape from being cultural creatures and having favored value orientations embedded into our ways of doing and thinking.

While it is important for us to understand our differences with others and to adapt, it is also important for us to recognize our boundaries. While it is our responsibility to maximize communication and mutual understanding, it does not follow that we should adopt the value orientations of the other person. There will be situations in which we will adapt easily and even adopt a cultural practice that seems to make sense to us. There will be other situations in which we will feel there is a line we cannot cross. Some value orientations are closer to the core of who we are and should not be compromised. This should also be the case with the shared values of the company. Spend time to reflect on your adaptability.

- **Cultural differences can add value.**

Paying close attention to cultural differences in business is not an issue of political correctness. The most compelling reasons are economic. As we saw with Procter & Gamble, culture impacts the bottom line. Toshiba is making use of cultural differences to better understand customers, improve design, and shorten lead times. ICI is bringing cultural differences to the surface to improve the productivity and effectiveness of its multicultural managers.

Competitive advantage is complex. Culture can facilitate or hinder the development of advantages in the marketplace. We can increase our chances of global success by increasing cultural learning throughout the organization. As Hoecklin makes clear, we do this by:[48]

Making cultural knowledge explicit.

Agreeing on outcomes.

Defining the approach(es) most likely to achieve the outcomes.

Reviewing results and modifying approaches to find a better fit.

At the interface of business and culture, the most important criterion for choice of approach is not "correctness" or "superiority" but the generative process of creating added value. See Figure 2–8.

SUMMARY INSIGHTS

As we expand trade across borders, form strategic alliances and joint ventures with foreign partners, and develop new relationships with overseas suppliers and distributors, we are beginning to understand the impact of culture on the formation and maintenance of competitive advantage. Companies that are paying attention to culture are seeing the results on their bottom lines.

Cultural competence is no longer a nice skill to have, it is an economic necessity. Cultural competence begins with open attitudes, which facilitate the development of self- and other-awareness, which need grounding in cultural knowledge for translation into cross-cultural skills. Recruiting and developing culturally competent managers is now a top priority for many companies.

Numerous researchers have provided us with insights into the value orientations that underpin much cultural behavior. These value orientations are preferences for certain outcomes over others. Our cultural orientations framework focuses attention onto orientations associated with 10 key variables: environment, time, action, communication, space, power, individualism, competitiveness, structure, and thinking. Business practices, such as conflict management, planning, and staffing, are conducted within a culture's primary set of orientations. It is the challenge of every global manager to create synergy out of cultural differences and sometimes to devise creative new ways that are workable across cultures.

A culture is not one thing, but many. While we may be able to identify dominant value orientations within a culture, we must always remain open to varia-

FIGURE 2–8
A Model of Cultural Learning

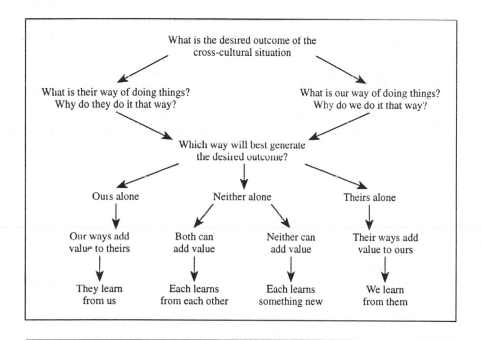

Source: Lisa Adent Hoecklin, *Managing Cultural Differences for Competitive Advantage* (London: The Economist Intelligence Unit, Special Report No. P656, 1993), p. 46.

tions and cultural change. Numerous factors influence groups and individuals within a culture, including family, region, education, and religion. We always need to pay attention, listen, observe, and have the flexibility to adapt. Unfortunately, stereotypes tend to lock us into well-worn channels of perception.

As we do business across the globe, it is important for us to understand that while we need to adapt to other cultures, we do not need to adopt other cultures. We all have boundaries we cannot cross, values we cannot violate. Our primary goal in coming to understand other cultures is not the achievement of some vague notion of political correctness, but the generation of *added value*.

DISCUSSION QUESTIONS

- To what extent is your company doing business across different cultures?
- What is your company doing to help managers develop intercultural competence?

- What are your primary cultural orientations? What are those of your main-stream culture? How do you account for the differences?
- In what ways do you think your mainstream culture is changing? What are the primary factors driving the changes?

NOTES

1. Louis E. Boone, *Quotable Business* (New York: Random House, 1992), p 188.

2. Laurie Freeman, "Japan Rises to P&G's No. 3 Market," *Advertising Age,* Dec. 10, 1990, p 42.

3. Edwin Artzt, "Winning in Japan: Keys to Global Success," *Business Quarterly,* Winter 1989, pp 12–16.

4. Annetta Miller et al., "No Cheer for Procter & Gamble," *Newsweek,* July 26, 1993.

5. Lisa Adent Hoecklin, *Managing Cultural Differences for Competitive Advantage,* Special Report No. P656 (London: The Economist Intelligence Unit, 1993), pp 10–11, 47–48, 92–96.

6. Edward T. Hall, *The Silent Language* (New York: Doubleday Books, 1990), p xv.

7. Joann S. Lublin, "Young Managers Learn Global Skills," *The Wall Street Journal,* March 31, 1992.

8. Bob Hagerty, "Trainers Help Expatriate Employees Build Bridges to Different Cultures," *The Wall Street Journal,* June 14, 1993.

9. Connie Leslie et al., "Global Market by Degrees," *Newsweek,* March 8, 1993, p 65.

10. Clifford Geertz, *The Interpretation of Cultures* (New York: Basic Books, 1973), p 13.

11. F. Kluckhohn and F. L. Strodtbeck, *Variations in Value Orientations* (Evanston, IL: Row, Peterson, 1961), p 340.

12. Clyde Kluckhohn, "Universal Categories of Culture," *Anthropology Today,* ed. S. Tax (Chicago: University of Chicago Press, 1962), p 317–318.

13. Talcott Parsons, "The Pattern Variables," in *On Institutions and Social Evolution: Selected Writings,* ed. Leon H. Mayhem (Chicago: The University of Chicago Press, 1982), pp 106–114.

14. Edward T. Hall, "The Silent Language in Overseas Business," *Harvard Business Review,* May–June 1960, p 92.

15. Boone, *Quotable Business,* p 186.

16. Geert Hofstede, *Culture's Consequences: International Differences in Work-Related Values* (Newbury Park, CA: Sage Publications, 1980), pp 70–73, 111–118, 149–154, 177–183.

17. Charles Hampden-Turner and Alfons Trompenaars, *The Seven Cultures of Capitalism* (New York: Doubleday, 1993), p 4.

18. Edward C. Stewart and Milton J. Bennett, *American Cultural Patterns: A Cross-Cultural Perspective,* rev. ed. (Yarmouth, Maine: Intercultural Press, 1991), pp 28–30.

19. Ibid., p 34.

20. Stephen H. Rhinesmith, *A Manager's Guide to Globalization: Six Keys to Success in a Changing World* (Homewood, IL: Business One Irwin, 1993), pp 77–79.

21. Hampden-Turner and Trompenaars, *Seven Cultures of Capitalism,* p 34.

22. Selected excerpt from *Who Prospers?* by Lawrence E. Harrison. Copyright © 1992 by Lawrence E. Harrison. Reprinted by permission of Basic Books, a division of HarperCollins Publishers, Inc.

23. Joel Kotkin, *Tribes: How Race, Religion, and Identity Determine Success in the New Global Economy* (New York: Random House, 1993).

24. Derald Wind Sue and David Sue, *Counseling the Culturally Different: Theory & Practice,* 2nd ed. (New York: John Wiley & Sons, 1990), pp 140–143.

25. Harrison, *Who Prospers,* p 12.

26. R. L. Wing, *The Tao of Power: Lao Tzu's Classic Guide to Leadership, Influence, and Excellence* (New York: Doubleday, 1986), passage 16.

27. Charles Lemart, ed., *Social Theory: The Multicultural and Classic Readings* (Boulder, CO: Westview Press, 1993), p 2.

28. Hall, *Silent Language,* p 2.

29. Ibid., p 7.

30. Ibid., p 6.

31. Nancy Adler, *International Dimensions of Organizational Behavior,* 2nd ed. (Boston: PWS-Kent, 1991), p 31.

32. Kluckhohn and Strodtbeck, *Variations in Value Orientations,* p 14.

33. Stewart and Bennett, *American Cultural Patterns,* p 156.

34. Yuko Tsushima, "The Silent Traders," in *Stories from the Rest of the World,* ed. Scott Walker, The Graywolf Annual Six (Saint Paul, MN: Graywolf Press, 1989), p 10.

35. Richard Mead, *Cross-Cultural Management Communication* (New York: John Wiley, 1990), pp 134–135.

36. Stephen H. Rhinesmith, *Cultural Organizational Analysis: The Interrelationship of Value Orientations and Managerial Behavior,* Publication Series Number 5 (Cambridge, MA: McBer and Company, 1971), p 35.

37. Hoecklin, *Managing Cultural Differences,* p 22.

38. Hall, *Silent Language,* p 176.

39. Hagerty, "Trainers Help."

40. Hampden-Turner and Trompenaars, *Seven Cultures of Capitalism,* p 22.

41. Ibid., p. 106.

42. Stephen H. Rhinesmith, *Cultural Organization Analysis,* p. 40.

43. Peter M. Senge, *The Fifth Discipline: The Art and Practice of the Learning Organization* (New York: Doubleday, 1990), p 3.

44. Stewart and Bennett, *American Cultural Patterns,* p 41.

45. Hoecklin, *Managing Cultural Differences,* p 49.

46. Miriam Erez and P. Christopher Earley, *Culture, Self Identity, and Work* (New York: Oxford University Press, 1993), p 221.

47. Erez and Earley, *Culture,* pp 222–223.

48. Hoecklin, *Managing Cultural Differences,* p 46

Chapter Three

Success in Crossing Cultures

A smaller world creates a bigger agenda for business. There are more cultures to understand, more social responsibilities to master, more time pressures to juggle, and more relationships to rethink.

Rosabeth Moss Kanter
Transcending Business Boundaries:
12,000 World Managers View Change

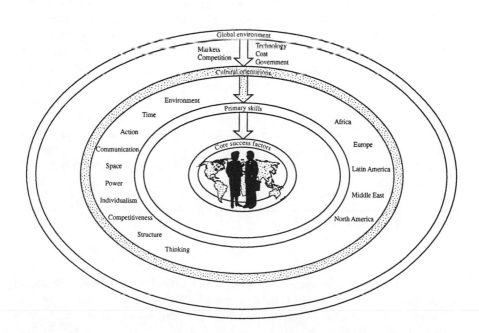

INTRODUCTION

You are about to begin a journey across six of the most fascinating regions of the world: Africa, Asia, Europe, Latin America, the Middle East, and North America.

In this book, you will be flying over these regions at a very high altitude and at great speed. Don't expect to gain more than an outline of the cultural landscape. To develop a deeper understanding, you need to land and spend time. The cultural orientations model presented in the last chapter provides you with a mental framework for identifying differences within and between each region.

And so, fasten your seatbelts, and enjoy the trip.

SETTING OUT ON A CULTURAL JOURNEY

Why is one culture different from or similar to others? Is it simply a question of location? There is no easy answer to this question. In May–June 1991, the *Harvard Business Review* published the results of a survey conducted among 12,000 managers from 25 countries.[1] They found that cultural affinity—more than geographic proximity—is a major factor in shaping a manager's views. The world does not divide into neat cultural packages that can be labeled, sorted, and inspected with ease. There are cultural allies and islands that owe their primary value orientations to history rather than simply geography. See Table 3–1.

While location is secondary to historical influence, we find that most international businesspeople think in terms of geographic regions rather than cultural allies and islands. They ask questions like, "I'm going to be doing business in Latin America: what do I need to know?" In line with this thinking, we have chosen to organize this chapter by regions. These regions are somewhat arbitrary, and each one is diverse in terms of culture, politics, economics, social structure, and so on. Yet, at a macro level, they do have defining characteristics that set them apart from each other. When we think of "Asia," we think of such belief systems as Buddhism, Zen, Taoism, and Confucianism. When we think of the Middle East, we think of Islam and Judaism. Understanding the predominant belief systems in a region helps us make sense of the behaviors and values we find on our cross-cultural journeys.

Primary Belief Systems

Buddhism

Influence.   Some 300 million people around the world are considered Buddhist. From 6th century BC India, it spread over Asia and has had a profound influence on the cultural orientations of the Eastern world. There are basically two schools of Buddhist thought:

TABLE 3–1
Cultural Allies and Islands

Cultural Allies	
Group 1:	Australia, Canada, Great Britain, New Zealand, Singapore, United States.
	Common traits: A preference for family over work, and the least "cosmopolitan." (Cosmopolitan is defined as being multilingual and having international experience.)
Group 2:	Argentina, Brazil, Italy, Mexico, Spain, Venezuela.
	Common traits: More privately held companies, fewer joint ventures, and a higher reliance on trade policy for industry protection.
Group 3:	Australia, Belgium, Finland, France, Germany, the Netherlands, Sweden.
	Common traits: Most cosmopolitan, more close partnerships, and more pessimistic about the future.
Cultural Islands	
Japan:	The strongest work ethic, the greatest concern about the work ethic of the rest of the work force, and strongly in favor of "free trade."
South Korea:	Strongly favors protectionism, puts country ahead of company, a strong sense of corporate responsibility toward employees, and more optimistic about the future.
India:	More optimistic about the future and strongly favors protectionism.
Hungary:	Organizationally different from companies in other countries and very focused on economic regeneration.

The above allies and islands were determined by statistical analysis. This clustering technique compares the responses by country for each survey question and evaluates the degree of overall country difference.

Theravada Buddhism is predominant in Burma, Cambodia, Sri Lanka, and Thailand. It is the most conservative school focusing directly on the life and teachings of Siddhartha Guatama (c. 563–483 BC), the Buddha (enlightened one).

Mahayana Buddhism is influential in China and Japan. Less conservative than the Theravada school, it stresses the importance of each individual's attempting to be a bodhisattva (enlightened being) through contemplation, compassion, and action.

Beliefs and Practices. The Buddha taught a "Middle Path" between self-denial (or asceticism) and the indulgence of the worldly life. It is a path that detaches the individual from worldly things and desires. The core of Buddhist belief is presented in writings known as "Three Baskets." The essence of Buddhist belief is captured in the Four Noble Truths:

Life is suffering and disappointment.

Suffering originates in desire for pleasure, power, and the intense craving to live and possess.

Desire must be overcome.

Desire is overcome by applying the Noble Eightfold Path (the path that leads to no desire). This path consists of the following steps: right belief (the Four Noble Truths); right aspiration or purpose (overcoming sensuality, having the right love of others, harming no living being, and suppressing all desires that produce suffering); right speech and right conduct (not indulging in hurtful talk or ill-will, and loving all creatures in word and action); right means of livelihood (choosing the correct occupation and working in ways that are in line with Buddhist principles); right effort (being alert to appropriate desires and attachments); right mindfulness (disciplined thought habits); right meditation or absorption (trance states that lead eventually to sainthood, i.e., arahatship and then to Nirvana).[2]

Like Hindus, Buddhists believe in a reincarnation cycle of existence. This cycle of death and rebirth is ended by the state of Nirvana, which brings contentment and release from the human condition.

Christianity

Influence.   From its origins in the Middle East, Christianity has spread around the world. Over 1.5 billion people are classified as Christian, one in every three. It is the primary religious belief system in Europe, North and South America, Australia, New Zealand, and the Pacific Islands.

A major division in Christianity occurred in 1054 AD when the Eastern (Orthodox) church and the Western (Roman) church broke apart. Another major division occurred in the 16th century when Martin Luther and others broke from the Roman church to establish Protestantism.

Today, the Roman Catholic church is very influential in the countries of Southern Europe and South America. The Eastern Orthodox church predominates in parts of Eastern Europe, the former Soviet Union, and Greece. Protestantism is the major religious force in Northern Europe, North America, Australia, and New Zealand. Protestantism is divided into numerous denominations.

Beliefs and Practices.   The Bible, both the Old and New Testaments, is the holy book of Christianity. The Old Testament books were originally written in Hebrew, while the New Testament books were written in Greek and tell the story of Jesus Christ and his disciples.

God is embodied in three entities: God the Father, God the Son (Jesus), and God the Holy Spirit. A fundamental belief of Christianity is that Jesus—through his death and resurrection—is the Savior of humankind.

Regardless of denomination, most Christians conduct baptisms of infants and new converts and perform some form of Communion (Eucharist) ritual.

Protestantism, which includes Lutherans, Presbyterians, Moravians, the Church of England, and nonconformist sects, such as, Baptists, Congregationalists, Methodists, and Evangelicals, is based on the fundamental belief that the individual is directly responsible to God rather than to the Church. Each person, therefore, seeks direct communication with God through prayer.

Catholicism recognizes the Bishop of Rome (the Pope) as the head of the Christian Church and the rightful successor of Saint Peter. Rather than having a direct relationship with God, the Catholic relationship is a mediated one in which the priesthood and a strong, authoritarian church play a major role.

Confucianism

Influence. Confucianism has had a profound influence on the cultural life of China and other areas of Asia. Some 5 million people in east Asia are said to be Confucianists. Its influence is particularly strong in Taiwan, Hong Kong, Singapore, and North and South Korea.

Beliefs and Practices. Confucius (K'ung-Fo-Tzu), born in approximately 551 BC in the Shantung province of China, was a contemporary of Buddha. While the Buddha propounded a metaphysical philosophy, Confucius sought to establish a practical social code—based on forms of etiquette, law, and ritual—and most of his energies were devoted to reforming the feudal governments of his day. He tried to teach by example, believing that the example set by the ruler influences the subjects.

Much of the Confucian code is aimed at promoting harmony in relationships both at the level of state and the family. Heaven ordains universal obligations or duties. According to Confucius, there are five primary relationships: between ruler and minister, father and son, husband and wife, elder and younger brother, and between friends. Each relationship has reciprocal obligations; if these obligations are met, tranquility will prevail. His primary task was not the creation of a new ethical code, but the preservation of those qualities he argued were displayed by the ancient sages. Leaders must act with an example of virtue because, "The relation between superiors and inferiors is like that between the wind and the grass. The grass (inferiors) must bend, when the wind (leader) blows across it."[3] Duty to parents and elders, propriety, obedience, faithfulness, sincerity, hard work, education, abstinence, frugality, modesty, kindness, generosity, earnestness, seriousness, and harmony are key to this interpersonal code.

Hinduism

Influence. With close to 650 million followers, Hinduism is the third largest religion in the world (following Christianity and Islam). Practicing Hindus are found primarily in India, although there are also notable Hindu communities in Malaysia and Singapore. The Hindu nationalist party—Bharatiya Janata—is very strong in India, and represents a growing Hindu fundamentalism.

Beliefs and Practices.   Hindu doctrines are derived from a number of ancient sacred books including the Veda, the Brahmanas, the Upanishads, and the Bhagavad-Gita.

Hinduism is a polytheistic religion (many gods), and its gods include: Brahma, the creator; Vishnu, preserver and defender of the world; and Shiva, god of destruction. Shiva's wife, Uma, is goddess of motherhood, but as Kali or Durga she is destructive. Hindu gods may demonstrate creative and destructive powers, good and evil.

To a Hindu, the divine is present in all things, but everything is subject to change. Two doctrines dominate the Hindu belief system: karma and transmigration. Existence consists of a cycle of lives (samsara), and one's destiny is determined by deeds (karma). Release from this cycle can be achieved through various ascetic practices or Yoga (bodily and mental exercises to further meditation). If one does not achieve release (or absorption into the absolute, known as atman or Brahman), the soul is reincarnated to a higher or lower form of life.

Respect for nature is fundamental to Hindu thought. The cow is considered a holy animal, and killing a cow for meat is a very serious offence.

While there are no Hindu congregations as such, temples have been built to honor a god or gods, and many homes have a shrine.

Though the Hindu caste system was abolished in 1950, its influence is still felt throughout the society of India. The four major castes were: Brahmans (priests), Kshatriyas (princes, soldiers), Vaisayas (merchants, landowners), and Sudras (farmers, workers).

Below these castes were the untouchables. Brahmans were able to marry women from other castes, and so a very complex system of subcastes evolved.

Islam

Influence.   Islam is the second most influential religious belief system in the world (after Christianity), and has a very active and powerful fundamentalist movement in many countries. There are approximately 800 million Muslims in the World. Islamic countries include Morocco, Iran, Egypt, Iraq, Saudi Arabia, Pakistan, Indonesia, and the republics once part of the Soviet Union.

Within Islam, there are two primary divisions: the majority Sunnites (Orthodox) and the minority Shiites. The division between the two branches is based on beliefs as to the rightful succession to Mohammed. The Shiites recognize descendents of Mohammed's daughter and son-in-law—Fatimah and Ali—as the successor (Caliph) to the Prophet. The orthodox group promotes the election of Caliphs by a vote of qualified followers.

Beliefs and Practices.   Islam (meaning submission to the will of God) considers itself to be an absolute and final faith. Orthodox Muslims relate to the Qur'an (Koran) as the word of God (Allah). Mohammed (570–632 AD), the last prophet, drew inspiration from the Old Testament and recognized Jesus as a prophet (but not the Son of God).

The Qur'an contains 114 chapters or suras (said to have been spoken to Mohammed by the angel Jibrail), and all but one begin with "In the Name of Allah, the Compassionate, the Merciful." Devoted Muslims will memorize much or all of the text.

Every Muslim has five primary duties:

To say with conviction, "There is no God but Allah, and Mohammed is his Prophet."

Conduct prayer five times daily, with the face turned toward the holy city of Mecca.

Give alms to support the poor.

Keep the fast during Ramadan, the ninth month of the Islamic year (during which time Muslims should not eat, drink or indulge in worldly pleasures between sunrise and sunset).

Make a pilgrimage to Mecca.

Drinking, gambling, and the eating of pork are forbidden. Sex outside of marriage is also disapproved of. Women are expected to dress modestly, even to the extent of covering their faces in public places.

Judaism

Influence.   Approximately 17,800,000 people (4 percent of the world's population) are Jewish. The majority live in the United States (about 44.5 percent), and a further 22 percent live in the state of Israel. The next largest Jewish majority lives in the states of the former Soviet Union (about 17.5 percent).

The three main branches of Judaism are:

Orthodox: The most conservative group, observing traditional laws and customs relating to food and purification. This group includes the Hasidim sects (Pious Ones), traditionally from Eastern Europe.

Reform: The most liberal Jewish group. While following the spirit of Judaism, they do not practice many of the traditional rituals or rules of conduct. The Reform group is strong in the United States.

Conservative: The most recent of the three groups, conservatives try to follow a middle path between Orthodox and Reform Judaism. Conservatives are also strong in the United States.

Beliefs and Practices.   Judaism is the oldest monotheistic (one God) religion. The Jewish scriptures are the books of the Old Testament Bible, and the

Old Testament father (patriarch) of the Jews is Abraham. The first five books of the Old Testament are known as the Torah (Law of Moses or Pentateuch); these sacred books describe the covenant made between God and the Jewish people, and relate the laws—including the Ten Commandments—communicated by Moses from Mount Sinai. The Talmud contains the civil and canonical laws of orthodox Jewish belief and practice.

The Jewish faith recognizes one omnipotent God, the creator of all things. The Old Testament prophets told of the coming of a Messiah anointed by God. The Christian Messiah—Jesus Christ—is not recognized in Judaism as the awaited Messiah.

Judaism places great emphasis on social relationships and the home and family. Jewish beliefs and practices reach into all aspects of daily life.

Shintoism

Influence.   The Shinto religion is the native religion of the Japanese islands.

Beliefs and Practices.   Shinto means "The Way of the Gods," and it expresses a religious faith about the divine nature of Japan and its people. The Emperor of Japan, according to ancient myths, is a direct descendent of the sun goddess Amaterasu, and the Japanese people are descended from lesser gods. The land itself is said to be divine, and gods and goddesses reside in natural forces such as the wind and objects such as mountains (for example, Mount Fuji).

Closely associated with patriotism and ancestor worship, Shintoism was embedded into Japanese life until the American occupation in 1945. At that time, Emperor Hirohito abdicated his divinity.

Closely related to Shinto is the Bushido code or "Way of the Warrior" practiced by the Samurai (one who serves). The code promoted loyalty to Emperor and lord, gratitude, courage, justice, truthfulness, politeness, reserve, and honor. The warrior who was humiliated or disgraced was expected to commit ritual suicide (harakiri). The principles of the code are still influential in modern Japan.

Sikhism

Influence.   While centered in the Punjab region of India, Sikhism has been spreading its influence across countries in the former British Empire. Militant Sikhs are aiming to establish their own independent state of Khalistan (Land of the Pure). There are estimated to be 16 million Sikhs around the world.

Beliefs and Practices.   Sikhism derives from the teachings of Guru Nanak (1469–1539). It teaches the existence of One God or Guru (the true teacher). The primary beliefs of Sikhism are a fusion of Islam and Hinduism.

Time is cyclical, as in Hinduism, but being human indicates the soul is close to the end of the cycle of rebirth. If the soul is still attached to the world, then rebirth takes place. If the soul is released from attachment, then the soul will join God.

The primary religious text of Sikhism is the Guru Granth Sahib. Produced in the 16th century, it contains writing and hymns from 10 Gurus, as well as Muslim and Hindu writings.

Taoism

Influence. Taoism ceased to be a recognized religion when the Chinese republic was founded. Its influence, however, is great in its native China, in other countries of Asia, and increasingly in the West. Numerous translations of its primary text, the *Tao Te Ching* (The Way of Life), have made it one of the most widely known Eastern religions in the world.

Beliefs and Practices. Taoism is a mystical—yet practical—philosophy. It recognizes the primary forces in nature as yin and yang. The tension between these opposites keeps the world in motion. The founder is thought to be Lao-tze ("the old philosopher" or "old sir"), born in the Honan province of China about 604 BC.

In response to the chaos and violent decay of the Chou dynasty, Confucius recommended a strict ethical code of duties and obligations. Lao-Tze's response was diametrically opposed and can be summed up in the expression *wu wei* ("not doing" or inaction).

Most actions, in this view, simply produce a reaction or the opposite of what was intended by the action (i.e., force defeats its own ends). Existence is what it is, and to disturb the natural state only creates resistance. The inaction of wu wei, is not passivity but action based on an understanding of natural law and living in harmony with the rhythms and cycles of nature. The Tao is the operating principle within the natural world.

The way to be followed is the natural way, the way of harmony, and of original order. To know the way is to cast off externally imposed ideas and be receptive to undivided existence—night and day, light and darkness, hot and cold, yin and yang. Yin (femininity) represents darkness, cold, wetness, withdrawal, and passivity. Yang (masculinity) represents brightness, heat, expansion, and procreation. Rather than being separate opposites, in Taoism they are dependent polarities representing unity. To live in obedience to the Tao is to live in harmony.

Zen

Influence. Zen is a very important belief system in Japan; its influence is felt in such arts as flower arranging, the tea ceremony, swordsmanship, archery, poetry calligraphy, and the art of self-defense.

Beliefs and Practices. Zen is primarily a Buddhist sect that stresses an intuitional quest for Buddha-reality, the experience of *satori* (a sudden insight into the essential, unified nature of reality, sometimes known as the diamond thunderbolt). This insight cannot be reached by the path of reason: classifying, analyzing, defining, questioning. In effect, words are useless for discussing absolute reality. Concepts are dualistic by nature, and the seeker of truth must go beyond dualisms to the essential oneness of reality.

Faith is placed in the inner self and spontaneous action. One tool used to help the student move beyond reason is the *Koan,* an insoluble riddle: for example, "What is the sound of one hand clapping?" or "A girl is walking down the street, is she the younger or the older sister?" A true response requires an emptying of the mind, a breakdown of habitual patterns of thought.

The emphasis on spontaneity rather than reason was influential with the Samurai warrior class in Japan, particularly in their practice of archery and swordsmanship. For example, in archery, the aim is not to master the bow, but to allow the arrow to shoot itself from the bow.

Zen also entails a disciplined form of meditation called *zazen,* aimed at stilling and concentrating the mind. As David Rearwin points out, one objective of this training is to focus the mind on paying attention, to enable the student to perceive small changes so that, "Even if you have done something before, don't assume it will be the same next time. Pay attention. You may see something that escaped your notice on previous occasions, or you may find that there has been a change."[4]

Understanding the primary belief systems of the areas in which you are working is critical for at least two reasons. First, it gives you a sense of what is sacred to the people you are working with. Secondly, it enriches your understanding of why a culture is as it is. For example, Buddhist, Hindu, and Sikh cultures have a cyclical view of time. Patterns are repeated over and over again. A constraint orientation to the environment is very likely. Cultures that recognize only one God may tend to be absolutist in their thinking style, recognizing only one way of doing something or only one correct answer.

AFRICA

In discussions of globalization, Africa is the forgotten continent. Very few American businesspeople are excited about opportunities in Africa, with the exception of South Africa (since the lifting of UN sanctions).

Africa is associated in Western minds with famine, extreme poverty, disease, illiteracy, political instability, corruption, and massive foreign debt. Undoubtedly, the prospects for Africa are bleak. Writing in the Foreign Affairs Quarterly, Marguerite Michaels says that the collapse of the Soviet Union "set America free to pursue its own interests in Africa—and it found it did not have any."[5] Invest-

ment opportunities are few, and demand for the continent's major natural resources, such as copper and cobalt, have dwindled. Most Africans are still reliant
on subsistence farming. The last U.S. president to visit sub-Saharan Africa was
Jimmy Carter in 1978.

Steven A. Holmes, writing in the *New York Times,* makes a valid point when
he writes:[6]

> But to view Africa as nothing but a bleak landscape is to miss the blossoms among
> the weeds. "If you look from one week to the next, the cup is more empty than full,"
> said a State Department Official. "But if you look over the last few years, the overall
> trend is in the right direction. The number of democratic elections is going up. The
> number of economic liberalization programs is going up."

Peace is holding in Mozambique and in Namibia, which won independence in
1990 after decades of rule by South Africa in defiance of the United Nations.
Kenya, Zambia, Ethiopia, Mali and Benin are inching or in some places running
toward multi-party democracy after decades of one party rule or military dicta-
torship. Under prodding by the World Bank, 26 countries have restructured their
economies and are expanding their trade.

During the 1980s, Cameroon's economy grew by 8 percent per year, and
Mauritius' economy grew by over 5 percent per head.[7]

One of the most difficult issues facing anyone looking at the cultural landscape of the continent is that many countries were formed as a result of colonialism. Cultures are more often associated with traditional kingdoms or tribes (some
3,000 in Africa) rather than existing national boundaries. Uganda is a prime example of a country formed out of rival ethnic and linguistic groups that have
never been successfully unified.[8] The power of tribalism can still be seen in
South Africa, where the Xhosa-dominated African National Congress and the
Zulu-dominated Inkatha Freedom Party have been fighting a bloody battle for the
past 10 years or so.

Culturally, Africa is a mix of Islamic, Christian, and traditional indigenous beliefs. Most Africans find themselves caught in a strange cultural mixture of Western values and ancestral and tribal loyalties and obligations. The principal
countries in Africa are listed in Table 3–2.

*Environment©**

The dominant mode toward the environment is one of constraint, even fatalism.
This isn't surprising given the history of colonialism over the past five centuries
and the predominance of subsistence farming and extreme poverty. Per capita income is lower now than it was 30 years ago.[9] Minimal educational opportunities

*©Training Management Corporation (TMC), *Doing Business Internationally: The Cross-Cul-
tural Challenges,* Seminar and Coursebook (Princeton, NJ, 1992).

TABLE 3–2
Principal Countries in Africa

Angola	Madagascar
Benin	Mali
Botswana	Malawi
Burkina Faso	Mauritania
Burundi	Mozambique
Cameroon	Namibia
Central African Republic	Niger
Chad	Nigeria
Congo	Rwanda
Equatorial Guinea	Senegal
Ethiopia	Sierra Leone
Gabon	Somalia
Gambia	South Africa
Ghana	Swaziland
Guinea-Bissau	Tanzania
Guinea	Togo
Ivory Coast	Uganda
Kenya	Zaire
Lesotho	Zambia
Liberia	Zimbabwe

for much of the population, the lack of adequate administrative and physical infrastructures, the dependence on foreign aid, and the relatively small middle class on the continent hinder the emergence of a control orientation. The majority of the population cannot help but see their lives as governed by external forces: the climate, foreign governments, internal—often authoritarian—governments, and so on. To some extent, this is changing. Steven Holmes writes:[10]

> Perhaps the most significant development is the willingness of Africans to admit their own past mistakes—to stop placing the blame for the continent's underdevelopment entirely on the West and the legacy of colonialism, and instead condemn gross abuses by incompetent or venal leaders . . . The shift in African attitudes first became evident in 1990, when West African states concluded that if they didn't do something about the strife in Liberia to ensure the stability of the region, no one else would; a Nigerian-led peace force intervened.

Change in Africa has mostly been externally driven. This state of affairs may alter as the West becomes increasingly indifferent to the greater part of the continent, and African countries are forced to come to terms with their own destinies.

Some guidelines:

Be realistic. Don't raise expectations too high.

- Don't try to force change. Facilitate change by persistence.
- Show empathy for perceived constraints, while keeping a focus on objectives.

*Time©**

Time in most of Africa is fluid. Relationships are given priority over schedules and deadlines. Being hurried may only breed resistance or mistrust.[11] Relationships are built by sitting and talking, with business being postponed until comfort is established. In Africa, as David Lamb says, "Patience is more than a virtue; it is a necessity for survival."[12] Life is not lived by the clock. Punctuality is defined loosely, particularly among friends and in rural areas. Africans living and working in urban areas—and meeting with foreigners—will try to hold meetings on time.

Most Americans and Europeans will find themselves frustrated in Africa, and Africans are confused about the impatience of their visitors. David Lamb tells stories of passengers being stranded on Wednesday only to be told, "I don't understand why you're so upset . . . there's another flight Saturday." Or being told that a flight is being delayed for two days because the president of the country has borrowed the plane.[13]

Time is one of the few items that seem to be in abundance in Africa. The future, however, has little place in African thought. John S. Mbiti states:[14]

> The linear concept of time in Western thought, with an indefinite past, present, and indefinite future, is practically foreign to African thinking. The future is virtually absent because events which lie in it have not taken place, they have not been realized and cannot, therefore, constitute time . . . *Actual time* is, therefore, what is present and what is past. It moves 'backward' rather than 'forward;' and people set their minds not on future things, but chiefly in what has taken place.

The impact of Christianity and Western-style education is changing the concept of time. A concern for the future has developed in many countries and manifests itself in national plans for economic growth and a concern for educational opportunities.[15]

Some guidelines:

- Don't show impatience or try to hurry. You may be perceived as trying to cheat your African counterpart.

---

*©Training Management Corporation (TMC), Doing Business Internationally: The Cross-Cultural Challenges, Seminar and Coursebook (Princeton, NJ, 1992).

- Slow down and be flexible. Put your watch in your pocket and don't try to fight against local time.
- Show respect for traditions.

*Action©**

African societies—in general—are more being than doing oriented. Traditionally, change has not been valued for its own sake. Work gets done after sincere, trusting friendships have been established. Many Africans are experiencing the transition from village to city and, as a consequence, are losing some of their reliance on close relationships. But for most the importance of relationships is still paramount. An aggressive focus on the task at hand may be perceived as trying to demonstrate superiority.[16] Work is not the central component of a good life. Leisure and family are extremely important.

Some guidelines:

- Spend time developing personal relationships. Don't be aloof or insincere.
- Don't appear to be too task oriented and never condescending or arrogant.
- Expect to do business one-on-one. Any other method may result in your being perceived as being less than serious.
- Always make good on your promises.
- Build connections.

*Communication©**

Communication in Africa is often high context, indirect, and inexpressive. David Lamb says, "It is rare that he [the African] will reveal his inner emotions or talk about his beliefs in more than superficial terms. As often as not, he will tell you what he thinks you want to hear rather than risk offending you with an opinionated view."[17] Politeness and protocol are highly valued, and hospitality is generous. Forms of address are often related to status and seniority. One sure way to destroy a relationship in Africa is to communicate any feelings about Africa being "backward." Africa is very proud of its achievements. Both Afrikaners and South Africans of British descent tend to be rather reserved and dislike loud and boisterous behavior.

Some guidelines:

- Communicate formality and respect.
- Soften directness. Listen for meanings not always spoken directly.

---

*©Training Management Corporation (TMC), *Doing Business Internationally: The Cross-Cultural Challenges,* Seminar and Coursebook (Princeton, NJ, 1992).

- Be open to receiving and giving hospitality.
- Always use titles.
- Be assertive, but avoid arrogance.
- Avoid political discussions.
- Demonstrate a genuine interest in African culture. Don't keep comparing Africa with your own culture.

Space©*

Personal space tends to be closer than most Westerners are used to. Space is more oriented to being public than private. This fits with the collective nature of much of African society and the reliance on friendship and trust. Friendly touching is common.

Some guidelines:

- Be warm and genuine when greeting others.
- Expect to shake hands a great deal.
- Don't refuse hospitality.
- Show respect by dressing in a very professional manner.

Power©*

Africa is often home to authoritarian leaders—"Big Man" as they are sometimes called. Authority is rarely questioned. Free expression is not given a high value. It helps to do business in Africa if relationships can be developed with top officials. Age can also be an asset, as wisdom is associated with the elderly. Connections are the key to success in many parts of Africa. Loyalty is highly valued and plays a significant role in decision making.

Some guidelines:

- Show respect at all times.
- Whenever possible, work through a respected third party with high-level connections.
- Expect decisions to be made in a centralized manner.

---

*©Training Management Corporation (TMC), *Doing Business Internationally: The Cross-Cultural Challenges,* Seminar and Coursebook (Princeton, NJ, 1992).

*Individualism©**

For the most part, African cultures are collectivist. The extended family and tribes are powerful groups that shape individual behaviors. Family loyalties en‑ courage nepotism, and kinship ties swell the ranks of bureaucracies across the continent. In a very informative book about Africa, Blaine Harden says:

> Not only does family loyalty gum up African governments, it can hobble the careers and limit the achievements of individual Africans. Jealous relatives often harm each other. Gossip, curses, land disputes, homicide, and witchcraft are aimed at successful relatives whose remittances to the family fail to meet expectations.[18]

The pressures of family/tribal obligations have been associated with the wide‑ spread corruption in many African countries.[19] While some bribery money will stay in the individual's pocket, a significant proportion may be channelled back to relatives in the rural areas. Tribes provide individuals with acceptable guide‑ lines for almost every aspect of life: birth, marriage, and death rituals, inheri‑ tance, succession, and so on. Laws derived from tribal custom may be more powerful than those of the nation.

African cities are some of the fastest growing in the world. The Africans in those cities have often made an abrupt switch from collective rural tradition to urban life with its more Western-oriented attitudes and individualistic values.

Some guidelines:

- Show respect for kinship and the importance of obligations.
- Pay attention to family/tribal as well as national loyalties.
- Expect rules, policies, and procedures to be applied in a particularistic rather than universalistic fashion.

*Competitiveness©**

Rapid change in Africa is increasing the emphasis placed on material success and prosperity. This is particularly the case in some countries of southern Africa, for example, Botswana, Namibia, South Africa, and Zambia. These countries con‑ tain much of the world's mineral wealth and are seeking to establish democratic, market-driven economies. Many of the countries in the region are talking of a southern African economic community to create bigger markets for local prod‑ ucts, to stimulate exports, and attract foreign investments. Elsewhere, competi‑ tiveness varies from low to moderate levels.

---

*©Training Management Corporation (TMC), *Doing Business Internationally: The Cross-Cultural Challenges,* Seminar and Coursebook (Princeton, NJ, 1992).

Some guidelines:

- Be competitive, but avoid being perceived as exploitative.
- Expect to be asked for concessions and favors.

Structure©*

Life in most of Africa is neither rigid nor highly regulated. David Lamb puts it this way:

> Africa has taken all the worst aspects of European bureaucracy, combined them with ignorance and indifference, and come up with a system that is as undirected, as lethargic as a rudderless dhow in a rough sea. Niceties aside, Africa just doesn't work very well.[20]

African bureaucracies are, on the whole, large and inefficient. Red tape can hinder any project.

Some guidelines:

- Build connections that can navigate you through the complexity.
- Expect to work from a broad agreement rather than a detailed plan or contract.

Thinking©*

If you spend time in Africa, "you quickly realize that all those things you learned in the West about punctuality, efficiency, and rational thought processes don't have much to do with Africa. Africa can only be explained in terms of Africa." So says David Lamb in *The Africans*.[21] But what is "African" thought?

Edgar J. Ridley, an African-American international management consultant, offers us interesting insights in his *An African Answer: The Key to Global Productivity.*[22] Ridley argues that Africa's socioeconomic progress and effectiveness are being impeded by decision making based on symbolic, mythological thought. A heavy dependence on symbolic thinking encourages superstition, and, in Ridley's view, a refusal to see things as they really are. He feels there is a confusion of symbol and substance. In his view, this is like living in a world of virtual reality. "The person has a sense of being part of a world that doesn't really exist."[23]

Ridley distinguishes between natural sign and symbol. Wet streets, for example, are a sign that rain has fallen, and smoke indicates fire. These are symptoms

---

*©Training Management Corporation (TMC), *Doing Business Internationally: The Cross-Cultural Challenges,* Seminar and Coursebook (Princeton, NJ, 1992).

of an actual state. Symbolic thinking goes beyond these symptoms to try to find something more real. While every people engages in symbolic thinking, he sees Africans as the "most symbolic-behaving people on earth, and such behavior is inadequate for doing world-class business."[24] While Ridley's thesis may be too sweeping, it does point to an Africa that Western businessmen and women may have trouble relating to.

Some guidelines:

- Withhold your critical judgment.
- Present arguments in small chunks in a clear, precise style.
- Expect decisions to be based on more than a consideration of data and presented facts.

ASIA

The Asian-Pacific region is one of wide cultural diversity, profound economic opportunity, and competitive challenge. The principal countries in the region are listed in Table 3–3.

With the largest continental land mass—over 17,400,000 square miles (over 30 percent of the world's surface)—Asia also has the highest percentage of the world's population, over 56 percent. China alone has over 1.1 billion inhabitants (21 percent of the world's population), and India's population is expected to reach 1 billion by the end of the century.

Asia-Pacific represents a region of deep contrasts. It has provided the most stunning economic growth since World War II, and yet also retains its roots in very ancient philosophical and religious traditions. Asia-Pacific provides U.S. business with vast market opportunities, access to new capital sources and technologies, lower-cost labor markets, expertise, and a profound cross-cultural challenge.

Apart from Australia and New Zealand, the Asian-Pacific region is very foreign to the vast majority of Americans. Having their roots in British cultural traditions, the majority of Australians and New Zealanders speak English, and Christianity is the dominant religious belief system. Americans tend to feel at home with the directness, informality, and individualism in both countries. Moving out of Australia and New Zealand, the situation becomes more problematic for most Americans.

To most Westerners, Asian cultures appear to be similar to one another. This perception has been amplified by the superficial Westernization of many Asian cities. While there is a cultural core within Asia (mostly derived from China), every country has a unique set of national characteristics. No West-

TABLE 3–3
Principal Countries in Asia-Pacific

Afghanistan	Macao
Australia	Malaysia
Bangladesh	Maldives
Bhutan	Mongolia
Brunei	Myanmar (Burma)
Cambodia	Nepal
China	New Zealand
Fiji	Pakistan
Hong Kong	Papua New Guinea
India	Philippines
Indonesia	Singapore
Japan	Sri Lanka
Korea (North)	Taiwan
Korea (South)	Thailand
Laos	Vietnam

erner should assume that Asia is becoming like the West. Anyone in the West who is of this opinion should keep in mind the words of Lee Kuan Yew, Singapore's former Prime Minister. He says this about Japan's change of government in 1993:[25]

> I do not see them becoming a fractious, contentious society like America, always debating and knocking each other down. That is not in their culture . . . Americans believe that out of contention, out of the clash of different ideas and ideals, you get good government. That view is not shared in Asia.

He goes on:

> If we follow the West in our social relations and family structures, we will be in deep trouble. In the West the Christian religion used to instill fear of punishment in hell or reward in heaven. Science and technology have eliminated that fear. So the controlling mechanism has gone awry. I am hoping that because Asian moral control is based on what is good in a secular this-world not a spiritual after-w ·ld, we will not lose our moral bearings . . . If you bring a child into the world in the West, the state caters for him. That's dangerous. If you bring a child into Asia, that's your personal responsibility.
>   As long as our society remains structured in this traditional way, we will be different. We will not allow muggers to clonk you on the head and grab your belongings . . . When you are ill, you will not be abandoned, because your family are required by culture to look after you or suffer shame.

Environment©*

Confucianism, Buddhism, Taoism, and Hinduism have instilled a harmony/constraint mix in Asia. Balance, harmony, order, and the establishment of correct relationships are of deep significance in those Asian countries most influenced by Confucian China: Korea and Japan. Harmony should not be confused with submission, peace and tranquility, or passivity. *Budo,* the Japanese word for martial arts, means "the way to stop the spear."[26] The aim of these highly disciplined activities is conflict avoidance through carefully controlled aggression rather than the elimination of conflict through brute force.

Part of the harmony orientation is quickly adapting to changed circumstances. Life is in continual motion, and the wise individual pays very close attention to even the smallest differences in circumstance. The Westerner who feels he or she has made an agreement with some Asian counterparts may be shocked to dis cover that because of changed circumstances the agreement has been changed or ignored. As David Rearwin says in *The Asia Business Book:*[27]

> Abstract concepts like right and wrong, or truth and untruth, depend on the circumstances, rather than being absolute. Behavior that is acceptable in one situation may be unacceptable in another. Both morally and legally, individuals and governments have no compunctions about changing the rules at any time to fit a new set of circumstances (including newly discovered needs or newly defined objectives on the part of the Asian in question).

Harmony is also reflected in Asian decision making, particularly in Japan's *inghi* system. All parties affected by a decision are consulted. While decision making may take longer than in the West, implementation is likely to be faster (everyone has been consulted and much of the preparatory work will have been done in the decision-making phase).

Some guidelines:

- Don't push. Be patient, and understand the need for consensus building.
- Pay attention, and be prepared for the unexpected.
- Don't be passive. Weakness will not be respected.

Time©*

In industrial East Asia, the orientation toward time is single focused. In the less developed countries of Southeast Asia, the orientation is more multifocused.

---

*©Training Management Corporation (TMC), *Doing Business Internationally: The Cross-Cultural Challenges,* Seminar and Coursebook (Princeton, NJ, 1992).

Throughout Asia, there is both a strong past and a long-term future orientation. Current decisions and plans are related to the past and the future. The sense of urgency is less than in the United States, and American negotiators often find themselves at a disadvantage because of self-imposed time pressures and impatience.

Due to their strong connection with the past, Asians (including corporations) generally have a highly developed sense of personal identification with national, business, and family histories One of the implications of the emphasis on the past and on family and national cohesion is that Asian cultures are more collectivistic than individualistic. Also, because Asians are generally oriented to the long term, they are particularly interested in getting to know you and your company. As a consequence, negotiations can take a relatively long time.

Some guidelines:

- Be punctual.
- Respect tradition and long-term commitments.
- Don't expect immediate payoff.
- Sell the reputation of your company and its success over time.
- Be patient. Don't force yourself into an impossible situation by setting arbitrary deadlines.

Action©*

Asian cultures display both a being and doing orientation. There is an emphasis on working hard and achieving success and on developing trust in relationships. Asians need to understand the context of doing business, including who you are and your company's status and reputation. It is very important to take time to develop a relationship through personal contact and not rush to discuss price, delivery dates, and so on. Who you are is as important as what you are selling.

Entertaining is a vital part of doing business in Asia and is critical to building and maintaining relationships. Entertainment or relationship-building activities should not be considered as necessarily leading to a deep relationship. If circumstances change, the relationship is likely to change.

Some guidelines:

- Focus on personal contact and relationship-building before getting down to business.
- Sell your company as well as yourself.

---

*©Training Management Corporation (TMC), *Doing Business Internationally: The Cross-Cultural Challenges,* Seminar and Coursebook (Princeton, NJ, 1992).

*Communication©**

Formalities are important to observe throughout Asia (for example, the Japanese tea ceremony) and they extend to all aspects of doing business: greetings, business card exchange, gift giving, terms of address, negotiation protocol, dining, and entertaining. Formality with those outside of one's immediate group is especially important.

Asians, on the whole, tend to be indirect, high context, and self-controlled in their communication style. They tend to avoid overt conflict, avoid the expression of anger, and when disputes arise, an intermediary who knows both parties may be asked to help resolve the conflict. Indirect and vague expressions are common in formal situations. Direct questions, however, are often posed in both Japan and Korea. Chinese expression is more controlled.

Some guidelines:

- Be low-key, polite, and formal. Use formal titles until a relationship is developed.
- Take your lead from your Asian counterparts on whether to bow or shake hands.
- Treat business cards with great respect. Study the ones given to you, and don't put them in your pocket (use a card holder). Give and receive cards with both hands while standing.
- Resist showing emotions; communicate seriousness.
- Be persistent without being overly aggressive.
- Lower the voice as a sign of respect.
- Pay attention to details.
- Avoid legalism. The legal process is a last resort, especially in Japan.
- Think before speaking. Don't rush to fill silences. And avoid talking with your hands.
- Help others to save "face" by always providing a way out.
- Communicate discipline and learning.
- Don't make overly prolonged eye contact. It may be mistaken for aggressiveness.
- Don't make jokes. They rarely translate well.
- Expect an indirect no (particularly in Japan): for example, "It will be difficult," "We'll study that option."
- Never criticize, not even the competition, and avoid open confrontation.

---

*©Training Management Corporation (TMC), *Doing Business Internationally: The Cross-Cultural Challenges,* Seminar and Coursebook (Princeton, NJ, 1992).

Space©*

Personal space requirements are similar to those in the United States, but more distant than those of Latin Americans or Middle Easterners. Office spaces tend to be quite public. Private offices are rare. Touching is avoided.

In Asia, the language of space is highly complex. Sitting positions are sometimes a clue to power relationships. For example, in Japan the seat farthest from the door is likely to be the "power seat." In a car, the seat directly behind the driver is considered the most prestigious.

In China, it is well to be aware of the notion of *feng shui* (wind and water). *Feng shui* principles act as guides to good fortune, and they seek harmony with the influences of the natural world. For example, a dwelling with trees planted near the front gate will come under the spell of evil influences; a building on a site at a "Y" junction is likely to suffer misfortune.[28]

Some guidelines:

- Pay close attention to who is sitting where.
- Be highly restrained in touching others.

Power©*

Asian orientations to power tend toward hierarchy, or "soft authoritarianism" and "authoritarian pluralism" as the power structure is sometimes called.[29] Democracy has played a very limited role in the history of the region. Democracy came to Japan, for example, only after the Second World War. Deference to older family members, particularly males, is widespread, and observance of rank and status is very important. Differences in age, sex, and status are commonly acknowledged in deferential and honorific speech and behaviors. Paternalistic authority is often the norm. In China, management by committee is a popular method. In the large Korean industrial complexes (known as *chaebol*) orders flow from top to bottom, and loyalty and obedience are prized. In many Southeast Asian cultures, there is usually a large difference in power levels between managers and subordinates.

Some guidelines:

- Clarify rank and status differences early in your discussions.
- Communicate your reporting relationships clearly and precisely.
- Don't try to circumvent levels of authority, no matter how cumbersome.
- Form relationships with the powerful and well respected.

---

*©Training Management Corporation (TMC), *Doing Business Internationally: The Cross-Cultural Challenges,* Seminar and Coursebook (Princeton, NJ, 1992).

*Individualism©**

Individualism, in general, is not highly valued in Asia. In Taiwan, mainland China, and Hong Kong, however, there is a strong entrepreneurial spirit. This has been evident in Taiwan and Hong Kong for some time, but is only just being released in China. It has been a very strong trait in Chinese emigrant groups overseas.

Loyalty to the work organization is strong, as well as loyalty to parents, mentors, and past teachers. The collectivist orientation results in tighter teamwork, more consensual decision making, obedience, and more widespread information sharing than is generally found in the United States. This orientation, however, should not be overstated. The Chinese and Koreans tend to put personal and family concerns before organizational and societal concerns. In Japan, the stress is on the organization and society. As part of the collective orientation, government and nationalistic pressures tend to play a larger role in economic life. As Rearwin says, "Throughout Asia, business is subject to a high degree of control by government, and businesses are supposed to work for the good of the country."[30]

Korean business leaders can be quite individualistic, while those in Japan are much more closely integrated into the group.

Some guidelines:

- Expect decision making to be slow and involved.
- Expect high loyalty and identification with the social group.
- Use third parties to help you make introductions and contacts.
- Safeguard intellectual property. (Its protection has far less value in the more collective Asian environment.)

*Competitiveness©**

Competitiveness varies across Asia. Japan, Hong Kong, and the Philippines are highly competitive. Many Japanese children, from a very young age, are placed in competitive classes for entrance to high-status universities.

Yet even in the highly competitive Asian countries, there is rarely an emphasis on individual success at the expense of the group or team. Also, while promotion based on performance and merit is becoming increasingly important, seniority is still an important factor.

---

*©Training Management Corporation (TMC), *Doing Business Internationally: The Cross-Cultural Challenges,* Seminar and Coursebook (Princeton, NJ, 1992).

Some guidelines:

- Don't be lulled into a false feeling of international brotherhood.
- Expect hardball, sometimes motivated by ethnocentrism.
- Don't make threats.
- Be competitive, but avoid boasting and making extravagant claims.
- Recognize the competitiveness between Asian nations, and use it to enhance your position.
- Show great respect for seniority and age.
- Persevere.

Structure©*

Values regarding structure also vary. Japan, South Korea, China, Taiwan, and Thailand place a relatively high value on structure, order, and control. In general, the stronger the value placed on structure, the stronger the value placed on consensus. Confucianism places a high value on roles, obligations, and the correct ways of doing things. This is often manifested in a somewhat rigid formalism and bureaucracy. There is, however, a lower value placed on legalism. Contracts are, in many instances, simply an expression of willingness to do business rather than a set agreement.

Some guidelines:

- Expect a high level of rigidity and multiple levels of regulation and administrative procedure.
- Spend time making contacts who can get things done.
- Recognize the spirit of the agreement and not just the fine details.

Thinking©*

Asian thinking patterns are notoriously difficult for Westerners to comprehend. David Rearwin has the best description of any observer:[31]

> You will encounter refusals with no apparent reason, leaps of logic (or illogic) that lead to totally impossible conclusions, willingness to follow a course that already leads nowhere, cheerful acceptance of mutually contradictory statements, and a literal-mindedness that forces you to ask exactly the right question in order to get useful information . . . remember that Asian thinking tends to reach a given target by moving in a

*©Training Management Corporation (TMC), *Doing Business Internationally: The Cross-Cultural Challenges,* Seminar and Coursebook (Princeton, NJ, 1992).

spiral or by generating a holistic image centered on a general (and often rather amorphous concept) rather than a clearly discernible line of thought.

Some guidelines:

• Keep an open, skeptical mind, and be ready to adapt.

• Allow the Asian thought process to run its course. Be objective and avoid showing frustration.

• Be prepared to answer a wide range of detailed questions. Don't lose face by having to get back to them with answers.

EUROPE

Europe is undergoing radical change. The fall of the Berlin wall, the collapse of Communism and growth of free markets, German unification, ongoing ethnic struggles, and the evolving European Community are changing the economic, political, social, and cultural terrain.

Europe is a patchwork of cultures and is likely to be so until well into the foreseeable future. Increased economic cooperation will not eliminate the deep cultural identities that shape the continent. In what can be described as a Euro-novel, the British author Malcolm Bradbury has fun with some of the sharp cultural contrasts he observes:[32]

> High mountains replaced the Lombardy plain, Italian chaos began giving way to Swiss neatness, Italian noise to Swiss silence.
>
> The girl behind the desk was solemn, dour, and reserved. So were all the maps and guidebooks she handed me. "Here it is the quality of life that counts," said the first guide I opened. "Each district, street, park and shop attempts to outshine the others, but always in the best of good taste with due moderation." No doubt about it; we had definitely arrived in Switzerland.

While there is a superficial MTV (Music Television) European culture among the young, the historical patterns of national and regional culture are well embedded, and it will take many generations before a pan-European culture emerges. Some observers even talk of cultural fault lines stretching across Europe, for example, in Bosnia with its stark division between east and west. Cultural and ethnic divisions in eastern Europe are beginning to re-emerge after years of communist dominance. How the culture wars in the east will play out over the long term is anyone's guess.

Any cultural division of Europe will be arbitrary, but one of the most common (and useful) is to think in terms of the north (Norway, Sweden, Denmark, Finland, Iceland), west (France, Germany, the United Kingdom, Ireland, Belgium, the Netherlands), south (Italy, Spain, Portugal, Greece), and east (Russia, Poland, Hungary, Romania, Bulgaria, the Baltic States).

One factor to be aware of in dealing with Europe is that European feelings toward America are very ambivalent. On the one hand, there is a feeling of respect and partnership. On the other, many countries are resentful of an encroaching Americanization. This is particularly true of France. The principal countries in the region are listed in Table 3–4.

*Environment©**

There is a mix of mastery, harmony, and constraint, depending on the specific country. Scandinavia and the Netherlands show a particularly cooperative and harmonious orientation toward the environment. Western European countries tend toward a control orientation, while those in the east and south tend toward constraint. A constraint orientation is particularly noticable in the east, where life is uncertain and people associate control over their lives with government, fate, or foreigners. History weighs heavily on the whole of Europe. Whereas an American might say, "Let's do it!" a European is more likely to ask, "What *can* we do?" A Bulgarian Foreign Minister is quoted as saying, "Here we are completely submerged under our own histories."[33] This makes Europeans more risk averse and somewhat suspicious of change. You will even find this in a country like Britain; British reticence can appear to Americans as obstructive. Risk aversion can be difficult to deal with in the east. Post-communist bureaucrats can play havoc with markets. Seagrams, for example, was attracted to Ukraine because of tax holidays and other exemptions. The business environment, however, is one of heavy constraint. The parliament and the president's office continue to create decrees that make it very difficult for Seagrams to do business: a rule making companies change half their dollar earnings into local currency at an artificially low rate; an excise tax that triples the price of Seagrams' locally produced Vodka; a prohibition on markups of more than 50 percent of production costs; and abolition of the free-market currency auction.[34] The radical conversion from communism to capitalism can be overstated. "Homo sovieticus" is still alive and well in the bureaucracies of the east.

Some guidelines:

- Be aware of perceived constraints, and don't push too hard to break through them (at least initially).
- Beware of being perceived as always wanting to take control.
- Be aware, particularly in east Europe, of a tendency to perceive Americans as having unlimited resources and the capabilities to get anything done. Set realistic expectations.

---

*©Training Management Corporation (TMC), *Doing Business Internationally: The Cross-Cultural Challenges,* Seminar and Coursebook (Princeton, NJ, 1992).

TABLE 3–4
Principal Countries in Europe

Albania	Luxembourg
Austria	Malta
Belgium	Netherlands
Bulgaria	Norway
Czech Republic	Poland
Denmark	Portugal
Finland	Romania
France	Slovak Republic
Germany	Spain
Greece	Sweden
Hungary	Switzerland
Iceland	United Kingdom
Ireland	Yugoslavia (former)
Italy	

- Don't come across as being overly optimistic. You may appear naive. Europeans are likely to interpret their own view as being realistic and mature.

Time©*

There is a strong respect for tradition; progress and change are not accorded the same importance as in the United States. Change is not respected for its own sake. More long-range goals are taken into consideration. In general, there is not the degree of short-term future urgency that one sees in the United States, although in Russia, the emphasis is currently on the achievement of short-term goals.

Businesspeople from western, northern, and eastern Europe have, for the most part, a single-focus orientation to time, while southern Europeans have more of a multifocused orientation. Malcolm Bradbury makes the following observations about the British and Italian approach to time. "'We're already half an hour late,' I said to Miss Belli. 'Only in Britain,' said Miss Belli. 'In Italy when you are an hour late, you are already half an hour early.'"[35]

Western European cultures are close to the American time orientation. Meetings begin and end on time, and life is generally fast paced, but not so fast as in America. In southern European cultures, time is more fluid and defined in less-precise terms.

---

*©Training Management Corporation (TMC), *Doing Business Internationally: The Cross-Cultural Challenges,* Seminar and Coursebook (Princeton, NJ, 1992).

One important factor about the east is that they have developed a distaste for long-term planning. This is undoubtedly a reaction to their communist past as well as a response to the current conditions of uncertainty. However, while the present may be the current dominant factor in the east's approach to time, countries such as Slovakia, the Czech Republic, Poland, and Hungary are keeping one eye on the future. Other countries, such as Bulgaria, Romania, and Albania are still, to a large degree, focused on the past.

Some guidelines:

- Be aware that now is *not* always perceived as the right time. The right time is more likely to arise naturally in the course of events.
- Respect the past and demonstrate knowledge of the other culture's history, traditions, and contributions to civilization.
- Be punctual, even if it's not expected.
- In southern Europe, expect interruptions and delays. Don't take them personally.
- Slow down. Take your time.

*Action©**

Europeans value the quality of life. Family life is extremely important; leisure time is spent with the family, and month-long vacations are the norm. There are also an average of 12 civic and religious holidays per year in most of western Europe. Relationships and affiliations are highly valued, particularly in the south and the east. While achievement is valued, activity is not valued for its own sake.

One notable difference between the United States and Europe is that business does not have equal status on the two continents. Europe, on the whole, gives business a lower priority. It is much more prestigious in Europe to be a professor, doctor, lawyer, or engineer than it is to be an executive.[36] Business tends to be associated with the mundane; it is a necessary evil rather than a noble or heroic pursuit.

There can also be a greater split between work life and social life. This may be expressed in a phrase like, "There's a time and place for everything." The British, in particular, are very protective of the gap between office and home. The French are intolerant of business discussions over a meal. If you really enjoy power breakfasts, stay in the United States.

The development of relationships with outsiders has not been a high priority in the east, while relationships with family, friends, and colleagues have been critical. As the communist system breaks down, this state of affairs is changing.

**©Training Management Corporation (TMC), *Doing Business Internationally: The Cross-Cultural Challenges,* Seminar and Coursebook (Princeton, NJ, 1992).

Many east Europeans are recognizing the importance of relationship-building in negotiations and other business activities. Poland and Hungary in the east have maintained a higher degree of individualism than many others under Soviet influence. As a consequence, both countries are more action-oriented in style.

Some guidelines:

- Work at communicating who you are as a person (character, beliefs, values, etc.) and not just what you do for a living.
- Let people know the value of your own social networks—family, friends, and so on.
- Share stories. Be willing to stay up until the late hours discussing ideas, opinions, and relationships.
- Try to do as much business as you can on a face-to-face basis rather than the telephone or fax.
- Be sure to follow up.
- Pay attention to when work is appropriate and when pleasure is appropriate.

*Communication©**

Communication style varies throughout Europe. The British tend to be indirect. Where an American might say, "He really screwed up. I'll kick his butt," an Englishman would say, "Let me look into it, and I'll have a quiet word in his ear." The French, on the other hand can be quite direct and confrontational. Their educational system promotes debate and argument. Part of building credibility with the French is a willingness to engage in intellectual discussion. "I think, therefore I am" was derived by the French philosopher, René Descartes. There is a disconnect here with the American "I work, therefore I am."

Cultures in southern and eastern Europe can be very expressive in style. Hand and arm movements are common among Italians, Greeks, and Spaniards. The expressive style matches a desire to do business through relationships rather than simply focusing on tasks.

The higher level of formality throughout Europe is well known. Protocol and manners are critical to the building and maintenance of business relationships. Proper titles should be used, interruptions should be kept to a minimum when others are speaking, and proper respect should be given to defined roles and responsibilities. Malcolm Bradbury shows us that there are differences in levels of formality throughout Europe:[37]

---

*©Training Management Corporation (TMC), *Doing Business Internationally: The Cross-Cultural Challenges,* Seminar and Coursebook (Princeton, NJ, 1992).

Also in Austria we do not have the habit of inviting the utter passing stranger into the pristine quiet of our homes. I know you come from an informal country (Britain), but here, even in these difficult days, we like to preserve a certain formality, with proper introductions and so on.

Communication styles in the east vary from country to country. Czech and Slovak individuals can be self-effacing and indirect when making demands. The Poles and Russians, on the other hand, can be very direct and emotionally expressive.

One critical point about European formality is that it should not be overstated. The reserve and politeness of Europeans lie at the surface of life. Once trust is built, the formalities are dropped, and the relationship becomes close and binding.

Some guidelines:

- Be polite.
- Always communicate respect by recognizing status levels.
- Work at building a genuine, long-term relationship, not one that is "here today, gone tomorrow."
- Tone down any tendency to be direct and "in your face."
- Avoid becoming emotional, but demonstrate warmth and concern.
- Recognize that in the south and east, "objective" job appraisals may not always be appreciated. Given their expressive and collective orientations, "objective" criteria may appear as demeaning and irrelevant.
- Avoid hype—exaggerated communication. It can make the European suspicious.

Space©

Personal space requirements vary with the country. Generally, people tend to be more intimate and stand closer to one another in the Mediterranean and east European countries, and are more distant and reserved in the northern and western European countries.

Some guidelines:

- Respect privacy.
- Don't back away if people stand or sit close to you.

---

*©Training Management Corporation (TMC), *Doing Business Internationally: The Cross-Cultural Challenges,* Seminar and Coursebook (Princeton, NJ, 1992).

Power©*

Power orientations also vary by country. In general, power in organizations flows from the top down, and hierarchy is pronounced. German companies are controlled by major executive committees comprised of shareholders, worker representatives, and management. Below that is a hierarchical structure comprised of managers who are also technical experts in their fields. French companies, on the other hand, tend to be controlled by a single individual. British companies are organized in a similar fashion to U.S. companies, although the British pay a great deal more attention to levels of authority. "Knowing your place" is critical to the British way of doing things.

East Europeans can also be highly sensitive about levels of authority and social position. It is ironic that communism—the great equalizer—created so many social divisions and levels of status and power.

Negotiations in the east can be difficult and lengthy. The decision-making process is often obscure to the outsider, and there is a continual checking with higher levels of bureaucratic authority.

The work force is generally well trained and educated, and long tenures exist within the same company. Company loyalty and hard work are rewarded, and lateral moves between different companies can be viewed with disfavor. European managers tend to be older than their American counterparts, primarily because they do not leapfrog ranks as many American managers do.

Higher education is respected and conveys social and professional prestige. Status and class consciousness are prevalent, but less so in the Nordic countries.

Some guidelines:

- Respect the need for consensus building in many cultures.
- Build time into plans for a lengthier decision-making process.
- Demonstrate loyalty to your own company.
- Communicate your own status, authority, education, expertise, and so on, but without self-promotion.
- Whenever possible, build credibility by using highly respected references.
- Don't assume equal access to information.
- Be careful of imposing equality on your hosts, for example, by socializing with all levels You may be perceived as someone who can't be trusted.
- Recognize that the in-built controls and levels are thought to be in everyone's best interest for example, by reducing ambivalence between people.

---

*©Training Management Corporation (TMC), *Doing Business Internationally: The Cross-Cultural Challenges,* Seminar and Coursebook (Princeton, NJ, 1992).

*Individualism©**

Most European countries place a high value on individualism. Throughout Europe, there is a distinction between one's core of intimate associates and those outside that core. This finds linguistic expression in the formal and intimate forms of address (for example, the German use of *du* and *Sie,* and the French use of *vous* and *tu*).

It is important for Americans to realize, however, that the term "individualism" may mean different things to different cultures. In the United States, individualism is associated with self-reliance, independence, and a strong personal identity. The British are individualists as well, but for them individualism has different associations. As John Mole says:[38]

> "Individualism" in the English sense means eccentricity and nonconformism rather than self-reliance. They are uncomfortable taking individual initiatives or making a commitment unless they are confident that there is a group consensus behind them.

To a greater or lesser extent, the same is true of many other European countries. It is perfectly acceptable to be an individual, but within the context of strong group affiliations, such as family and class.

Although there have been dramatic changes in the east, the primary orientation is still collectivist. Social networks are critical, and individuals can feel uncomfortable outside of their primary social groups. Decision making is group oriented, and loyalty is a key factor in personal success. This is less so in the more individualistic cultures of Poland and Hungary. Decentralization is making an impact in both cultures.

Some guidelines:

- Expect high value to be placed on loyalty and connections in the collective cultures of southern and eastern Europe.
- Recognize that pride is often associated with group affiliation rather than individual accomplishment.
- Be cautious about overly using "I." You may appear to be a maverick without wider support and respect.
- Communicate respect for the "common good" and not just personal/organizational needs.

*Competitiveness©**

German-Swiss countries, Belgium, Greece, Italy, and the United Kingdom place a high value on competitiveness. The remaining northern European countries are quite low in competitiveness, and place a high value on the quality of life and in-

---

*©Training Management Corporation (TMC), *Doing Business Internationally: The Cross-Cultural Challenges,* Seminar and Coursebook (Princeton, NJ, 1992).

terdependence. It is interesting to observe the role that Nordic countries have played in world politics over recent decades. Helsinki, Finland, was the site of the SALT Treaty and major discussions on human rights; Reykjavik, Iceland, was the site chosen by Ronald Reagan and Mikhail Gorbachev for their negotiations in 1986; and, more recently, we have learned of the major role played by the Norwegians in bringing Israel and the Palestinians together. Although we should not push this notion of Nordic cooperativeness too far, they do inject their dealings with a sense of fairness and equality.

Competitiveness in the east can often tend toward the destructive. The Russians, in particular, see negotiation as a process in which they should maximize their gains at the loss of the other side. It seems to be associated with high-stakes gambling and game playing. As a result, Russian negotiators can be confrontational, blunt, and combative.

Some guidelines:

- Tone down any "winner takes all" aggressiveness.
- Look for a win-win outcome, if possible.
- Don't mistake politeness for an absence of competitiveness.
- Beware of competitive game playing, particularly in the east.

*Structure©**

Southern Europe, Belgium, France, and Germany place a high value on structure and are generally risk averse. In the United Kingdom and Scandinavia, there is a higher tolerance for ambiguity, and, consequently, less need for a high level of structure. The Germans and Swiss are well known for placing great reliance on structure. German negotiators are always very well prepared with data, reports, and so on, and view conflict as a symptom of being unprepared. They are also low risk takers and shy away from intuitive and spontaneous decision making.

The concept of "structure" is highly relative. Most Americans, because of their attachment to legalistic solutions, tend to think of themselves as highly structured. Most Europeans, however, find Americans to be somewhat anarchistic. Garrison Keillor, the popular American radio broadcaster, makes some acute observations about himself and the Danes: "The Danish sense of order makes me uneasy of course. I come from a nation of jaywalkers . . . This [Denmark] is a nation of people who wait for the green light before they cross the street, even if it's 2 A.M. and the streets are deserted."[39]

---

*©Training Management Corporation (TMC), *Doing Business Internationally: The Cross-Cultural Challenges,* Seminar and Coursebook (Princeton, NJ, 1992).

Americans often find British planning too highly structured for their taste. Whereas Americans will often trust in trial and error to reach a goal, the British will want to define every contingency.

East Europeans tend to be very uncomfortable without a high degree of structure. Failure is to be avoided and uncertainty reduced to a minimum. Observance of protocol is very important in the negotiation process.

Decision making in Germany entails a thorough analysis of the facts and may require more time than in the United States. The German emphasis on precision permeates much of their culture; there is an emphasis on discipline, caution, and concern for detail.

Some guidelines:

- Provide as much structure as is needed: reports, memos, documentation, policies, and procedures, and so on.
- Don't expect activities like brainstorming to be appreciated in high-structure societies; such activities can be perceived as irrational or immature.

*Thinking©**

Every possible thinking style is represented in Europe. The French are highly deductive in their approach. They will often want to begin with a theory of how something would work (or should work). Only after a framework for understanding has been established can matters proceed. Even then, they will continually debate the meaning and application of principles and ideas. The French also tend toward holistic, big picture thinking.

The British style tends to be more deeply pragmatic and linear in approach. John Mole captures the essence of British thinking when he says the British have[40]

> An aversion to working within a rational and systematic framework. They take pride in "mudding through," in "getting there in the end" . . . British thinking is interpretive rather than speculative. It prefers tradition and precedent and "common sense," in other words the interpretation of experience untrammelled by theory or speculation.

Although the British will develop "rules of thumb," they will, if possible, avoid abstract generalizations. This can make working relationships between the British and Americans very strained. Americans gather data from experience or experimentation in order to generate working generalizations. The British will often challenge such constructs.

---

*©Training Management Corporation (TMC), *Doing Business Internationally: The Cross-Cultural Challenges,* Seminar and Coursebook (Princeton, NJ, 1992).

In general, European thinking styles are more deductive and holistic than the American style. Apart from the Germans and east Europeans, Americans are likely to find less of a reliance on data for decision making and problem solving, and a greater reliance on thinking *per se*.

Some guidelines:

- Recognize the potential role of theory in "doing things the right way."
- Demonstrate a balance between concepts and facts and figures. Be sure you have your facts at hand, and that you can explain the assumptions underlying the data collection.
- Don't just ask questions that only require numerical answers.
- Be prepared to discuss the "whys" and not just the "hows."
- Don't accept a *fait accompli* no matter how much data or logical reasoning supports the argument.

LATIN AMERICA

Much of the cultural heritage in Latin America is derived from Spain, Portugal, and other European countries. Countries in the region that have been heavily influenced by European cultures include Argentina, Chile, most of Colombia, Costa Rica, and Uruguay. Indian-based cultures include those of Guatemala, El Salvador, Ecuador, Peru, Bolivia, and Paraguay. One common mistake is to think of the region as homogeneous. There are a number of variations of Spanish in the region, and Brazilians speak Portuguese. The principal countries in the region are listed in Table 3–5.

Throughout the region, you will find an ambivalent attitude toward the United States. On the one hand, there is respect for American achievements, and on the other there is a fear of encroaching Americanization. Nationalism is a powerful force in the region, and cultural pride is a key ingredient.

While North and South America were both colonialized by Europeans, there is, as Frank Acuff points out, a critical difference:[41]

> Both Spain and Portugal dominated colonial Latin America, and status could be achieved only by adapting to their standards. While North Americans came to the New World to flee the oppression of the Old, the Spanish and Portuguese brought their traditional system with them, and they considered themselves still part of the mother country rather than colonizers. Their social and economic style was based on the manorial lifestyle of Europe, a system where status is connected to birth and bloodlines, and where loyalty is primarily to individuals rather than to laws or the constitution of the land.

This explains many of the critical differences found in Latin America, for example, the strong emphasis on obligations to family and friends and the existence of hierarchical power structures.

TABLE 3–5
Principal Countries in Latin America

Argentina	Haiti
Belize	Honduras
Bolivia	Mexico
Brazil	Nicaragua
Chile	Panama
Colombia	Paraguay
Costa Rica	Peru
Cuba	Puerto Rico
Dominican Republic	Uruguay
Ecuador	Venezuela
El Salvador	The Guianas
Guatemala	

*Environment©**

There is a prevailing belief that human beings are controlled by forces of nature and the environment and that success is obtained not just by hard work but also by fate and luck.

Roman Catholicism has been a major religious force in the region with its conception of a God-ordained order to the world. This situation is changing as Protestantism gains ground. In Brazil, for example, 20 percent of the population describe themselves as Protestant (up from 4 percent in 1960). Approximately 72.5 percent of Brazilians identify themselves as Catholic, which is down from 93 percent in 1960. Overall, the Protestant portion of Latin America has tripled to 12 percent over the last 30 years—51 million compared to 67 million in 1960.[42] As James Brooke, columnist for the *New York Times*, points out:[43]

> Millions of poor people are turning away from the Catholic church and the class-based "liberation theology" to embrace a storefront Protestantism that offers fervent spiritualism and a pro-capitalist ideology of hard work, sober living habits, and individual advancement.

While the constraint orientation to the environment is changing—particularly in urban areas—it is best to assume that you will be met with a more fatalistic posture than the one you may be used to in the United States. Adjustment, rather than change, may be the primary working principle.

---

*©Training Management Corporation (TMC), *Doing Business Internationally: The Cross-Cultural Challenges,* Seminar and Coursebook (Princeton, NJ, 1992).

Some guidelines:

- Don't make too many assumptions about constraints. Spend time listening to your counterpart and gathering data on his or her perspective on what is or is not feasible.
- Be flexible in formulating more or less detailed plans and schedules.
- Be open to the unpredictable, which will be determined by God's will.

Time©

History and traditions are highly valued in the region. There is a strong multifocus as well as a past and present orientation toward time. Change may not always be viewed as positive. There is also pronounced overlap between business, social, and family spheres. Time also tends to be seen as fluid, with schedules adapted easily to shifting priorities. Time tends to flow in agricultural seasons rather than industrial seconds and minutes.

The will of God determines when something will be done, which, of course, affects plans and schedules. Meetings may start well after the scheduled time, and family issues may interrupt business transactions.

The importance of building trusting relationships adds time to doing business, but provides a firmer foundation for the long term. Whether or not deadlines are met may well depend on the strength of the relationship.

The Latin American approach to time can be frustrating. A report for the journal *Global Production: Manufacturing and Sourcing in the America's* said:[44]

> The mañana syndrome hangs on. In fact, culture and language can present some of the biggest challenges to U.S. manufacturers in Central America. Our sources say it is essential, in most of the region, to hire managers who speak Spanish. And the mañana attitude—which roughly translates into, "Why do today what can be put off until tomorrow?"—is difficult to overcome, according to most of the manufacturers interviewed for this report.

Some guidelines:

- Don't get angry if meetings begin late or are interrupted.
- Be punctual, even if a meeting is not expected to begin on time.
- Schedule extra time when doing business in the region.
- Expect business deadlines to take a lower priority than those of family and close friends. Social obligations and allegiances are paramount.
- Show a respect for the past as well as the present and long-term future.

---

*©Training Management Corporation (TMC), *Doing Business Internationally: The Cross-Cultural Challenges,* Seminar and Coursebook (Princeton, NJ, 1992).

Action©*

Throughout the region, there is a strong being orientation. In business, trust is critical, and is established by developing long-term relationships—not just by fulfilling contracts and executing tasks in the most efficient manner.

The basis of mutual trust is "being simpatico"—having shared feelings and understandings. You stand a greater chance of success if your counterpart feels you can be a loyal compadre and not just a business associate. This takes time; you cannot expect to develop this relationship overnight.

Work is not the primary focus of life as it is for many in North America. Leisure and companionship are critical to a full life; work and money are a means to a full life, not ends in themselves.

Some guidelines:

- Demonstrate empathy and sincerity.
- Be personable. Be willing to share your thoughts, feelings, background, and so on.
- Think relationship before business.
- Expect to spend time socializing, visiting local sites, and so on.
- Spend time building a network of influential individuals who can possibly act as intermediaries.

Communication©*

Given the high-context nature of the culture, you may miss many of the subtleties that exist for promoting social harmony between individuals and groups. Much of the understanding that passes between individuals will be implicit. This makes use of the telephone for doing business unpopular. Mark Vaughan writes, "In Latin America, 95 percent of your work cannot be done by phone—a telephone mentality is not part of the culture. So plan on putting a lot of resources into on-site legwork."[45]

The communication style in the region tends to be formal, indirect, serious, subjective, expressive, and sometimes argumentative. Formality is an important part of doing business. Customs regarding hospitality, deference to authority, and establishing relationships are particularly important.

The expressive style may appear to an American as long-winded and rhetorical. An American may become frustrated by a seeming reluctance to get to the point. But eloquence is highly valued. It reflects your status and position, and is considered to be a sign of one's intellectual prowess and wisdom. Many Latin

*©Training Management Corporation (TMC), *Doing Business Internationally: The Cross-Cultural Challenges,* Seminar and Coursebook (Princeton, NJ, 1992).

Americans have a love of language that is somewhat foreign to North Americans. They are very proud of their world-renowned writers, such as Gabriel Garcia Marquez and Jorge Luis Borges.

Some guidelines:

- Don't be insulted by interruptions. Your host is simply anxious to express ideas and perspectives with you.
- Respect formal titles and status positions.
- Be willing to listen to topics that may appear to be unrelated to business, for example, literature and the arts. If possible, familiarize yourself with some South American writers and artists before you leave.
- Be a little more expressive in your gestures. Smile and enjoy your host's hospitality.
- Be prepared to reveal more of yourself than you would to a North American client.

Space©*

Latin Americans are comfortable doing business at closer distances than Americans, Canadians, northern Europeans, and many Asians. Latin American distance should not be interpreted as "intimate" distance.

Physical contact is more frequent in Latin America, and handshakes may be longer lasting.

Office areas in the region tend to be more public, except at higher levels where they become more private.

Some guidelines:

- Don't appear cold and impersonal by backing away from your host's closeness. Stand your ground.
- Expect long, relatively soft handshakes and more frequent touching.
- Show professionalism in your dress.

Power©*

The majority of Latin American countries place a high value on hierarchy and rank. In general, predetermined and traditional roles according to age, sex, and rank are strictly adhered to. Leadership style often is autocratic and authoritarian. Leaders tend to be highly experienced, well-connected senior males. Managers

---

*©Training Management Corporation (TMC), *Doing Business Internationally: The Cross-Cultural Challenges,* Seminar and Coursebook (Princeton, NJ, 1992).

demand respect because of their rank, which conveys authority. There is little face-to-face questioning of authority. Conflicts are resolved by those in power. Persons in power are treated deferentially, and subordinates may be reluctant to offer suggestions for improvement or be included in decision making.

The issue of face saving is very important. To consult with those of a lower rank could be very damaging to an individual's credibility. To challenge a high-ranking individual's decision may cause him a great deal of face and lose you business. Such a challenge displays a lack of respect and a lack of confidence.

One consequence of this orientation is that information may be purposely withheld from all employees except those actually making decisions.

Some guidelines:

- Always show respect for levels of authority.
- Don't try to work around the hierarchy.
- Protect the other person's self-esteem.
- Don't try to force egalitarianism by mixing hierarchical levels in meetings or elsewhere.

Individualism©*

Individualism is highly valued, but within the context of loyalty to and involvement with groups, particularly family groups. Individual identity—often defined in social/educational terms—is the foundation of self-esteem, and self-esteem translates into charisma, personal power, and inner worth. Rather than self-reliance or task accomplishment, an individual is defined by unique qualities of character and connection.

In general, obligations to the family supersede all other obligations. Social relations are with family and friends, and the employer can be part of the extended family. A business may be involved with the everyday lives of its employees. Nepotism is considered natural; family and friendship considerations can, to some extent, determine employment. An individual's close social network may be much more important than his or her technical knowledge or qualifications. Job tenure tends to be long, as firing may involve great loss of prestige.

In conducting business, rather than a teamwork approach, dependent workers execute tasks under the manager's direction. Loyalty, however, is a primary concern.

Work and family are often intertwined in the region. Mahatma Davies writes, "In the Dominican Republic, for instance, the workplace is considered an extension of one's family. The company is expected to participate in the marriages, funerals, birth celebrations, and other family events of its employees."[46]

---

*©Training Management Corporation (TMC), *Doing Business Internationally: The Cross-Cultural Challenges,* Seminar and Coursebook (Princeton, NJ, 1992).

Some guidelines:

- Protect an individual's unique sense of self and self-esteem.
- Respect the network of social relations in which the individual operates.

Competitiveness©*

Competitiveness varies across the region. Panama, Chile, Costa Rica, Guatemala, Peru, and Uruguay are relatively low in competitiveness, emphasizing concern for people and the quality of life. Venezuela, Mexico, Ecuador, Argentina, and Colombia are relatively high, tending more toward material success and achievement.

Even with these relatively high-competitive Latin American countries, there is still a concern for quality of life (working to live, not living to work) that is not particularly manifest in other high-competitive countries such as the United States or Japan. In general, competition is perceived as destructive and leading to disharmony.

A key element of Latin American competitiveness is *machismo:* masculine power and courage aimed at attracting respect. A *macho* man will always display confidence; undertake tasks that test his capabilities; and express disdain for rules, regulations, policies, and procedures that constrict his maverick style.

Some guidelines:

- Don't mistake a formal yet friendly politeness for a lack of competitiveness.

Structure©*

The Latin American orientation toward structure is ambivalent. Uncertainty, change and risk are generally avoided and, if faced, are dealt with by centralized or authoritative decision making. At the same time, while a great many laws, rules, and regulations exist in the region, the emphasis placed on the particular versus the universal means that laws, policies, procedures and regulations, are often applied differentially according to who is involved, or they are not applied at all.

Documentation is often considered a waste of time. This fits with the emphasis placed on machismo and on relationships before formal business procedures.

Some guidelines:

- Don't expect highly detailed contracts or agreements.
- Be prepared for dealing with ambiguity.

---

*©Training Management Corporation (TMC), Doing Business Internationally: The Cross-Cultural Challenges, Seminar and Coursebook (Princeton, NJ, 1992).

*Thinking©**

Latin American thinking styles tend toward the deductive and holistic. They are less concerned with facts and figures than with concepts and ideas. Decisions are often based on intuition and judgment rather than painstaking analysis. It is not uncommon for Latin Americans to place ideals before realistic goals.

Some guidelines:

- Don't push data. Put your proposal within a conceptual framework that gives meaning to raw facts and figures.
- Engage in dialogue without seeming to question the competence of your counterpart.
- Respect the other person's point of view and withhold your critical judgment.

MIDDLE EAST

How can we begin to understand the Middle East? For many of us in the West, the very term "Middle East" conjures up images of hostages, terrorist bombings and shootings, holy wars, stone-throwing mobs, and Ayatollahs. The first thing we need to understand is that the real Middle East is far more complex than the one portrayed in the media.

The principal countries in the Middle East are listed in Table 3–6.

Edward Said, a celebrated professor of comparative literature at Columbia University—who also happens to be an Arab, had this to say about the region after a recent visit:[47]

> What struck me, not for the first time, was the extraordinary richness and many-layered quality of the terrain: The Arab world today remains turbulent and interestingly unpredictable and, in my opinion, quite resists any weak attempt to compress it into little boxes labeled "Islamic" or "non-Islamic." Most of these societies—Egypt's certainly, but also Lebanon's and Jordan's—are still largely secular despite the clamorings and debates over Islamic government. The texture of everyday life, with its infinite number of transactions and processes, from the post office to the public transport system, from currency to electrical power, clothes, medical treatment, diet, construction, television, radio, publishing—all these are worldly (that is to say secular) developments, the result not of foreign occupation, imperialism, or Zionism, but of willing adaption, education, and history.

In line with many other areas of the world, a tension exists between modernity and secularism and between traditional religious beliefs and new cultural prac-

*©Training Management Corporation (TMC), *Doing Business Internationally: The Cross-Cultural Challenges,* Seminar and Coursebook (Princeton, NJ, 1992).

TABLE 3–6
Principal Countries in the Middle East

Algeria	Libya
Bahrain	Morocco
Cyprus	Oman
Egypt	Qatar
Iran	Saudi Arabia
Iraq	Syria
Israel	Tunisia
Jordan	Turkey
Kuwait	United Arab Emirates
Lebanon	Yemen

tices. Sometimes, this debate is framed as Arab versus the West, but more often it is categorized internally between secular powers and fundamentalists. Algeria and Egypt are—at the time of this writing—undergoing fierce internal conflicts. Iran's fundamentalist (non-Arab) revolution is ongoing, but there is now considerable discussion about seeking a new rapprochement with the West (Western investment, including American, is returning). Turkey—a secular democracy—continues to look toward Europe rather than the East, but there is a significant portion of the population that see their roots in the East.

Many of the elites in the Middle East have been educated in the West. The influence of French culture is particularly felt in the former colonies of Algeria, Tunisia, Lebanon, and Morocco.

One fact we need to be clear about: Middle Eastern culture and religion are inseparable. Every Arab country in the region except Lebanon recognizes Islam as its state religion.[48] Approximately 90 percent of the people living in Middle Eastern countries are Muslims. Jewish and Christian strands weave themselves throughout the region. While there are secular forces in the region, religion is the primary cultural factor shaping perceptions and influencing behavior. It will pay you to do your homework on religion in the Middle East.

*Environment©**

There is a prevailing belief that human beings are controlled by forces in nature and the environment. The emphasis on fate and the will of God has significant implications for business. Because of the prevalence of religious fatalism, the

---

**©Training Management Corporation (TMC), *Doing Business Internationally: The Cross-Cultural Challenges,* Seminar and Coursebook (Princeton, NJ, 1992).*

suggestion that one can control the events of one's life might be viewed as arrogant or blasphemous.

The idea that life is what you make of it is foreign to most people in the Middle East. One of the authors once asked for the weather forecast in Morocco only to be told, "Only Allah knows." To take on the future is considered highly presumptuous and dangerous.

Some guidelines:

- Don't push for plans that can't be given. Work with broad outlines rather than specifics.
- Familiarize yourself with the constraints imposed by religion. For example, during Ramadan—the ninth month of the Islamic lunar calendar—there is a reduction of work activity as well as fasting.
- Downplay talk about the future.
- Expect contracts to be general rather than specific.

Time©

The Middle East is strongly rooted in the past. Preserving traditions and customs is emphasized over progress and change. Little emphasis is placed on developing modern management techniques. The pace of business is slower than in the United States.

Middle Easterners, like Latin Americans, tend to be multifocused regarding time. Great flexibility is demonstrated regarding deadlines and schedules, and interruptions in meetings are very common. For Muslims, time is in the hands of God. Past, present, and future flow together in a divine continuum. Whatever is to be accomplished will be done so in God's time. Punctuality for meetings is not highly valued.

It is difficult to determine when Allah's will in regard to time is sincerely religious, and when it is simply a delaying tactic. Idries Shah tells the following story:[49]

> Nasrudin had saved up to buy a new shirt. He went to a tailor's shop, full of excitement. The tailor measured him and said: "Come back in a week, and—if Allah wills—your shirt will be ready." The Mulla [Nasrudin] contained himself for a week and then went back to the shop. "There has been a delay. But—if Allah wills—your shirt will be ready tomorrow." The following day Nasrudin returned. "I am sorry," said the tailor, "but it is not quite finished. Try tomorrow, and if Allah wills—it will be ready." "How long will it take," cried the exasperated Nasrudin, "if you leave Allah out of it?"

---

*©Training Management Corporation (TMC), *Doing Business Internationally: The Cross-Cultural Challenges,* Seminar and Coursebook (Princeton, NJ, 1992).

To hurry is insulting. There needs to be time for deliberation and consideration.

Some guidelines:

- Don't keep looking at your watch. Your Arab counterpart may take this as a sign of personal rejection.
- Be flexible in your scheduling.
- Don't push for deadlines, but persist in keeping the business in front of your Arab counterpart.
- Expect work to be interrupted at prayer times.
- Never show impatience. Be calm.
- Don't be surprised to find yourself in the middle of several conversations.

*Action©**

There is much more of a being than doing orientation in the Middle East. Who a person is—and what sort of character and connections he or she has—may be considered more important than technical merit or achievement in terms of hiring or buying.

Relationships and religion come before business. Any issues that relate to family are given a very high priority. Neil Chesanow places Arab loyalties in the following order of importance:[50]

- Nuclear family
- Extended family
- Muslim Arab friends
- The Arab Islamic community
- Country
- Non-Arab Muslims

Arab hospitality fits with the priority given to relationships. It conveys respect and mutual obligations.

While the family is very important to Arabs, it is inappropriate to inquire about female members of the family. Privacy is very important in this area.

Some guidelines.

- Don't rush into talking business.
- Work hard at building trust. Sell yourself before anything else, but avoid boasting.

---

*©Training Management Corporation (TMC), *Doing Business Internationally: The Cross-Cultural Challenges,* Seminar and Coursebook (Princeton, NJ, 1992).

- Expect to make several trips in order to build a relationship. Keep in touch between trips.
- Accept hospitality, but only after giving a polite refusal.
- Reciprocate hospitality to the same degree as it was given. To be more generous would throw the relationship out of equilibrium.
- Give great respect to family honor.
- Demonstrate respect by dressing well. Aim for a great first impression.
- Recognize that while the first meeting may be relaxed and social, you are still being assessed. Your hosts are asking, "Can we do business with this person?"
- Think in terms of a long-term relationship, not just a deal.

*Communication©**

Face-to-face discussion or the interview is the preferred mode. Raising the voice or displaying emotion indicates sincerity, although when dealing with foreigners emotions may be restrained.

Speaking tone depends upon the person's social position and family influence. Negotiation, bargaining, and persuasion are highly developed in the Middle East, and it is certainly advisable to work with someone who knows the cultural terrain.

Communication in Israel tends to be very direct. Elsewhere, it can be quite indirect. It may be necessary to infer what is actually being said; specifics may be lacking. A direct straightforward "no" is uncommon, and the acceptance of "no" is also uncommon. Politeness is important, and only a slight hesitation may give you a clue as to whether the other person agrees with you or not.[51]

Gestures are often quite dramatic, language is often exaggerated in content and tone, eye contact is direct, and touching and embracing are common among Arab men.

Formality is critical; titles reflect status and power, and they should always be used. The "dos and taboos" related to Islam are particularly critical.

Some guidelines:

- Don't be too objective and unexpressive. Demonstrate your sincerity by showing some emotional commitment, but without yelling.
- Know your product/service inside and out. You could quickly lose credibility if you have to find out information from headquarters.
- Don't be surprised by Arab men holding hands in public. It simply denotes friendship.

---

*©Training Management Corporation (TMC), *Doing Business Internationally: The Cross-Cultural Challenges,* Seminar and Coursebook (Princeton, NJ, 1992).

- Avoid conflict in front of others. Face saving, dignity, honor, and self-respect are highly valued.
- Keep probing to ascertain whether a "yes" is actually "yes" or "maybe" or nothing at all. But bear in mind, a solid "yes" is still uncertain.
- Expect silences for reflection. Don't rush to fill them.

Space©*

Middle Easterners are comfortable conducting business at a close distance (18 inches)—a distance that would be deemed as "personal" or "intimate" by American standards.

If the conversation becomes lively, the distance may be reduced even further. This helps gain and maintain attention. Looking into the eyes is a means to "read" the other person.

Other body language is also important within the interpersonal space. For example: Don't show the soles of your feet to an Arab or pass anything with your left hand (reserved for personal hygiene). Also, don't point or turn your back on an Arab or sneeze loudly in public.

The codes for body language are quite elaborate, and the reader is advised to refer to a specialist book on the Middle East.

Some guidelines:

- Spend time in face-to-face contact. Don't try to do business just over the phone or by fax.
- Don't confuse touching with sexuality; it is merely associated with friendship.
- Be aware that the Arab gesture for "no" is similar to the American gesture for "yes"—an upward nod of the head.

Power©*

Middle Eastern cultures value hierarchical position. Status and affiliation are based on familial connections. Group and family connections determine one's role in society.

Organizational structure is highly bureaucratic, with power and authority resting at the top. Leadership is authoritarian in tone, and there are many management directives. A rigid chain of command exists. Leaders often deal with intermediaries or contact makers. The top manager makes all the decisions and prefers to deal only with outside executives who have decision-making power.

---

*©Training Management Corporation (TMC), *Doing Business Internationally: The Cross-Cultural Challenges,* Seminar and Coursebook (Princeton, NJ, 1992).

This emphasis on hierarchy makes for highly centralized business structures. Leaders are unlikely to be technical people who have worked their way up the organization. They deal at the strategic level rather than with the details.[52] Subordinates advise and counsel and provide the necessary technical support.

In many ways an Arab business leader is like a father figure. He is expected to care for his employees in exchange for loyalty and trust.

Some guidelines:

- Seek out influential people to be your agents, for example, members of a royal or elite family or high-level government officials.
- Recognize status and power. Don't try to work around authority figures. You'll lose.
- Keep presentations to decision makers brief and, if possible, visual.

Individualism©*

The Middle East places a low value on individualism. Identity is based on the attributes of the family and other in-groups more than on individual attributes. Primary obligations are to parents and other family members. Individual rights and opinions are not emphasized.

Working your way up the organization is not the Arab way of doing things. The decision makers at the top are those whose wealth, power, and connections place them in positions of authority. This is changing as those educated in the West come into more positions of power. But, for the most part, assume that decisions are in the hands of a few powerful men.

Some guidelines:

- Pay attention to who is who and connect with the most powerful.
- Stress the loyalty and commitment of both yourself and your company.
- Stress your own rank and influence.
- Help your counterpart save face.

Competitiveness©*

The Middle East is a mix between concerns for quality of life and material success. Success in business depends to a large extent on education and on being a member of a well-known and influential family. Personal contacts rather than

---

*©Training Management Corporation (TMC), *Doing Business Internationally: The Cross-Cultural Challenges,* Seminar and Coursebook (Princeton, NJ, 1992).

qualifications are key for advancement, and major positions tend to be filled by those with respected social origins.

Arab competitiveness is often most visible in the rituals of negotiating. Bargaining (or haggling) is a key part of the culture. Often, initial demands are very high, and then the negotiations proceed through a series of concessions.

Some guidelines:

- Work with an agent who has influential connections.
- Don't be insulted or react strongly to high initial demands. Recognize those as part of a competitive process.
- Don't try to hard sell.

Structure©*

Structure is highly valued. Structure is preserved more by autocratic decision making than by elaborate rules and regulations. Roles and responsibilities also tend to be well defined (implicity rather than explicitly). Uncertain or ambiguous situations can appear as threatening, although contracts are likely to be broad and always open to negotiation.

The distinction between men's and women's roles is part of the value placed on structure. In general, women will not be involved in any business dealings. Women are related to the private life of home and family.

Some guidelines:

- Observe protocols.
- Don't show impatience.
- Work through an agent who understands the local conditions.

Thinking©*

Thinking styles in the Middle East tend toward the deductive and systemic with a high degree of intuition. The big picture, rather than details, is important to most Arab decision makers.

Chesanow makes a very valid point when he says:[53]

> The Arab's love of his language rivals that of the French. It's a rhythmic, musical tongue, full of color, variety, and nuance of sound. But it's also a language that encourages hyperbole and elaborate verbal rhetoric spoken with great flourish. *How* some-

**©Training Management Corporation (TMC), *Doing Business Internationally: The Cross-Cultural Challenges,* Seminar and Coursebook (Princeton, NJ, 1992).

thing is said may matter as much as or more than its actual content. In Arabic, the medium often *becomes* the message. Observes one scholar: It is characteristic of the Arab's mind to be swayed more by words than by ideas, and more by ideas than by facts.

Arabic is respected as a divine language. As a consequence, an Arab is likely to approach a text differently from a Westerner. Richard Mead argues:[54]

In Muslim cultures, Arabic is revered as the language of the Koran and is held to have divine origins. It is believed to be precise and hence no useful distinction can be drawn between the dictionary definition of a word and its significance. The reader is not trained to interact with a text as in Anglo cultures, mentally editing and disputing points. He or she does not easily distinguish more or less significant points. This reverence for written texts extends to newspapers . . . At university level, students pass examinations by learning and regurgitating set texts and notes. These students are unlikely to change their attitude to text when they take up business careers and assume responsibilities for writing and interpreting contracts.

Some guidelines:

- Expect data to play a secondary role in decision making. A decision is likely to be based on informed intuition (based on the "feel" of the relationship) rather than the persuasiveness of data and logical conclusions.
- Present arguments in small chunks to allow for reflection (as well as possible interruptions).
- Respect Arabic. Use skilled translators who can communicate your meaning precisely.

NORTH AMERICA

In late 1993, one of the authors delivered a brief presentation to a major U.S. company on the importance of cultural differences to global business success. The New York audience responded well, but then became skeptical when another consultant suggested that economic considerations would always overcome differences in culture.

As the day wore on, the importance of culture seemed to fade into the background. The last presentation was given by a young woman in charge of a major business alliance between the U.S. company and a partner in Canada. No one expected cultural differences to be raised as a significant issue. In fact, her whole presentation stressed how the economic desirability of the venture had been in danger several times because of a lack of attention to culture. Suddenly, the importance of culture was highlighted (one story is worth a thousand abstractions). If Americans and Canadians can get into cultural difficulties, what problems might arise when the differences are much more profound?

The predominant cultures of North America (by which we mean the United States and Canada) are rooted in Europe: the United Kingdom and Ireland, France, Italy, Germany, the Scandinavian countries, eastern Europe, and so on. Today, this picture is changing—particularly in the United States—as new immigrants make their way from Asia and Latin America (see Table 3–7).

Currently, one out of four Americans is from a minority ethnic group and, if current immigration and population growth conditions continue, the United States will be a nation with no ethnic majority during the 21st century.

The new immigration will change the cultural profile of America. How? It's very hard to say. Immigrants eventually assimilate but also bring lasting cultural traits that affect the wider population. As America moves into the global marketplace, its diverse population could be its greatest asset.

The separate cultural distinctiveness of Canada is a source of continual debate, especially among Canadians. This isn't surprising when you consider the ignorance of most United States citizens about their northern neighbor. Al Capone is reported to have said, "I don't even know what street Canada is on."

*Environment©**

The prevailing North American belief is that human beings are superior to, and set apart from, the rest of the environment. Rather than working in harmony with the natural world, Americans try to take control and shape nature to their purposes. Often, they seem to be at war with nature, and they are less accepting of natural rhythms and processes than people in many other cultures. While the environmental movement has had an impact on this control orientation, the predominant view is still one of dominance through the application of a pragmatic intelligence (often given form and substance in a new technology). In Canada, the prevailing attitude is more a combination of mastery and harmony.

This strong control orientation can be perceived by some as a form of naive optimism or extreme innocence. The strong self-help worldview in which men and women are capable of profound change and able to direct their personal fates, is somewhat unique in the world. The older business cultures of Europe, in particular, may show a reluctance to entertain American ideas because of how they appear to simplify the change process and reduce complex reality to a set of generalizations. Americans, however, look to ideas to be levers of change rather than just descriptions of reality. American culture—driven by entrepreneurship—seeks change, while many cultures of the Old World seek to defend against changes that appear imposed from the outside.

---

*©Training Management Corporation (TMC), *Doing Business Internationally: The Cross-Cultural Challenges,* Seminar and Coursebook (Princeton, NJ, 1992).

TABLE 3–7
Sources of Legal Immigrants 1971–91

Asia			35.2%	Central and		11.1%
Philippines	6.7%	Vietnam	4.7%	South America		
Korea	4.7%	India	3.5%	El Salvadore 2.2%	Colombia	1.6%
China*	4.7%			Canada		1.8%
Mexico			23.7%	Europe		12.0%
Caribbean			13.1%	Britain	2.0%	
Cuba	3.3%	Jamaica	2.8%	Soviet Union	1.3 %	
Dominican	3.2%			Rest of world		3.1%
Republic						

*Includes Taiwan and the People's Republic of China.

Source: Reprinted from July 13, 1992 issue of Business Week by special permission, © 1992 by Mc-Graw-Hill, Inc.

Some guidelines:

- Project a confident take-charge attitude.
- Set measurable goals and objectives.
- Be prepared to present detailed plans and schedules.
- Demonstrate self-reliance and independence.
- Show commitment to change and continuous improvement rather than stability and predictability.
- Respect the power of technology in introducing and maintaining change.

*Time©**

American businesspeople value time, and there is no time like the present. Time is seen as a limited resource that must be spent wisely and profitably. Americans are always perceived to be in a frantic hurry. As the English author, Jessica Mitford, once said, "Things on the whole are much faster in America. People don't *stand for election,* they *run for office.*"[55]

A businessperson's day is likely to be conducted at a swift, rapid-fire pace, and packed with appointments and deadlines. Efficiency and punctuality are considered virtues, and schedules create the necessary action framework for achieving goals.

Americans have a single-focus orientation to time and emphasize the present and the short-term future (a five-year plan is considered to be a long-term plan).

---

*©Training Management Corporation (TMC), *Doing Business Internationally: The Cross-Cultural Challenges,* Seminar and Coursebook (Princeton, NJ, 1992).

For the most part, Americans consider the past and the long-term future to be irrelevant. Results are measured in quarters, and investments are expected to show quick returns. Unlike Asian companies, American companies seek short-term profitability over the gradual building of market share.

Canadians also tend to have a single-focus orientation, but conduct business at a less urgent pace. Canadians, on the whole, like to differentiate themselves from Americans. A Canadian told one of the book's authors that many Canadians will not ask for the bill in a restaurant; this would make them appear to be in the same hurry as Americans.

Some guidelines:

- Be a little early rather than a little late.
- Focus on one thing at a time.
- Adopt the attitude that time is money, and demonstrate a sincere concern with efficiency and productivity.
- Focus on the present and short-term future.
- Commit to deadlines and deliver.
- Stress speed as a priority.

*Action©**

Americans are "doers." The United States is arguably the most doing-oriented culture in the world. Results, behaviors, and actions are believed to speak louder than words. "Getting things done" is a virtue. One of the authors remembers his introduction to this cultural trait during his early days in an American corporation. He was spending a longer amount of time than was thought desirable on making a decision. Taken to one side by his boss, he was told, "It doesn't matter what decision you make. The important thing is to be seen making a decision."

Canada is also more of a doing- than a being-oriented culture, although Canadians as a rule do not define themselves in terms of measurable accomplishments as much as Americans.

Some guidelines:

- Be diligent in demonstrating your work ethic.
- Show decisiveness and initiative in your actions.
- Demonstrate your commitment to "getting the job done," or "doing whatever it takes."

---

*©Training Management Corporation (TMC), Doing Business Internationally: The Cross-Cultural Challenges, Seminar and Coursebook (Princeton, NJ, 1992).

- Be prepared to spend long hours in the workplace regardless of the work to be done.
- Get to the bottom line quickly, and be prepared to back up your conclusions.

Communication©*

Both Canada and the United States are low-context cultures, with the United States being the lower context of the two countries. The emphasis in the United States is on task accomplishment rather than relationship building.

Business communication in the United States is often informal, direct, and instrumental. The focus is on accuracy and getting fast results. The freedom to express opinions is valued, and conflict is viewed as an inevitable result of individual differences and interests. Most Americans expect, and some even encourage, the face-to-face expression of disagreement. In fact, conflict is often considered to be a positive, healthy force, leading to progress.

Business communication in Canada, particularly among French Canadians, tends to be more formal in tone, but still confrontational.

Some guidelines:

- Be open, direct, and relatively informal.
- Don't be overly emotional.
- Be prepared to deal with conflict and argument.
- Expect to be interrupted when you're in a reflective thinking mode.
- Be explicit.
- Show optimism.
- Use adjectives that stress quality, size, strength, and so on. Don't understate your position.
- Practice being persuasive.

Space©*

Both Canadians and Americans tend toward a private-space orientation, and are not comfortable conducting business at too close a distance.

Some guidelines:

- Try to maintain at least three feet between yourself and others.
- Give firm, brief handshakes.

---

*©Training Management Corporation (TMC), *Doing Business Internationally: The Cross-Cultural Challenges,* Seminar and Coursebook (Princeton, NJ, 1992).

- Expect very little touching.
- Respect private space.
- Look people in the eye, but don't stare.

Power©*

While Canada and the United States do not place a high value on hierarchy *per se,* businesspeople from both countries respect the authority of those of higher management levels and maintain professional distance from subordinates. While there is an acceptance of hierarchical business structures, decisions are increasingly based on input from different levels within the organization. The goal of many North American companies is to create flatter structures, eliminate bureaucracy, and empower employees.

Some guidelines:

- Show respect, but not deference, to superiors.
- Learn to question proposals and to provide constructive alternatives.
- Actively identify problems.
- View challenges as opportunities.

Individualism©*

North American heroes are loners, individuals who "go it alone" and refuse to follow the collective. Henry Fonda in the movie *Twelve Angry Men* is a case in point. He is the only person on a jury who believes the accused is innocent. The entire film consists of his battle to overcome the prejudices and ill-formed opinions of the other jurors. Gregory Peck, the attorney in the movie *To Kill a Mocking Bird,* is a similar example. Ask a multicultural group to name an American hero and they will often say John Wayne or Clint Eastwood—further examples of strong, independent individuals who will not take no for an answer, and who struggle to shape their own destinies.

Rugged individualism has been a characteristic orientation of American life since at least the conquest of the West. The earlier Americans relied more, perhaps, on the power of communities. The image of the heroic pioneer battling a hostile world is now embodied in the risk-taking and adventurous entrepreneur. Personal achievement is now seen as a result of the application of individual effort and ability within the context of a free enterprise system. Rewards are based

---

*©Training Management Corporation (TMC), *Doing Business Internationally: The Cross-Cultural Challenges,* Seminar and Coursebook (Princeton, NJ, 1992).

primarily on performance rather than need, group membership, heritage, or personal connections.

Unlike more collective societies, Americans will often negotiate alone rather than in teams, and decision making is individualistic rather than consensual. While work teams have been introduced into American business, they have not settled easily into the American system.

Some guidelines:

- Stress your personal achievements rather than loyalty.
- Demonstrate your willingness to take risks and to be creative.
- Position yourself as a self-starter.
- Accept personal responsibility for success or failure.
- Show motivation for accepting challenging tasks.

Competitiveness©*

The United States and Canada are very high in competitiveness. Stress is placed on material success and achievement, and competition between individuals and groups is taken as a given.

Some guidelines:

- Be assertive, but not excessively aggressive.
- Show determination in aiming to meet personal and organizational goals.
- Demonstrate to others how you can help them be more competitive.
- Be energetic and industrious.
- Take business seriously.
- Focus on risk taking rather than saving face.

Structure©*

Both countries place a relatively low value on structure and do not fear uncertainty and ambiguity as much as many other countries in the world. Increasingly, stress is placed on creating flexible structures and on empowerment. At the same time, there is a tendency toward legalism—highly detailed contracts and agreements that try to cover all contingencies.

---

*©Training Management Corporation (TMC), *Doing Business Internationally: The Cross-Cultural Challenges,* Seminar and Coursebook (Princeton, NJ, 1992).

Some guidelines:

- View policies and procedures as a framework rather than as a rigid system.
- Continually seek new, more productive ways of doing things.
- Stress the result rather than the process.
- Demonstrate flexibility.

*Thinking©**

North American thinking styles are primarily inductive and linear. Conceptual arguments without supporting quantitative data lack credibility. Practicality and efficiency are stressed over intellectual "correctness" or theory; the key tests are "Will it work?" and "Will it work well?" Thought is rooted in concrete evidence rather than intuition or the cut and thrust of ideas.

Some guidelines:

- Be prepared to present comprehensive—usually quantitative—data.
- Analyze problems into small cause and effect relationships and present arguments in a logical fashion.
- Emphasize the practical over the ideal.

SUMMARY INSIGHTS

How can we summarize such a quick trip around the world? We should, perhaps, start with a very important principle. In all your dealings with other cultures, seek to **minimize regret.** Prepare for a cross-cultural encounter with purpose and thoroughly. Take nothing for granted. As you prepare, keep the following points in mind.

Don't:

- Assume similarity.
- Try to adopt the orientations of the other culture. Adaption does not mean adoption.
- Keep comparing the other culture with your own.

---

*©Training Management Corporation (TMC), *Doing Business Internationally: The Cross-Cultural Challenges,* Seminar and Coursebook (Princeton, NJ, 1992).

- Keep evaluating the other culture in terms of "good" or "bad."
- Assume that just being yourself will be enough to bring you cross-cultural success.

Do:

- Set realistic expectations for yourself and others.
- Accept that you will make mistakes, but remain confident.
- Be patient with yourself and your counterparts.
- Slow down. Aim to make relationships, not just deals.
- Keep your sense of humor.
- Keep your integrity. Know what you stand for and your limits.
- Stay objective and minimize blame.

Most importantly:

- Develop your cultural self-awareness.

The 10-variable framework presented in the last two chapters provides you with a simple tool for understanding yourself and others in cultural terms. It offers you a mental model for identifying and organizing your cultural experiences. Your goal should be to sit in a meeting in an unfamiliar culture and be able to determine the other side's dominant cultural orientations in relation to your own. When you can do this, you can pinpoint areas of potential conflict and, if possible, make the necessary adaptions in order to build and maintain relationships.

The first, and most important, step is becoming aware of your own cultural orientations and the impact they can make in doing business across cultures.

To help build your cultural self-awareness, we have included several exercises after the discussion questions.

DISCUSSION QUESTIONS

- With what cultural regions might you be doing business in the foreseeable future?
- What cultural differences do you think you would have most difficulty adapting to and why?
- How will you prepare yourself to be most effective in the other culture?

EXERCISE 1: SELF-AWARENESS

Identify your dominant cultural orientations.
For example,

1. Environment										
	1	2 ✔ 3	4	5	6	7	8	9	10
	Control environment			Harmony with environment			Constrained by environment		

indicates that you think and act on the assumption that the world around you can and should be controlled.

1. Environment										
	1	2	3	4	5	6	7	8	9	10
	Control environment			Harmony with environment			Constrained by environment		
2. Time	1	2	3	4	5	6	7	8	9	10
	Multifocus							Single focus		
	1	2	3	4	5	6	7	8	9	10
	Fixed									Fluid
	1	2	3	4	5	6	7	8	9	10
	Past				Present					Future
3. Action	1	2	3	4	5	6	7	8	9	10
	Being									Doing
4. Communication	1	2	3	4	5	6	7	8	9	10
	High context							Low context		
	1	2	3	4	5	6	7	8	9	10
	Direct									Indirect
	1	2	3	4	5	6	7	8	9	10
	Expressive								Instrumental	
	1	2	3	4	5	6	7	8	9	10
	Formal									Informal

5. Space										
	1	2	3	4	5	6	7	8	9	10
	Private									Public

6. Power										
	1	2	3	4	5	6	7	8	9	10
	Hierarchy									Equality

7. Individualism										
	1	2	3	4	5	6	7	8	9	10
	Individualistic									Collectivist
	1	2	3	4	5	6	7	8	9	10
	Universalistic									Particularistic

8. Competitiveness										
	1	2	3	4	5	6	7	8	9	10
	Competitive									Cooperative

9. Structure										
	1	2	3	4	5	6	7	8	9	10
	Order									Flexibility

10. Thinking										
	1	2	3	4	5	6	7	8	9	10
	Deductive									Inductive
	1	2	3	4	5	6	7	8	9	10
	Linear									Systemic

EXERCISE 2: CULTURAL IMPACT

- In the left-hand column, indicate (with a check mark) your dominant orientations.
- In the right-hand column, indicate how your dominant orientations affect your actions and attitudes.

For example:

My dominant orientations	How do these orientations show themselves in my actions, attitudes, etc.?

1. Environment
   Control ✔
   Harmony
   Constraint
	I believe I can plan for the future and make things happen.
	Life is what you make of it.
	I can set goals, monitor my progress, and move forward.
	Problems are opportunities waiting for my solutions.

My dominant orientations	How do these orientations show themselves in my actions, attitudes, etc.?

1. Environment
   Control
   Harmony
   Constraint
2. Time
   Multifocus
   Single focus
   Fixed
   Fluid
   Past
   Present
   Future
3. Action
   Being
   Doing
4. Communication
   High context
   Low context
   Direct
   Indirect
   Expressive
   Instrumental
   Formal
   Informal	

My dominant orientations	*How do these orientations show themselves in my actions, attitudes, etc.?*
5. Space *Private* *Public* 6. Power *Hierarchy* *Equality* 7. Individualism *Individualistic* *Collectivist* *Universalistic* *Particularistic* 8. Competitiveness *Competitive* *Cooperative* 9. Structure *Order* *Flexibility* 10. Thinking *Deductive* *Inductive* *Linear* *Systemic*	

EXERCISE 3: CONFLICTING PERCEPTIONS

- In the left-hand column, indicate (with a check mark) your dominant orientations.
- In the middle column, briefly describe how you perceive people with the other orientations.
- In the right-hand column, briefly describe how others might perceive you.

For example:

My dominant orientations	How I perceive others	How others might perceive me

1. Environment
  Control ✔
  Harmony
  Constraint
	Harmony: Conformist Superstitious.
	
	Constraint: Backward. Lazy.
		Harmony: Very aggressive.
		
		Constraint: Naive. I don't understand the complexities of the world.

My dominant orientations	How I perceive others	How others might perceive me

1. Environment
  Control
  Harmony
  Constraint
2. Time
  Multifocus
  Single focus
  Fixed
  Fluid
  Past
  Present
  Future
3. Action
  Being
  Doing
4. Communication
  High context
  Low context
  Direct
  Indirect
  Expressive
  Instrumental
  Formal
  Informal		

My dominant orientations	How I perceive others	How others might perceive me

5. Space
   Private
   Public
6. Power
   Hierarchy
   Equality
7. Individualism
   Individualistic
   Collectivist
   Universalistic
   Particularistic
8. Competitiveness
   Competitive
   Cooperative
9. Structure
   Order
   Flexibility
10. Thinking
   Deductive
   Inductive
   Linear
   Systemic		

EXERCISE 4: ADAPTATIONS

Exercise 3 gave you a sense of the conflicting perceptions to be faced when doing business internationally. In this final exercise, think about a specific region of the world you may be doing business with in the future. Consider the similarities and differences you might find between yourself and people in the region, and then think about what you could do to minimize possible conflict.

For example:

Region: Middle East	Me	What I can do?

1. Environment
   Control
   Harmony
   Constraint
	1. Environment
	   Control
	   Harmony
	   Constraint
		• Work with less-detailed plans.
		• Show respect for perceived constraints.
		• Be flexible, but keep my own work under control.

Region:	*Me*	*What I can do?*

1. Environment
   Control
   Harmony
   Constraint
2. Time
   Multifocus
   Single focus
   Fixed
   Fluid
   Past
   Present
   Future
3. Action
   Being
   Doing
4. Communication
   High context
   Low context
   Direct
   Indirect
   Expressive
   Instrumental
   Formal
   Informal
	1. Environment
	   Control
	   Harmony
	   Constraint
	2. Time
	   Multifocus
	   Single focus
	   Fixed
	   Fluid
	   Past
	   Present
	   Future
	3. Action
	   Being
	   Doing
	4. Communication
	   High context
	   Low context
	   Direct
	   Indirect
	   Expressive
	   Instrumental
	   Formal
	   Informal	

Region:	Me	What I can do?

5. Space
   Private
   Public
6. Power
   Hierarchy
   Equality
7. Individualism
   Individualistic
   Collectivist
   Universalistic
   Particularistic
8. Competitiveness
   Competitive
   Cooperative
9. Structure
   Order
   Flexibility
10. Thinking
   Inductive
   Deductive
   Linear
   Systemic
	5. Space
	   Private
	   Public
	6. Power
	   Hierarchy
	   Equality
	7. Individualism
	   Individualistic
	   Collectivist
	   Universalistic
	   Particularistic
	8. Competitiveness
	   Competitive
	   Cooperative
	9. Structure
	   Order
	   Flexibility
	10. Thinking
	   Inductive
	   Deductive
	   Linear
	   Systemic	

NOTES

1. Rosabeth Moss Kanter, "Transcending Business Boundaries: 12,000 World Managers View Change," *Harvard Business Review,* May–June 1991, p 164.

2. John B. Noss, *Man's Religions,* 3rd ed. (New York: Macmillan, 1956), p 176.

3. James Legge, *Confucian Analects, The Great Learning and The Doctrine of the Mean* (New York: Dover Publications, 1971), p 105.

4. David Rearwin, *The Asia Business Book* (Yarmouth, ME: Intercultural Press, 1991), p 11.

5. Steven A. Holmes, "Africa, from the Cold War to Cold Shoulders," *New York Times,* March 7, 1993, p 4E. Copyright © 1993 by The New York Times Company. Reprinted by permission.

6. Ibid.

7. David Aronson, "Why Africa Stays Poor, and Why It Doesn't Have To," *Humanist,* March/April 1993, p 10.

8. Ibid., p 11.

9. Blaine Harden, *Africa: Dispatches from a Fragile Continent* (Boston: Houghton Mifflin, 1990), p 15.

10. Holmes, "Africa," p 4E.

11. Philip R. Harris and Robert T. Moran, *Managing Cultural Differences: High Performance Strategies for a New World of Business,* 3rd ed. (Houston, TX: Gulf Publishing, 1991), p 515.

12. David Lamb, *The Africans* (New York: Vintage Books, 1985), p 226.

13. Ibid., p 231.

14. John S. Mbiti, *African Religions and Philosophy,* 2nd ed. (Oxford: Heinemann, 1990), pp 16–17.

15. Ibid., pp 211–22.

16. Harris and Moran, *Managing Cultural Differences,* p 517.

17. Lamb, *The Africans,* p 235.

18. Blaine, *Africa,* p 69.

19. Harris and Moran, *Managing Cultural Differences,* p 515.

20. Lamb, *The Africans,* p 226.

21. Ibid., p 226.

22. Edgar J. Ridley, *An African Answer: The Key to Global Productivity* (Trenton, NJ: Africa World Press, 1992), pp 26–27.

23. Ibid., p 42.

24. Ibid., p 26.

25. Lee Kuan Yew, quoted in *The Economist,* "A Survey of Asia," October 30, 1993, pp 21–22.

26. *The Economist,* "A Way to Stop the Spear," May 15, 1993, p 114.

27. Rearwin, *Asia Business Book,* p 55.

28. Evelyn Lip, *Feng Shui: A Layman's Guide to Chinese Geomancy* (Union City, CA: Heian International, 1992).

29. *The Economist,* "A Survey of Asia," October 30, 1993, p 21.

30. Rearwin, *Asia Business Book,* p 35.

31. Ibid., p 104.

32. From *Doctor Criminale* by Malcolm Bradbury. Copyright © 1992 by Malcolm Bradbury. Used by permission of Viking Penguin, a division of Penguin Books USA, Inc.

33. Robert D. Kaplan, *Balkan Ghosts: A Journey through History* (New York: St. Martin's Press, 1993), p xxi.

34. Jane Perlez, "A Mean Political Hangover for Seagram in Ukraine," *New York Times,* January 27, 1994, p D1.

35. Bradbury, *Doctor Criminale,* p 137.

36. Marlene L. Rossman, *The International Businesswoman of the 1990s: A Guide to Success in the Global Marketplace* (New York: Praeger, 1990), p 66.

37. Bradbury, *Doctor Criminale,* p 53.

38. John Mole, *Mind Your Manners: Managing Culture Clash in the Single European Market* (London: Nicholas Brealey 1993), p 105.

39. Garrison Keillor, "The Tidy Secret of Danish Freedom," *New York Times,* September 5, 1993, p E11.

40. Mole, *Mind Your Manners,* p 98.

41. Frank L. Acuff, *How to Negotiate Anything with Anyone Anywhere around the World* (NY: Amacom, 1993), p 202.

42. James Brooke, "Pragmatic Protestants Win Catholic Converts in Brazil," *New York Times,* July 4, 1993, p 1.

43. Ibid., p 10.

44. Erich E. Toll, "Is Low-Cost Labor Supreme?" *Global Production: Manufacturing and Sourcing in the Americas,* November–December, 1993, p 21.

45. Mark Vaughan, "Making Your Way in Latin America's Leading Markets," *Global Production: Manufacturing and Sourcing in the Americas,* November–December, 1993, p 7.

46. Mahatma G. Davies, "Cracking Caribbean Business Culture," *Global Production: Manufacturing and Sourcing in the Americas,* November–December, 1993, p 27.

47. Edward Said, "The Phoney Islamic Threat," *New York Times Magazine,* November 21, 1993, p 62. Copyright © 1993 by The New York Times Company. Reprinted by permission.

48. Ibid., p 64.

49. Reproduced by permission from *The Pleasantries of the Incredible Mulla Nasrudin* by Idries Shah (The Octagon Press Ltd., London).

50. Neil Chesanow, *The World-Class Executive: How to Do Business like a Pro around the World* (Toronto: Bantam Books, 1986), p 116.

51. Acuff, *How to Negotiate Anything,* p 241.

52. Chesanow, *World-Class Executive,* p 139.

53. Ibid., p 122.

54. Richard Mead, *Cross-Cultural Management Communication* (Chichester, UK: Wiley & Sons, 1990), p 87.

55. Louis E. Boone, *Quotable Business* (New York: Random House, 1992), p 185.

Chapter Four

Success in Communicating across Cultures

Don't overlook the importance of worldwide thinking. A company that keeps its eye on Tom, Dick, and Harry is going to miss Pierre, Hans, and Yoshio.

Al Ries, *Chairman, Trout & Ries Advertising, Inc.*

Boy, those French! They have a different word for everything.

Steve Martin

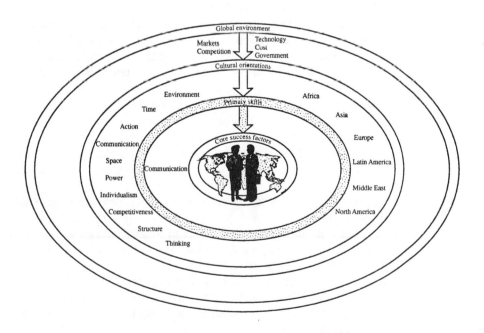

INTRODUCTION

As the cultural anthropologist Clifford Geertz says, we are "tumbled" into a world of "endless connection" in which "it is increasingly difficult to get out of each other's way."[1] Connection is a key word as we make our way into the international marketplace. Our contact with others from different cultures has increased dramatically, but our ability to *connect* with them remains tenuous at best.

The British novelist E. M. Forster, author of such books as *A Passage to India* and *Howard's End,* wrote that the antidote to a confusing and chaotic world is summed up in the phrase, "Only connect." In other words, the building of a foundation of personal relationships cuts through those things that divide us, such as class and culture.[2] This is particularly useful advice for American managers, who as we saw in an earlier chapter, tend to want to get down to business without having to build trust or to focus on compatibility or the development of long-term relationships. As business comes more and more to rely on multicultural teams and engage in international projects and alliances, the issue of communication is at the heart of competitive advantage.

The United States is somewhat ambivalent about cultural differences. On the one hand, there is a tendency to dismiss them as irrelevant or, at best, as only temporary phenomena until the whole world is Americanized in a global melting pot or salad bowl. On the other hand, there is an increasing feeling among many Americans that cultural differences are not going to go away (internally or externally), that they are a powerful component of individual and group identity, and that we had better learn how to work with them rather than against them. Global companies are finding that they not only need to create standardized products to maximize efficiencies, but need to customize the product and marketing and sales strategies to be responsive to the local customer. Global managers are also finding that they cannot impose forms of management onto people culturally unable to accept them. The imposition of universal products, services, and management styles may simply lead to confusion and resistance. We have to learn to communicate in ways that can derive value from differences, not that assume similarity or impose conformity.

We find ourselves in the middle of what at least one domestic commentator describes as the "culture wars,"[3] and the secret to not only surviving these wars, but coming out of them stronger and more able to compete and grow, is connection, which in turn is based on communication. The world is a network of computers and telecommunication systems that relay information around the world in seconds. But the really important business communication that takes place is still, and is likely to remain so for decades into the next century, at the face-to-face, personal level. This is the level where deals are made or lost, and where reputations are built or destroyed.

COMMUNICATION PROCESS LEVELS

As pointed out in the first chapter, corporations are reinventing themselves in order to compete successfully in global markets. The emerging business organization is reengineering to cope with (and even create) continuous change, focus intensely on customer needs rather than simply quick profits, tap into the generative power of multifunctional teams and a multicultural workforce, manage work through complex networks and matrices rather than rigid hierarchies, capitalize on knowledge generated inside and outside of the company, integrate processes to optimize cost effectiveness and time competitiveness, and maximize quality of products and services. Such a radical reinvention of business organization places huge strains on internal and external communication processes.

A company's communication processes can be thought of on three interrelated levels: the macro level, the organizational level, and the micro level (see Figure 4–1).

FIGURE 4–1
Communication Process Levels

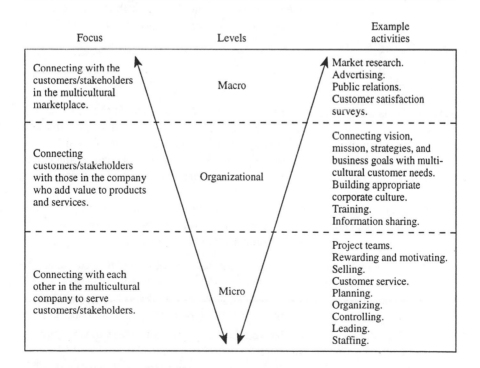

Focus	Levels	Example activities
Connecting with the customers/stakeholders in the multicultural marketplace.	Macro	Market research. Advertising. Public relations. Customer satisfaction surveys.
Connecting customers/stakeholders with those in the company who add value to products and services.	Organizational	Connecting vision, mission, strategies, and business goals with multicultural customer needs. Building appropriate corporate culture. Training. Information sharing.
Connecting with each other in the multicultural company to serve customers/stakeholders.	Micro	Project teams. Rewarding and motivating. Selling. Customer service. Planning. Organizing. Controlling. Leading. Staffing.

Source: © Training Management Corp. (TMC), *Doing Business Internationally: The Cross-Cultural Challenges,* Seminar and Coursebook (Princeton, NJ, 1992).

At the macro level, the company reaches into the multicultural marketplace to communicate with and understand its customers and other stakeholders (including shareholders, suppliers, and distributors). This customer/stakeholder understanding needs to feed into the organization's vision, mission, strategies, and so on, which shape the activities of those who can add value to the customer. In order to serve customers/stakeholders most effectively, individuals within a multicultural company must also be able to communicate with each other with mutual understanding and respect.

This is not a simple one-way process from macro to micro. At the micro level, individuals also deal with customers/stakeholders. They come to understand specific customers in ways that can supplement and/or question information gathered at the macro level. The sales force, for example, often has information gathered from its daily contact with customers that can add richness to the high-level data gathered through surveys. It is very important, therefore, that information flow freely between the levels and that it not be jammed up by protective levels of management or jealously guarded by functional specialists more concerned with territory than serving the customer.

While we will focus our discussion on communication at the micro level, we will first give some attention to the macro and organizational levels and the role culture plays in each.

Macro

Advertising is a key method for connecting with customers at the macro level. While companies seek to reap the benefits of standardization and mass marketing, customers force companies to pay attention to the demands of local culture. If there has been one lesson learned by global companies, it is that products and services, brands, and marketing messages are perceived differently, depending on cultural context.

Neglecting culture can be embarrassing and costly for a company concerned with protecting its brand equity. There are numerous examples of communication blunders at the macro level; we will mention only a few:

- Pepsi-Cola translated its slogan "Come Alive with Pepsi" into German. The translation actually read, "Pepsi brings you back from the grave."[4]
- A manufacturer in Singapore received an order for 100,000 trombones for the U.S. armed forces in Vietnam. Trombone is the French word for paper clip.[5]
- General Motors (GM) tried to sell the Chevy Nova in Mexico. GM quickly found out that "no va" in Spanish means "won't go."[6]
- Pillsbury introduced its Jolly Green Giant brand into Saudi Arabia; the brand name was translated as "Intimidating Green Ogre."[7]
- Kentucky Fried Chicken used its slogan "It's finger-lickin good!" in Iran only to find it had translated as "It's so good, you will eat your fingers."[8]

These are just small examples of how inattention to language differences can disconnect us from our customers. Such differences can destroy the usefulness of market research and customer satisfaction surveys. Of more importance, perhaps, are those differences in underlying value orientations that can sabotage our best efforts and communicate meanings at odds with those we intend.

For example, in the 1980s, Heineken beer decided to aim the same message to consumers across Europe on the assumption that a Euro-consumer was emerging. A further assumption was that the European consumer was "shifting away from pretentiousness toward more 'authentic,' 'pure,' yet sophisticated behavior."[9] One of the advertisements shows a young woman searching for a formal dress to put on. Her male companion is already dressed in a formal dinner jacket. The ad shows him leaving the room and then returning in very casual clothes. He hands her a pair of jeans, and instead of having a formal night out, they visit a place with an informal, pub-like atmosphere where they can be more natural.

In some European cultures, the intended message was the one received. However, in Greece and Spain there was an unintended disconnect with the customer. The Greeks and the Spaniards saw the couple settling for less, and Heineken as being downgraded to a very ordinary beer. We learn from this that while the product or service may be standardized, the message needs to be adapted to the cultural orientations of the different audiences (in this case, higher and lower levels of formality).

As Hoecklin points out, understanding differences can facilitate the communication of differences.[10] Steelcase Strafor, a French office furniture design and retailing company, developed an advertising campaign for delivery in 10 countries. In Britain, the text and tag line ran as follows:

Text: "If you are still smiling when you leave the office, it was designed by Steelcase Strafor."
Tag line: "Steelcase Strafor. More than a partner, a partnership."

In France, it read:

Text: "For this smile, Strafor designed the office."
Tag line: "Steelcase Stafor. More than a partner."

In Italy, it read:

Text: "For this smile, Strafor designed the office."
Tag line: "Steelcase Stafor. More than a partner, a friend."

The differences are subtle, but highly significant. In relation to our cultural orientations framework introduced in Chapter 2, we can highlight the following:

Britain

- There is a higher emphasis on words than in the French and Italian versions, indicating a lower-context culture.

- The ad is direct rather than indirect in its communication style.
- The language is instrumental rather than expressive; emotion is very much in the background.
- The stress on "partnership" rather than "partner" indicates a high degree of formality and structure.

France

- The ad is higher context and more indirect than the British version. The words used aim more at suggestion and possibility rather than precision and transfer of information.
- The ad is less instrumental and hints at expressiveness with its compressed and enigmatic "For this smile."
- "More than a partner" again leaves the interpretation ambiguous and highlights the importance of relationship.

Italy

- The Italian version, like the French, is high context.
- The only difference between the two versions is in the tag line, which adds "a friend." This places even higher stress on relationships—relationships that are particularistic rather than universalistic.

These illustrations are used to show that connecting with customers across cultures is not easy. The cultural fragmentation in Europe is particularly pronounced. Electrolux, a Swedish-based company, found this out when they assumed that European culture was converging and that Europeans would want to buy very similar refrigerators. They bought the Zanussi Group in Italy and built the largest appliance manufacturing company in Europe. Unfortunately, the assumption of a common culture was mistaken. Electrolux found that:

- Customers in northern Europe want very large refrigerators because they only shop once a week in supermarkets. Northerners also like their freezers on the bottom.
- Customers in southern Europe want small refrigerators because they shop very regularly in street markets. Southerners like their freezers on top of the refrigerator.
- Customers in Britain want 60 percent freezer space in their refrigerators because of their heavy consumption of frozen food.

To meet the diverse tastes across Europe, Electrolux produces 120 refrigerator designs with 1,500 variations.[11] There are numerous pitfalls in international markets, and every company is bound to make mistakes. One of our key success factors must be a tolerance for making mistakes (as long as we learn from them).

Organizational

As Hampden-Turner argues in *Corporate Culture for Competitive Edge,* a corporate culture is a cybernetic system—it allows the company to process feedback about conditions in its environment and make necessary corrections.[12] In our view, corporate culture is the system that connects the dynamic needs of customers and other stakeholders with those in the company who bring value to the customer (ideally, this would be everyone in the company; what are people doing if they are not creating value for the customer?).

Faced with constant change, the organization needs to be responsive and adaptable. As Stephen Rhinesmith puts it:

> Developing a global corporate culture involves forming the integrating values, mechanisms, and processes that allow a company to successfully manage constant change in a competitive marketplace.[13]

A global corporate culture is the primary integrative web that connects the components of a business. It does this by communicating the vision, mission, values, strategies, and goals of the company, by establishing standards for professional behavior and job performance, by defining appropriate internal and external relations, and by optimizing the flow of information through the global network. As such, it provides the critical context in which management decisions are made, plans are formulated, resources are allocated, people are hired and motivated, and performance is evaluated. If this culture is not focused on customers and stakeholders, then it is focused in the wrong place. Corporate culture becomes destructive when it becomes rigid and unresponsive to changing conditions. Paul Carroll, in *Big Blues: The Unmaking of IBM,* discusses how IBM's culture didn't adjust to the fast changes in technology and decline in customer loyalty.[14] As a result, IBM has lost $75,000 billion in stock market value and 150,000 jobs.

As Peter Drucker says, "Information is replacing authority."[15] As organizations seek to get closer to the customer and become more responsive, they get flatter. As organizations get flatter, individual responsibilities increase, jobs expand in scope, individuals need to network across organizations, and information becomes a major resource. Drucker also points out that:

> Knowledge is power, which is why people who had it in the past often need to make a secret of it. In post-capitalism, power comes from transmitting information to make it productive, not from hiding it.[16]

When information flows, the global company is in a better position to define strategies, identify and solve problems, adapt to local conditions while maximizing global efficiencies, shift resources and technologies to where they can add the most value, and time decisions to gain optimal benefits.

How can we enhance the communication process at the organizational level? We need to develop and implement practical techniques for building a collective learning mind-set. Learning and communication are not two separate processes; where there is actual communication there is also actual learning. But this collective learning mindset is not aimed at learning for its own sake; its goal is the creation and delivery of added-value, not some vague notion of "truth" or intellectual purity. Businesspeople cannot spend years determining the correctness of a theory or the validity of data or a methodology. While this is no excuse for sloppy work or thinking, we must always remember that the business agenda is not the academic agenda.

Building and sustaining a collective learning mindset is created by managers who establish receptive open dialogue between the company and customers/ stakeholders, and between levels and functions within the organization. Everyone in the organization needs to be encouraged to:

- Learn by listening and observing.
  What are customers/stakeholders saying?
  What are they doing?
  What are competitors saying and doing?
  What are business analysts saying?

- Learn by experimenting.
  What happens if we transfer this from here to there?
  What happens if we offer these customers this service?
  What happens if we change this process?
  What happens if we remove these boundaries?

- Learn by auditing.
  What can we measure in order to learn more about ourselves and others?
  What succeeded in the past? And why?
  What failed in the past? And why?

- Learn by researching.
  Whom can we benchmark?
  How does this market differ from our known markets?
  What are the primary cultural orientations of these customers, and how can we connect with them most effectively?

- Learn by broadening perspective.
  What can we learn by looking outside our industry and established markets?
  What can we learn by looking outside of our established ways of doing things?
  What can we learn by looking at the system and not just the parts?
  What can we learn by rotating jobs?

In a multicultural environment, a corporate culture that facilitates learning is critical. Existing habits, assumptions, and methods must always be open to question; at the same time, we must avoid the dangers of inaction and analysis paralysis.

David Garvin suggests the creation of learning forums, "programs or events designed with explicit learning goals in mind."[17] These include:

- Strategic reviews of the competitive environment, the company's products, its market positioning, and its technologies.
- Systems audits to review cross-functional processes and delivery systems.
- Internal benchmarking reports to identify best practices.
- Study missions to visit leading organizations around the world to analyze their performance and skills.
- Jamborees or symposia to bring together customers, suppliers, experts, and internal groups to promote the exchange of ideas and learning.

The communication and learning that takes place at the organizational level become increasingly important as we form partnerships, strategic alliances, and joint ventures with foreign companies. This is the primary global strategy of many U.S. companies, one fraught with obstacles. The success rate for such ventures is only estimated to be one-third to one-half.

A primary cause of failure is mismatched expectations, which often relate to cultural differences. If you think about the cultural orientations framework we introduced earlier, it isn't difficult to identify possible areas of conflict:

- Environment. Different views as to the need for or level of planning and control.
- Time. Different views as to the necessary speed for breaking even or producing results.
- Action. Differences as to whether business is done through developing relationships or simply by setting and completing tasks.
- Communication. Different levels of formality in conducting negotiations.
- Space. Different conceptions about the layout of new facilities.
- Power. Differences in the degree to which work can bypass levels of authority.
- Individualism. Differences in whether decisions are made by group consensus or individuals, and the circumstances to which decisions apply.
- Competitiveness. Different conceptions as to desirable levels of collaboration.
- Structure. Differences in the required level of contract documentation.
- Thinking. Different approaches to solving problems and developing strategies.

While such differences may not break an alliance, they can certainly contribute to the development of a stormy relationship.

Micro-Communication Explored

Communication is simply the exchange of meaning between individuals. If successful, this exchange involves little loss of meaning, establishes or maintains a relationship, and leaves open the possibility for further exchanges. The ultimate goal is synergy—the creative output of a whole that is greater than the sum of the individual contributions. Synergy comes from the Greek *synergos,* which means working together,[18] and it describes those benefits that can materialize from collaboration. According to Moran and Harris, working at developing cultural synergy is an investment aimed at increasing goal achievement through the "sharing of perceptions, insights, and knowledge."[19]

In the ideal communication process, information flows between the sender and the receiver, and the intended message is identical, or very close, to the received message (see Figure 4–2).

As you can see, there is no interference (noise) in the message flow from sender to receiver or in the confirmation flow in terms of feedback from the receiver to the sender.

Unfortunately, this ideal communication process is far from reality. Let us imagine two people from two different cultures: A and B. Their individual cultural profiles are listed in Table 4–1.

You can already see that communication may be difficult; the only cultural orientation they share is competitiveness (such profound difficulties exist even before the issues of language, gesture, and other barriers have been introduced). Both A and B have a configuration of value orientations that can be described as

FIGURE 4–2
The Ideal Communication Process

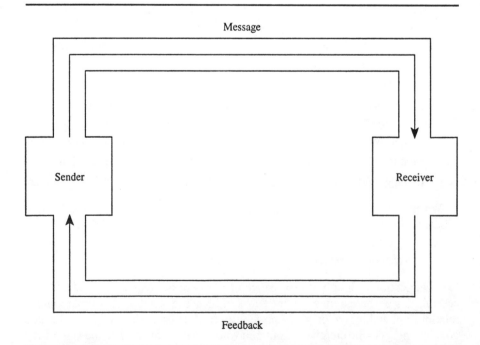

TABLE 4–1
Two Cultural Profiles

A	B
Control environment	Harmony with environment
Single-focus time	Multifocus time
Fixed time	Fluid time
Present time	Future time
Doing	Being
Low context	High context
Direct	Indirect
Instrumental	Expressive
Informal	Formal
Private space	Public space
Equality	Hierarchy
Individualistic	Collectivist
Universalistic	Particularistic
Competitive	Competitive
Flexibility	Order
Inductive thinking	Deductive thinking
Linear thinking	Systemic thinking

their *cultural frames.* A cultural frame is the perceptual window through which an individual defines him or herself, others, and the world. The perceptions filtered through the cultural frame are highly selective because each frame contains those classifications and categories determined by the culture to be necessary, relevant, and appropriate.

Glass windows can differ as to the amount and type of light they let in and the means by which they transform the light into patterns and colors. Our cultural frames perform a similar function. Our physical senses flood us with data; we can only make meaningful sense of it all by passing it through the selective filters derived from our value orientations embedded in our cultural frame. From birth, we are socialized by parents, schools, churches, friends, and so on into the "normal" patterns of thinking, feeling, and behaving. This makes it very difficult to determine *equivalence across cultures.* Are we talking about the same thing? And if we are, will we behave in the same manner toward it?

- Are blue and green different colors? They are to speakers of English. Speakers of Tarahumara, however, do not distinguish between blue and green.[20]

- Do we agree that children should be punished when they have done something wrong? Probably. Our culture, however, is likely to determine how that punishment should be carried out. For example, in England children who have misbehaved may be sent to their rooms. In America, they will also be "grounded," confined to the house. This punishes the child by denying them their individual freedom and independence. In Japan, the child will be punished by being kept out of the home. This denies the child access to the collective, the family.[21]

Suppose A is a salesperson and B is a customer. The differences in cultural frames may manifest themselves as follows (see Table 4–2 for a more complete list of possible differences):

Environment

Control versus Harmony

A: And what's more, this little device will cut through that mountain like a knife through butter.

B: But I don't want to build a road through the mountain. I want a road that blends in with the natural landscape and doesn't disrupt the animal sanctuaries. This mountain is sacred to us. To cut through it would be very wrong.

Time

Single-Focus Time versus Multifocus Time

A: Boy, I wish I could get his attention. I've never known such a rude person. Why doesn't he tell his father to call back after the meeting?

B: Why is he looking so upset? Interruptions are a fact of life. And I must see to my father's needs before anyone else's.

Fixed Time versus Fluid Time

A: When I set up this sales meeting to begin at 10 o'clock, I assumed that it would begin at 10 o'clock, not 10:45. I've got other appointments to get to. Unbelievable!

B: Typical! Always in a hurry to get somewhere else. Does he think I'm just another customer who will make do with "Hello. Buy this. Good-bye." I've lived without this gadget all my life. What's the rush now? Patience. Please take the time necessary to do this properly.

Present Time versus Future Time

A: With this device, you will be able to increase your current productivity figures by 5 percent, and reduce your staff by 15 percent. Just think what that will mean to your year-end figures.

TABLE 4–2
Cultural Orientations and Sales

1. Environment

Control	Client: "Will this product/service help me get more control of my life and environment?"
Harmony	Client: "Will this product/service be acceptable to others, or will it give offense and alienate me from others?"
Constraint	Salesperson can expect client to be skeptical of product claims.

2. Time

Single Focus	Salesperson can expect a client's undivided attention. Salesperson can also expect the prospect to be receptive to linear, point-by-point sales presentations.
Multifocus	Salesperson can expect interruptions. Salesperson can expect the prospect to manifest a more holistic buying approach.
Fixed	Client will want to begin and finish on time. Schedules will be tight and organized in blocks. Salespeople, however, should allow some flexibility in their time slots so as not to pressure the potential customer into buying.
Fluid	Client is less concerned with "clock time" than with "event time," taking the amount of time needed to do what needs to be done. Other appointments may have to wait. Sticking to the formally allocated time for its own sake is not appropriate.
Past	Client: "Does this product/service fit with what has gone before?" Emphasizing the company's history, experience, and reputation is effective.
Present	Client: "Will this product/service gratify my needs right now?" Emphasizing the company's immediate responsiveness and attention is effective.
Future	Communicating the company's commitment to serving the customer for the long term, as well as your personal commitment to maintaining the relationship, is effective.

3. Action

Being	Client: "How will this product/service improve my quality of life and relationships?" A "softer," more personal sales approach is appreciated.
Doing	Client: "How will this product/service help me be more productive and accomplish my personal goals?" An efficient, business-focused sales approach is appropriate

4. Communication

High Context	Client will be very concerned about building a relationship of trust with the salesperson. The salesperson should not expect to close a sale rapidly. However, once trust is gained, there is higher potential for obtaining repeat and referral business. The salesperson

TABLE 4–2 *(continued)*

	should provide contextual information leading up to an inevitable conclusion.
Low Context	Client will be very concerned with facts and figures and "straight talk" that gets to the point. The salesperson may want to start with the bottom line or conclusion and then provide the amount of contextual information defined by the customer. The salesperson can expect to close the sale relatively quickly.
Direct	Client will be confrontational and list many objections in a "no holds barred" manner. He or she is also likely to fire many questions at the salesperson: "How much?" "When?" "How?" A direct salesperson may be perceived as very aggressive in some cultures or forthright and refreshing in others.
Indirect	A client's questions and answers will be softened so as not to give offense or cause loss of face. A direct salesperson may be confused and frustrated at the seeming vagueness of response.
Expressive	Client will openly express positive and negative emotions. The possibility of embarrassment and conflict is to some degree higher. The salesperson may find it easier to know where he or she stands.
Instrumental	Client will keep emotions hidden. The salesperson may find the client difficult to read. How the client feels about the product may not be revealed until a sales close is attempted.
Formal	Salesperson will need to show respect by observing appropriate behaviors and customs. The salesperson should learn the specific customs of the prospect's culture pertaining to sales: buyer/seller status, greetings, conversational topics, do's and taboos, and so on.
Informal	Salesperson can dispense with a high level of protocol, although respect should be communicated at all times.

5. Space

Private	Sales meeting is likely to take place in a quiet, secluded location where privacy can be maintained. The prospect will most likely maintain a fairly distant social distance.
Public	Sales meeting may take place in a crowded, noisy location with little privacy. The prospect may feel most comfortable with a more personal social distance.

6. Power

Hierarchy	Client may be very concerned with deference to position and status both in the home and at work. The salesperson may or may not be meeting with the decision maker. The chain of authority is pronounced. The salesperson needs to command respect. The salesperson should expect negotiations to be formal and should communicate respect for the prospect.
Equality	Salesperson and client meet on relatively equal terms. Titles, status and formal position count for very little in the sales situation.

TABLE 4–2 *(concluded)*

7. Individualism		
	Individualistic	Decision making is likely to be fast and made on the spot. Selling to benefits that help the individual meet personal goals is very effective. Saving face is less of a concern.
	Collectivist	Decision making may take longer because of the client's need to confer with others. The collectivist prospect maintains close affiliations with various in-groups; selling to benefits that help these in-groups is very effective. Face-saving is paramount; the salesperson should do nothing to cause the prospect to lose face, especially in front of others.
	Universalistic	Client wants to feel he or she is being treated as fairly as everyone else. That the price, quality, and so on, are identical for all customers, under all circumstances.
	Particularistic	Client wants to be treated as an exception. A formal agreement is only a guideline. Agreements develop out of relationships rather than impersonal conditions applied to everyone.
8. Competitiveness		
	Competitive	Client may be highly aggressive in pursuing the "best deal" or outsmarting the salesperson in a competitive "battle."
	Cooperative	Emphasis on the shared quality of life and relationships. Consensus is valued above winning.
9. Structure		
	Order	Client will need a great deal of information and comprehensive documentation regarding the product/service and agreements. The prospect will be less willing to take risks. Selling benefits that communicate increased order, certainty, or security is effective.
	Flexibility	Client will be willing to make a decision with relatively little information or formal documentation. The prospect will be more willing to take risks or consider alternatives.
10. Thinking		
	Deductive	This type of client wants fewer statistics and more conceptual reasoning and debate about the ideas behind the product or service.
	Inductive	The client wants to see the factual data that relate to the product or service and to hear about prior experiences and then draw conclusions. The salesperson should always be prepared with product data and customer experiences.
	Linear	The client wants to see the argument for buying laid out in a logical manner with each small chunk of information leading smoothly to the next. This kind of thinking can appear to be impersonal.
	Systemic	The selling process is less direct and may involve "circling around" issues and looking at the wider implications of a buying decision.

B: I want to know how this will fit with my 15-year plan to expand my oper-
    ations in Latin America. Will it fit with those plans, and not just with
    what I'm doing now?

Action

Doing versus Being

A: This service is going to help you be more productive and meet your very
    challenging goals.
B: But what about my quality of life? With this approach, it looks like I'll
    never leave the office or see my family and friends again.

Communication

Low Context versus High Context

A: Well, let's not waste any time with fluff. Let me give you the straight
    talk and go directly to this comparison chart that shows our competitive
    advantages.
B: But who are you? Can I trust you? Tell me more about yourself. How
    long have you been with your company?

Direct versus Indirect

A: Well, I can see that you disagree with me. Let's be honest with each
    other, and lay our cards on the table. What don't you like?
B: What you offer is very interesting. Let me think about it for a while, and I
    will get back to you soon.

Expressive versus Instrumental

A: I don't believe it. Sounds like sales hype to me. Hype! Hype! Hype!
    All you people are probably in sales because you can't get real jobs.
    Right? Ha!
B: I think we should stay focused on the problem we're trying to solve with
    this product. If we follow these three practical steps, I believe we can in-
    crease your productivity threefold, and build increased flexibility into
    your manufacturing process. Let me lay out my plan in detail.

Informal versus Formal

A: Hi. Nice to meet you. What's happening?
B: Good morning. Won't you please sit down? Here is my card. May I offer
    you some tea? Are you always so impolite?

Space

Private Space versus Public Space

A: I was hoping we could meet in a place where we could be free from dis-tractions, especially people walking in and out, and telephones ringing off the hook.

B: What distractions? You mean your office isn't like this? I think I'd go crazy in a quiet office.

Power

Equality versus Hierarchy

A: I don't know what title you hold in this company. I don't think that kind of thing means very much in the real world. As far as I'm concerned, it's just you and me trying to make a deal that will benefit us both. Titles and all that other stuff just get in the way.

B: Doesn't he know who I am? I should have the guard throw him out. What impertinence!

Individualism

Individualistic versus Collectivistic

A: I think you should make the decision today and take advantage of this special offer that I'm making.

B: Doesn't he know that I need to consult with my colleagues? But, if I say so, I may look indecisive and weak and lose face.

Competitiveness

Competitive and Competitive

A: I can really come out a winner on this one.

B: She thinks she came out a winner on this one. I'll show her!

Structure

Flexibility versus Order

A: We can dispense with the paperwork. I'll put the order through myself, and that may cut some of the delivery time.

B: He can't be serious. I want the paperwork completed right here and now, and I want three copies for my files.

Thinking

Inductive versus Deductive

A: We've conducted extensive customer satisfaction research, and our results show quite clearly that we are the best in the business.
B: But what business are you actually in? Tell me something about your
   company's business philosophy and why you do what you do and some
   of the ideas behind this service you offer.

Linear versus Systemic

A: Let me present the benefits to your operation in a logical order, from A
   to B.
B: That sounds very interesting, but put it into the big picture for me. How
   will this fit into our total operation?

CROSS-CULTURAL COMMUNICATION BARRIERS

You can see that the cultural frame of each individual creates potential for conflict and misunderstanding. The challenge is to recognize one's own frame, identify the key characteristics of the other person's, and to the largest degree
possible, adapt. Before we can do this, however, there are certain myths that we
need to clear away.

Myth # 1: We're really all the same.

No, we're not. The differences in value orientations mentioned in this and previous chapters should convince you of that. The most important first step in developing cultural competence is to recognize difference without judging or
becoming defensive. Nancy Adler's advice should be taken to heart: *"Assume
difference until similarity is proven."*[22] At the same time, we need to recognize
that we do share orientations, and we are not unique.

Myth # 2: I just need to be myself, and everything will be OK.

Cultural differences run deep. Being a naive foreigner, but intelligent and
charming, may carry you for a time. Pretty soon, however, that will wear thin.

Myth # 3: I have to really like this other person before I can do business.

Like is the wrong word. You need to develop your understanding and respect
of differences rather than force yourself to like the other person.

Myth # 4: I have to adopt the practices of the other culture in order to succeed.

False. You need to adapt rather than adopt. "Going native" is not necessary
and may not earn you respect from members of the other culture. Some practices
of the other culture may be adopted if they seem useful, desirable, comfortable,
or satisfying.

We talked about the ideal communication process above. We now need to
add the cultural frames to our model (see Figure 4–3). The chances of a loss of

FIGURE 4–3
The Not-So-Ideal Communication Process

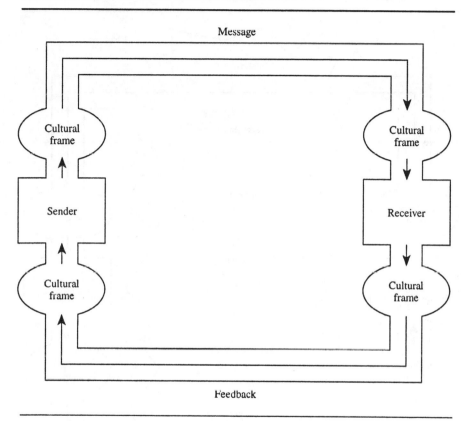

Source: © Training Management Corp. (TMC), *Doing Business Internationally: The Cross-Cultural Challenges,* Seminar Coursebook (Princeton, NJ, 1992).

meaning are now increased through ignorance, misinterpretation, and misplaced evaluations.

As you can see, the sender formulates the message in terms of a cultural frame. The receiver interprets the message in light of another cultural frame and then creates feedback based on that frame. The original sender now interprets that feedback from within his or her frame.

The process is messy and full of cultural static. Interference, and a consequent loss of meaning, grows when we add other possible noisemakers. These noisemakers (see Figure 4–4) or common communication barriers increase the possibility of distortion and misunderstanding. But we do have some degree of control over them. They are not so inherently a part of the communication process as the cultural frames we've spoken of. The one exception to this is language, but we will discuss this a little later.

FIGURE 4–4
The Closer-to-Reality Communication Process

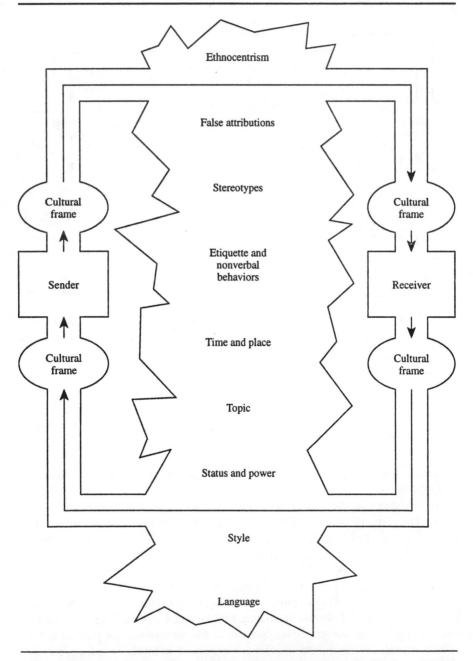

Source: © Training Management Corp. (TMC), *Doing Business Internationally: The Cross-Cultural Challenges,* Seminar Coursebook (Princeton, NJ, 1992).

While perhaps not destroying communication altogether, the barriers listed in Figure 4–4 can be very damaging unless brought under control.

Ethnocentrism

Given the intense feelings that experiencing a new culture can generate—fear, hate, confusion, and so on—it should be no surprise that we often degenerate into ethnocentrism, a belief in the inherent superiority and naturalness of our own culture. In this mode, we rate everyone according to our standards and our way of doing things. Although it can be highly destructive, it is a basic human response based on survival instincts; we all have ethnocentric tendencies. As David Hoopes says:[23]

> From birth we begin identifying with and affirming that which gives us sustenance, our parents, our families, our culture groups. To believe that one's group is right and must be defended provides or has provided human beings with one of their most effective defenses against the depredations of nature and of other human beings . . . Yet as civilization becomes more advanced and complicated, as the population increases and as culture groups become more accessible to each other . . . ethnocentrism becomes a threat.

Seeing ourselves as the center of the universe closes off our ability to relate. Instead of reflecting on our own and the other's behavior and thinking patterns, we are quick to jump to hasty evaluations and derogatory remarks: "That doesn't make sense," "That's stupid!" "Strange!" "Really weird!" "Unbelievable!" "They're so lazy." "They're devious." "I've never known such rude people." We are all prone to make such statements when we feel anxious or are afraid of losing face. These expressions may also make us feel closer to our own group.

When we catch ourselves thinking or making such remarks, we need to stop and ask ourselves: What is going on here? What are the underlying differences that are causing such a strong reaction in me? How would I see things if I were in their shoes? What is interesting and valuable in the way they see things? Such questions slow the judgmental process down, and provide a breathing space for thought and reflection. Some other actions that will help you avoid the destructive consequences of ethnocentrism are listed in Table 4–3.

False Attributions

When we witness behavior that is different from our normal expectations, we try to make sense of it by attributing a cause. For example, if we are negotiating with the Japanese, we might be made uncomfortable by the fact that they don't make prolonged eye contact with us. Anglo-Americans are raised to make eye contact with people they are dealing with. For example, parents and teachers often say,

TABLE 4–3
Avoiding Ethnocentrism

When experiencing a new culture, try to:

- Set realistic expectations for yourself and others.
- Be curious. Seek to learn all you can about the new culture. What are the primary value orientations? What makes the other culture tick?
- Look at problems and experiences from the other person's point of view.
- Keep your sense of humor.
- Keep judgments at bay.
- Be tolerant of yourself and others.
- Accept that you and the others are going to make mistakes.
- Be patient. Slow down.

Don't:

- Keep comparing the other culture with your own.
- Deny that you can be ethnocentric. Recognize it and move on to a deeper understanding.

Source: © Training Management Corp. (TMC), *Doing Business Internationally: The Cross-Cultural Challenges,* Seminar Coursebook (Princeton, NJ, 1992).

"Look at me when I'm talking to you." As children, we may have averted our eyes when we felt ashamed or had something to hide. In our negotiations with the Japanese, therefore, we associate their lack of eye contact with having something to hide, and we may revert to calling them sly or devious. For the Japanese, on the other hand, prolonged eye contact is a sign of aggressive behavior. So, on the one side of the table, you may have the Americans thinking, "These people are too devious to do business with," and on the other side the Japanese may be thinking, "These people are too aggressive. I can't do business with them."

One of our clients, an American accountant, was sent to Japan to teach members of an affiliate company the fundamentals of U.S. financial practices. Our client was surprised and delighted by the depth of knowledge among his Japanese counterparts. Wanting to convey how impressed he was, he said, "How did you get such good training in our methods?" The Japanese attributed aggressiveness to our client and reacted defensively, assuming that the American was attacking their authority and competence. It took some time for the communication bridge to be mended.

Usually such attributions are based on only a little knowledge about the other culture. We fill in the blanks by inserting our own meanings rather than digging out additional information. It helps to consider what the problem is from the other person's point of view. Seeing from the other side does not mean that you agree with them; it just means that you are in a better position to have a more complete understanding of the problem.

Stereotypes

Often our attributions may be based on stereotypes that we hold about other groups. We talked earlier about how our cultural frame contains specific classifications and categories that organize our experience. Stereotypes are closed categories that leave no room for individual differences or exceptions. Any new information is channeled into the existing category, which in turn strengthens the category and confirms our existing viewpoint. Let us be quite clear: There is no such thing as a positive stereotype; for example, African-Americans are great athletes. Such a view closes off our actual experience with individuals; we don't see people for who they are. Sikkema and Niyekawa offer some sound advice:[24]

> Each observation must be kept separate. Labeling and categorizing must be suspended. When certain things are observed repeatedly, when a recurrent pattern is noted, then one may tentatively create a category . . . until one has had enough exposure to and contact with the people of a new culture, no generalizations should be made.

We need to be aware that we all categorize others. We cannot cope with the complexity of experience in any other way. Generalizations can help us orient ourselves at the beginning of an interaction. But becoming trapped in categories closes off new experiences in a destructive fashion.

Also, be alert to the possibility that those you are interacting with may be working with stereotypes of you: "the brash American," "the arrogant Frenchman," "the English snob." If you feel a stereotype is being used against you, display behavior in contradiction to the expectations, and, if necessary, allude to the differences between yourself and the stereotype. For example, an American may want to slow down his or her rate of speech, soften directness, and demonstrate concern for the longer-term. Try not to become defensive; that will only cause the situation to degenerate. Focus on the problem, not the personalities.

Etiquette and Non-Verbal Behaviors

Does everyone know that the American gesture of "OK"—touching the index finger to the thumb and making a circle—is an obscene gesture to the Greeks, the Brazilians, and the Turks? It could bring conversation to a close very quickly.

Did you also know that the Japanese point with their middle finger, which is close to an obscene gesture for Americans?

And did you know that showing the soles of your feet to a Saudi is a definite insult, and that you would never pass anything with your left hand as that hand is reserved for personal cleanliness?

Business and social etiquette is a vast topic, and no other area of cross-cultural understanding has been more talked or written about. Several books in our bibliography deal with the do's and don'ts for specific countries and regions; and as you have already seen, we have included some in Chapter 3: Success in Crossing Cultures. Understanding the meanings associated with particular gestures, facial expressions, and positionings of the body requires specific knowledge of a culture. It can be a particular problem when the participants in a cross-cultural interaction are of different sexes. Some American women, for example, might misconstrue the physical closeness of Hispanic or Arab men as a sexual advance. For some general guidelines on business etiquette, see Table 4–4.

TABLE 4–4:
Etiquette Guidelines

Watch Your Manners	Be more polite and formal in a foreign culture than you would be in your own. It's a great temptation to drop the formalities when away from home. Resist the temptation. Don't lead with a first name or a casual phrase like "Hi." Stay formal until you are invited to use more familiar terms.
Communicate Respect	Take time to learn names and titles, and their correct pronunciations. Learn some of the host country's language, but make sure your pronunciation is good; small differences can have dramatic results. Don't insult the host by simply talking louder if he or she doesn't appear to understand. Learn the culture's customs regarding the giving of gifts (also know your company's policy toward gift giving as well as any legal restrictions of your own or your host's country). Particularly in Asia, avoid causing someone to lose face. Handle business cards with care. Take time to read the card after you are given it, use two hands for giving and receiving cards, and keep cards in a special holder. Dress somewhat conservatively; it's better to be safe than sorry.
Show Patience	The use and perception of time differs across cultures. Impatience may cause you and your host stress, damage the relationship, and lose you business. Don't expect to always be received on time, even if you have a scheduled appointment.
Be Gracious	You are a representative of your country, your culture, and your company 24 hours a day. Accept and give appropriate hospitality. When entertaining, understand local customs in relation to alcohol and appropriate foods. For example, Muslims don't drink alcohol or eat pork; Hindus don't eat beef.
Prepare Well and Seek Confirmation	Learn as much as you can about the foreign culture before making your visit. But don't assume too much, or make hasty attributions. Whenever you can, check that your understanding is correct.

Time and Place

We all know the old saying, "There's a time and place for everything." For example, when in France, avoid talking about business during meals, unless your host gives you the signal that it is OK to do so. The holiest time in the Muslim year is Ramadan, which lasts for 30 days. To be considerate, and avoid upsetting your hosts, don't eat, drink, or smoke in front of people during daylight hours.

Topic

In general, avoid conversations about politics, sex, religion, the cost of items, age, and comparisons with your own culture. Such topics can be controversial and can create a damaging first impression that may be very difficult to overcome. Try to find out in advance what conversational topics are appropriate. The British will always engage in a conversation about the weather, but it is probably wise to avoid making fun of the Royal Family, the troubles in Northern Ireland, the British affection for animals, or the local work ethic. Right-wing politics and World War II can be sensitive subjects in Germany, as can the Palestinian question in Israel, terrorism in Arab countries, and illegal immigrants to the United States in China and Mexico. Focusing on a country's stereotypical weak spots is not a good way to build relationships; you will probably be perceived as arrogant, ignorant, and offensive.

Status and Power

Observing status and power differences in most cultures around the world is very important. Deference to rank and respect for hierarchical levels is especially important in Latin American, Asian, and European cultures. If you want to severely damage a negotiation in East Asia, do not show any particular deference to the senior negotiator relative to the other members of the team.

Style

Earlier, we talked about the differences between high and low context, and direct/indirect, and formal/informal cultures. Unacknowledged differences in these styles can have very detrimental effects on the exchange of meaning. One other style characteristic that can affect communication is expressiveness. This includes the emotional level conveyed not only through word choice and tone, but through body movement and intensity of disagreement.

Language

Language is perhaps the greatest barrier of all, even when all of the participants in a cross-cultural encounter speak the same language. For example, in a meeting between English and American managers, one of the English managers says,

"And I'd like to *table* another item." The Americans think she wants to postpone talking about that issue or put it aside altogether. Instead she wants to bring it to their attention.

We should all try to learn at least the basics of the other language (greetings, expressions to apologize, please, and thank you), and we should stay simple and slow paced. Jargon, slang, unusual idioms, and colloquialisms should be avoided at all times. The following statements look innocent enough, but can cause problems:

- "I've been reviewing the materials you gave me, Mr. Neuru. You have a real cash cow here. Excellent."
  First of all, is Mr. Neuru going to have any idea what a "cash cow" is? And, if Mr. Neuru is a Hindu, isn't it possible he might take offence to the use of "cow" in this context?

- "I'll be sure to check with you in a week."
  What does the other person understand by the word "check"? He or she will receive money in a week?

- "Well, here's a ballpark figure for you. Chew on this for a while and give me a buzz." "Ballpark figure"? Does this refer to a shapely cheerleader? A park in the shape of a ball? "Chew on this." How does food fit into the discussion? "Give me a buzz." Does this have something to do with the drug problem in America? Or a beehive?

People in other cultures tend to learn standard, formal English in school, and ambiguous phrases can create all sorts of puzzlement.

Sometimes it will be necessary to make use of a translator or interpreter. If you do, you should follow these guidelines:

- Prepare the interpreter in advance. Make sure he or she understands the subject matter and your objectives.

- Speak in a clear, slow voice and be concise.

- Avoid obscure or difficult words.

- Repeat key ideas in different ways.

- Divide what you have to say into small chunks.

- Allow ample time for the interpreter to clarify points.

- Never interrupt the interpreter.

- Avoid long sentences, double negatives, or negative wording.

- Write out all agreements so both parties can confirm understanding.

- Ask interpreter for advice on proper wording.

OVERCOMING BARRIERS

There are many barriers to cross-cultural communication, but they are not impossible to overcome. There are several things we can do to limit the loss of meaning in the communication process.

Pay Attention to Feedback

Feedback is one of the central concepts in the science of cybernetics. *Cyber* is a Greek term for pilot, steersman, or governor, and feedback is what we learn about a system's past and present performance to help guide future performance.[25] If cross-cultural interactions were simple stimulus-response events, we would have very few problems. But, as we have seen, the stimulus (the message) is processed through different cultural frames as well as being shaped by the communication barriers we have just discussed. We don't, therefore, receive a predictable response. Instead, we need to judge the effectiveness of our communication by the feedback we receive. Only by analyzing the feedback can we determine what adjustments we need to make.

Take Responsibility for the Communication

Taking responsibility for communication means being actively engaged in limiting the loss of meaning. Some cross-cultural encounters can be difficult, and it is sometimes easier to take a passive role, to "tune out." When we do this, we fake comprehension, pretending to pay attention. We hear without listening and look without seeing. We hear words and watch behaviors, but fail to grasp *meaning*. Very often, we are too eager and are directing our energy to what we want to say next rather than focusing on what is being said. Or we may allow our minds to wander onto other topics and priorities, especially if the other person is slower in speech. We may also focus too hard on trying to analyze the cultural orientations of the participants in the encounter and lose track of our business objectives.

An active listener will ask questions: open-ended questions to gain as much information as possible ("Please tell me how you think I can be of most benefit to you?"); closed-ended questions that require a yes or no answer to gather specific facts ("So, Poland is now your fastest growing market?"); and summary questions to clarify what has been said or agreed to ("Now let me see if I understand you correctly . . . You're saying that . . . Is that correct?").

When we take responsibility for the communication, we work at getting the meaning, and we pay close attention to details and nuances. For tips on practicing active listening and observing, see Table 4–5.

TABLE 4–5
Tips on Active Listening and Observing

Listening	Observing
• Concentrate, avoid distractions.	• Learn the subleties of body
• Listen for central ideas.	language of the other culture.
• Ask questions.	• Focus clearly on the behavior
• Check yourself for cultural	and the setting.
assumptions.	• Avoid projecting your own
• Try to interpret from the	meanings onto the behavior.
other's cultural perspective	Keep an open mind.
as well as your own.	• Don't generalize from one gesture,
• Restate and paraphrase to	movement, or sign. Pay attention
confirm and clarify.	to consistent and repeated postures,
• Listen to content, not delivery.	eye movements, facial expressions,
• Respect silences. Don't rush to	and personal space requirements.
fill in the gaps.	
• Postpone evaluations.	
• Show interest.	

Limit Time in the Escalation Box

The escalation box is not a penalty box for those who have committed really serious ice hockey fouls. Rather, it is a cross-cultural encounter in which there is an escalating level of conflict due to misunderstanding or ignorance and no apparent way out. In a cross-cultural encounter it is always possible—and easy—to give or take offense. Let's assume we are in a multicultural team meeting. The team leader, Lee, an engineer from New York, is unhappy about some missed deadlines. He points to a Mexican member of the team, and says, "Please, Carlos, say something. Help us out with this." He doesn't wait for a reply, but moves on to chastise another member of the team for showing up late. Carlos feels the leader just caused him to lose face in the group, and is deeply annoyed. Later in the meeting, when the team leader is again complaining about members of the group for their lack of active participation and input, Carlos decides to confront the team leader (although somewhat indirectly). He says, "Lee, why don't we take a short break and calm ourselves. Then perhaps we can all reach agreement on how to proceed." The team leader bursts in with, "That's not the kind of help I'm looking for Carlos. I don't want to waste any more time." Carlos feels a further loss of face, and is now extremely angry and considering how he can get back at the team leader without losing his job. All of his work has been first-rate, and submitted on time. He doesn't know why the team leader should feel so aggressively toward him. Carlos says in an emotional voice, "I give you my best work.

I receive good feedback. No one has complained." This cycle of conflict could continue and deepen until the conflict becomes destructive and makes a significant impact on the morale and performance of the whole team.

The participants in this encounter need to perform a cultural check to examine what underlying orientations are at work in the conflict (see Figure 4–5). The team leader is annoyed with the team for missing deadlines, but he chooses to attack one of his best team members, Carlos. In a moment of stress, he has attacked the person in the team most unlike himself. The leader feels frustrated by Carlos' lack of participation in team meetings and seeming lack of independence and drive. Basically, Lee wants Carlos to be more American in his style—aggressive,

FIGURE 4–5
The Escalation Box

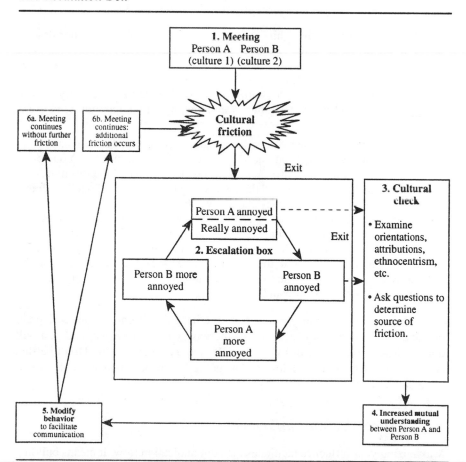

Source: © Training Management Corp. (TMC), *Doing Business Internationally: The Cross-Cultural Challenges,* Seminar Coursebook (Princeton, NJ, 1992).

driving, direct, and willing to express ideas in the team on an equal basis with everyone else. Carlos mostly communicates his ideas to the team through his excellent weekly reports, which are recognized by management and the team as being of very high quality. Carlos has great regard for the technical expertise of the team leader, but feels the leader doesn't respect him. Why else would he cause him to lose face in team meetings? Carlos isn't used to questioning authority or having to participate in informal, unstructured team meetings; he looks to a leader to lead, take charge, and give direction.

Apply Damage Control

We all make mistakes, even with the best of intentions. Damage control is recognizing that we have made a cultural *faux pas,* and doing what we need to do before the situation is beyond repair. Let's consider a few examples.

- You are meeting with a Chinese businessman. You decide to demonstrate your cultural sensitivity by using a few Mandarin phrases in your opening remarks. Your efforts are met with a blank stare and uncomfortable silence until he says, "I speak Cantonese."

     In this case, you can say something like, "I apologize. I recently learned a few words in Mandarin, and I've been looking for an opportunity to use them. I made a wrong assumption. I'm sorry."

- You are trying to close a deal with a Japanese company. The company's representatives seemed convinced of the merits of your product. You decide to assume a sales close, and ask when you can install the machine. You are met with silence, and then a few vague references about "needing more time" and "needing to find out if we are ready for this."

     You realize that you may have appeared too aggressive, and not understanding of their need to come to a consensus decision. In this case you might say, "I'm sorry. I don't want to rush you into making a decision. I appreciate that you need to discuss this further with your colleagues. Can I call you at a later date when you've had an opportunity to consult with other members of your team?"

Confidence in responding to members of other cultures only comes with practice and time. Each small success will increase your confidence, and you will only achieve those successes by taking risks and trying things out. Don't be shy. And don't be afraid to use apologies. An apology is the best damage control technique in the world.

Maximize Your influence

Maximizing your influence facilitates the communication flow. It means building and sustaining your credibility. Establishing your credibility is one of the most important tasks you face in doing business internationally. While it is difficult to generalize about how to be credible across the world, there are certain behaviors that will help you.

- Demonstrate preparation.
  Show that you have prepared to work with the other culture. Use phrases of the language to show good will, or speak in their language if you can. Demonstrate empathy and sensitivity to their culture, and be courteous at all times.

- Demonstrate flexibility.
  Be open to differences that don't fit into your expectations. Deal with the reality in front of you, not the reality you think should be there.

- Demonstrate your expertise.
  Be knowledgable about your business, current developments in your field, and leading figures. Ask questions that show the level of your understanding. We often demonstrate our credibility by the questions we ask, rather than the answers we give.

- Demonstrate ethical behavior.
  Never even hint at something that is less than honest. If approached to do something that you feel is dishonest, don't give a direct "No." Just say, "I'll see if my company would allow that," and move on.

- Demonstrate self-confidence.
  Be confident without being arrogant. No one wants to do business with someone who is insecure and nervous. Likewise, no one wants to do business with someone who doesn't listen to what anyone else says.

- Demonstrate reliability and commitment.
  Don't make promises you can't keep. To paraphrase an old saying from India: Integrity is keeping your promises. Wisdom is only making promises you can keep.

- Demonstrate patience.
  Slow down. Don't try to deal with those from other cultures at the same fast-paced, breakneck, everything-is-a-crisis speed you might be used to. They will resent your pushiness. It may also signify to them that you are not thinking about what you are doing.

- Demonstrate enthusiasm.
  Show that you care for them, for your work, and for the results you hope you can achieve together.

- Demonstrate respect.
  Perhaps the most important behavior of all. Many cultures around the world are often suspicious of Western intentions. Wars and colonialization have left scars on the cultural landscape. One of the authors recently asked a woman from the Philippines what she felt was the most important behavior an American should demonstrate when wanting to do business in Asia. Without a moment's hesitation she said, "Respect." "What else?" the author asked. "More respect," she said, followed by "trust and friendship."

SUMMARY INSIGHTS

As we enter the global marketplace, we must learn how to connect with our multicultural customers, stakeholders, and employees. Much of the business world outside the United States is relationship driven, and, as a consequence, cross-cultural communication is at the heart of international competitive advantage. We cannot hope to be successful if we try to standardize our products, our marketing and sales efforts, and our management systems, and fail to adapt to local cultures.

Cross-cultural communication must be planned for at three levels: the macro, the organizational, and the micro. At the macro level, the company reaches into the multicultural marketplace to communicate with and understand its customers and other stakeholders (including shareholders, suppliers, and distributors). This understanding must be translated into a global vision which, in turn, forms the basis for global strategies. Activities at the macro level include market research, advertising, public relations, and customer satisfaction surveys. Each activity must be fine-tuned to maximize our understanding of global and local customers.

At the organizational level, the challenge is to connect the global vision and strategies with those in the company most able to add value to customers. This is achieved by building a corporate culture that promotes adaptability and learning in the face of a constantly changing and highly competitive marketplace. A successful global organization needs a collective learning mindset that learns by listening to and observing its environment, by experimenting, by auditing what has happened in the past, by benchmarking, and by broadening its perspective. Techniques for encouraging the development of a collective learning mindset include strategic reviews, system audits, internal and external benchmarking studies, study missions, and jamborees and symposia aimed at encouraging the exchange of ideas and learning.

The challenge at the micro level is to increase person-to-person cross-cultural understanding in the company in order to maximize productivity and service to customers. Each individual has a *cultural frame* through which he or she perceives the world. Only by understanding and appreciating each other's cultural frame can we hope to make an effective connection with another person. An individual must also learn to overcome those barriers that interfere with the smooth flow of communication: ethnocentrism, stereotyping, false attributions, and style.

Only by meeting the cross-cultural communication challenges on all three levels will we be able to compete successfully in the global marketplace. We have to be better at communicating than the best in the world.

DISCUSSION QUESTIONS

- Think of an unsuccessful cross-cultural encounter you have had. What factors do you think caused the communication to fail?

- Have you ever experienced synergy in a group? What did it feel like? What factors do you think helped create the synergy?

- Which cross-cultural communication barriers do you think will be most difficult for you to overcome? What can you—or anyone else—do to minimize the difficulties?

- Think about a situation in which you felt someone with whom you were dealing was acting in an ethnocentric manner, putting you and your culture down. How did you feel? How did you respond? Can you recall situations when you have acted in an ethnocentric way?

- How would you rate yourself as an active listener and observer? What can you do to improve your listening and observing skills?

NOTES

1. Clifford Geertz, *Works and Lives: The Anthropologist as Author* (Stanford, CA: Stanford University Press, 1988), p 147.
2. E. M. Forster, *Howard's End* (New York: Bantam Books, 1985), epigraph.
3. Henry Louis Gates, Jr., *Loose Cannons: Notes on the Culture Wars* (Oxford: Oxford University Press, 1992).
4. Trenholme J. Griffin and W. Russell Daggatt, *The Global Negotiator: Building Strong Business Relationships Anywhere in the World* (New York: Harper Business, 1990), p 49.
5. Griffin and Daggatt, *Global Negotiator,* p 47.
6. Lisa Adent Hoecklin, *Managing Cultural Differences for Competitive Advantage,* Special Report No. P656 (London: The Economist Intelligence Unit, 1993), p 56.
7. Ibid.
8. Ibid.
9. Ibid., p 62.
10. Ibid., p 68.
11. William Echikson, "The Trick to Selling in Europe," *Fortune,* September 20, 1993, p 82.
12. Charles Hampden-Turner, *Corporate Culture for Competitive Edge: A User's Guide,* Special Report No. 1196 (London: The Economist Publications, 1990), p 7.
13. Stephen Rhinesmith, *A Manager's Guide to Globalization: Six Keys to Success in a Changing World* (Homewood, IL: ASTD/Business One Irwin, 1993), p 89.
14. Jolie Solomon, "America's Errant Empires," *Newsweek,* September 27, 1993, p 53.
15. T. George Harris, "The Post-Capitalist Executive: An Interview with Peter F. Drucker," *Harvard Business Review,* May–June 1993, p 116.
16. Harris, "Post-Capitalist Executive," p 120.
17. David Garrin, "Building a Learning Organization," *Harvard Business Review,* July–August 1993, p 91.

18. Herbert Kohl, *From Archetype to Zeitgeist: Powerful Ideas for Powerful Thinking* (Boston, MA: Little Brown, 1992), p 203.

19. P. R. Harris and R. T. Moran, *Managing Cultural Differences* (Houston, TX: Gulf Publishing, 1991), p 155.

20. Roy D' Andrade, "Some Propositions about the Relations between Culture and Human Cognition," *Cultural Pschology: Essays on Comparative Human Development,* eds. James W. Stigler et al. (Cambridge: Cambridge University Press, 1990), p 71.

21. Richard Brislin, *Understanding Culture's Influence on Behavior* (Fort Worth, TX: Harcourt Brace, 1993), p 88.

22. Nancy Adler, *International Dimensions of Organizational Behavior* (Boston: PWS-Kent, 1991), p 83.

23. David Hoopes, "Intercultural Communication Concepts and the Psychology of Intercultural Experience," *Multicultural Education: A Cross-Cultural Training Approach,* ed. Margaret D. Pusch (LaGrange Park, IL: Intercultural Network, Inc., 1979), p 18.

24. Mildred Sikkama and Agnes Niyekawa, *Design for Cross-Cultural Learning* (Yarmouth, ME: Intercultural Press, 1987), p 32.

25. Kohl, *From Archetype to Zeitgeist,* p 112.

Chapter Five

Success in Negotiating across Cultures

Negotiation is one of the single most important international business skills.

Nancy Adler

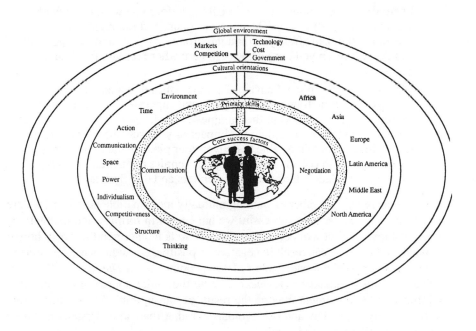

INTRODUCTION

Before getting into some of the intricacies of reaching agreements across cultures, it is important to highlight the Number One rule of negotiating: **Never, under any circumstances, underestimate the capabilities of the other party.** U.S. General John Sedgwick's last words at the Battle of Spotsylvania were, "They couldn't hit an elephant from this dist—."[1]

Conflict is an integral part of life. Bring together any two individuals from different cultures and you have the potential for conflict. For example:

- Structure
  Order: I want you to write detailed procedures for the new process.
  Flexibility: Well, it's really self-explanatory. You just . . .
  Order: I want detailed procedures. Better to be safe than sorry.

- Individualism
  Collectivist: My cousin is coming in this afternoon. I'd like you to hire him for a job in administration.
  Individualist: But what can he do? What are his qualifications and experience?
  Collectivist: What do you mean? He's family!

- Formality
  Formal: I would appreciate you knocking before you walk into my office.
  Informal: Hey, I'm sorry. The door was open, and I thought . . .
  Formal: Well, I'm afraid you thought wrong. My door may be open, but that doesn't mean you can just walk in here whenever you feel like it.

- Thinking
  Linear: As you can see, I have broken the issues down into a small series of steps, with time frames for each step, and suggested responsibilities.
  Systemic: I appreciate your thoroughness. But, it seems to me that you are neglecting to take into account the impact of your scheme on the total project. While you might be able to deliver your piece in the time frames you suggest, you also risk alienating our joint venture partner and possibly destroying our relationships with our suppliers and distributors.

If we perceive each other as wanting mutually incompatible outcomes, we are in conflict. No matter how successful we have been in forming and maintaining relationships, conflict will occur. Conflict *per se* is neither good nor bad; how it is handled, however, can result in negative or positive consequences. Agreement, also, is neither good nor bad. As Jerry Harvey points out in *The Abilene Paradox,* "The inability to manage *agreement* may be the major source of organization dysfunction."[2] Agreement may be the result of "groupthink," conformity pressures, anxiety, collusion, and risk avoidance, rather than an understanding based on an authentic meeting of minds.

CONFLICTING VIEWPOINTS

American managers are always in the business of conflict management and negotiation. Hardly a day goes by in the factory or the office without some kind of negotiation taking place—between manager and executive or with a union representative, managerial colleague, or employee. But as the globalization process accelerates, the negotiation environment expands and becomes more diverse. We find ourselves negotiating with others who relate differently to conflict and who perceive negotiation in different terms.

Americans view conflict as natural. Direct confrontation and even an aggressive "winner-take-all" viewpoint is not untypical. Both parties are expected to give their best and fight for what they want. Compromise can be frowned upon. Americans also tend to keep conflicts on a fairly impersonal, unemotional level and often discuss them in terms of problem solving. The French expect, and even enjoy, a fairly high degree of conflict. The French educational system encourages students to engage in debate. In addition, the style of individualism found in France is such that the surfacing of individual differences in a conflict situation is an integral part of communication and even communicates respect. The Mexicans, on the other hand, while accepting the inevitability of conflict, will attempt to deal with it indirectly, and will avoid it if possible. Face-saving to preserve honor and dignity is crucial. If the conflict is unavoidable, the approach is likely to be emotional and sometimes passionate. The Japanese value what they call *Wa* or harmony. They will communicate indirectly and avoid open conflict. Face-saving is paramount, and emotions should be hidden.

Such different approaches to conflict—tied to primary cultural orientations—affect the shape and tone of the negotiation process. In Japan, for example, negotiation is seen as a lengthy collaborative process; given their collective high-context orientation, there may need to be several meetings before substantive issues are on the table. To maintain harmony, the Japanese will stress assertiveness and persistence and avoid open conflict. Issues, positions, and counterpositions may not be stated directly, and the language is likely to be ambiguous and indirect. Americans, in particular, may find this approach frustrating. For the Germans, negotiation is a competitive rather than collaborative process. The negotiations will be planned, well organized, and direct in approach, with the discussion centered on facts. Conflict is seen as dysfunctional, a symptom indicating a lack of preparation; it wastes time that could be used for more useful discussion.

Whatever approaches are clashing in the negotiation process, the international manager needs to perceive conflict as both a challenge and an opportunity.

CONFLICT AS CHALLENGE AND OPPORTUNITY

The management challenge is to mold conflict into a constructive form (i.e., conflict that surfaces important issues; facilitates learning, growth, and creativity; and develops trust and openness) and then manage it over time. We avoid the term *resolution* as in "conflict resolution" because this is by no means always feasible. The differences across cultures are substantial, and if conflict does occur it is not always possible to arrive at a win-win outcome.

The general process of conflict management can be conceptualized in terms of five sets of interrelated issues, as shown in Figure 5–1.

Source Issues

As individuals and groups, we have different values, beliefs, and perceptions of self-interest; conflicting goals and priorities; contrasting methodologies; fundamentally different interpretations of events; and we have disparities in resources, cost and price expectations, schedules, knowledge, and levels of status and power.

The first task of the manager (if involved in the conflict, or acting as a third party) is to define the source of the conflict as precisely as possible. What type of conflict is it? Who is involved? What are the mutually incompatible desired outcomes of the parties? Is the articulated source of conflict the actual source, or is there another hidden source?

FIGURE 5–1
Conflict Management Issues

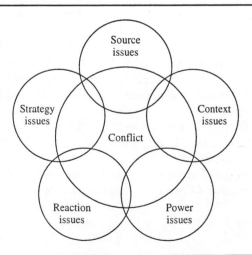

Context Issues

Conflict doesn't take place in a vacuum. What is the history of the conflict? How do cultural and organizational factors affect the conflict and to what extent? For example, you should ask: What are the shared values of the organization, and how do they relate to the conflict? What investment is the organization willing to put into international travel and communications in order to deal with the issue(s)? To what extent does the corporate culture support conflict management? What cross-cultural information resources (internal and external) could help provide us with the knowledge we need to understand the other side? What policies and procedures are in place that will help guide us through the conflict? Who in the organization has received appropriate cross-cultural training? What intermediaries are available, if needed?

You also need to ask: How dependent are the parties on each other? How serious is the conflict in relation to the parties involved and to the team or organization as a whole? Whatever the answers to these questions are, managers always need to be thinking about the following question: What can we learn from this conflict that may be to our competitive advantage?

How can conflict lead to competitive advantage? Conflicts can be thought of as having depth and width. Depth points to the intensity of the conflict, while the width describes its scope (see Figure 5–2).

FIGURE 5–2
Conflict Intensity and Scope

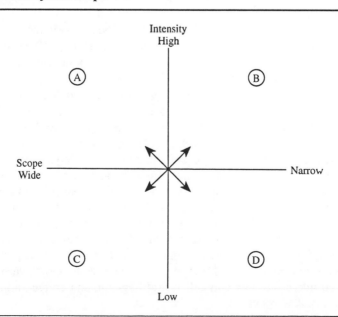

There are four major types of conflict situation highlighted in this simple model, and each type has the potential for moving into another quadrant.

A. High intensity, wide scope.

B. High intensity, narrow scope.

C. Low intensity, wide scope.

D. Low intensity, narrow scope.

The high intensity, wide scope (A) conflict may already be out of control, and may need to be narrowed before it becomes destructive to the organization and harms competitive advantage. For example, let's imagine a global company that has intense conflicts between its headquarters in London and its subsidiaries scattered across the world. Headquarters wants increased product standardization to maximize efficiencies; the subsidiaries, on the other hand, want greater customization of products to be responsive to local markets. The conflict goes on for months; executives line up on either side of the conflict. Several resignations of country managers ensue. The morale of the organization is at its lowest point. If the company is trapped in either/or thinking, it may seriously damage itself. If, on the other hand, it can narrow the conflict by breaking the issue down into specific issues by asking, for example, Which products could most benefit from standardization, and which from customization? Which markets are most responsive to customization and which to standardization? How can we organize ourselves to deliver such a mix? it may find not only that it improves its relations with its subsidiaries, but that its competitive advantage is enhanced by *optimizing* global efficiency and market responsiveness.

A high intensity, narrow scope (B) conflict may be of less immediate concern, but managers always need to be alert for *conflict spillover*. While the conflict may presently be confined, it is always possible that it could spill into other parts of the organization and create havoc. For example, imagine a company that creates consumer products. Currently, the organization is divided into business units that reflect specific product lines: toothpaste, mouthwash, coffee, tea. The toothpaste and mouthwash business units get into a dispute over market penetration. It seems that in some parts of the world, people are now brushing their teeth with the mouthwash (which is less expensive) and no longer buying the toothpaste. The business unit managers are furious with each other. On hearing the dispute, the manager of the coffee business unit conducts some research and is now concerned that the tea business unit manager is cutting into coffee sales in Latin America. As in the previous example, senior management needs to be asking, What can we learn from this conflict that may be to our competitive advantage? They may well learn that a reorganization is called for that will help create synergy between related products: for example, toothpaste and mouthwash could be reorganized into a business unit called oral hygiene, and coffee and tea into a business unit called beverages.

Power Issues

What is the balance of power in the conflict? There are many factors that affect this balance, for example:

- Time: Which party is under most pressure to reach an agreement? What are the deadlines? Which side is the most impatient? Which side has the most to lose if there is a delay?
- Money: What are the financial stakes? Who has most to gain? The most to lose? What investment is required? Who has the necessary capital?
- Knowledge and skill: Which side brings the most expertise and experience: In the industry? Of the problem area? Of negotiation strategies and tactics? Of cultural issues?
- Information: What information is available to everyone? Who has access to what information? How will information be presented?
- Authority: Who has the authority to make decisions? How can position and status be used to influence the negotiation?
- Legitimacy: Who has morality and/or the law on their side?
- Network: Which side brings the most powerful connections to the table?

Most of these are power issues that can be defined objectively; for example, who has the most financial resources to fund the project. But it must be remembered that power is also subjective. If you perceive the other party as having more power, they do.

In any negotiation there is usually a *power spread*—the sources of power are spread across the two parties. But ask yourself if the balance of power leans one way rather than another. What are the consequences of the balance for managing the conflict and reaching an agreement?

Reaction Issues

How aware are the parties of the source and contextual issues? How are the parties reacting to the conflict? With anger, fear, excitement, reason, moral outrage? How does the one party talk about the other? As enemy, intruder, menace? The language used often gives clues as to the nature and degree of the conflict. How likely is it the parties can be brought to the table to negotiate? What can be done to separate the personalities from the problem and bring the conflict back to substantive issues?

Strategy Issues

Dr. Marshall Sashkin identifies five strategies for dealing with conflict: fighting, smoothing, avoiding, bargaining, and problem solving (see Figure 5–3). Each complex negotiation is likely to involve several of these strategies at different

FIGURE 5–3
Strategies for Dealing with Conflict[3]

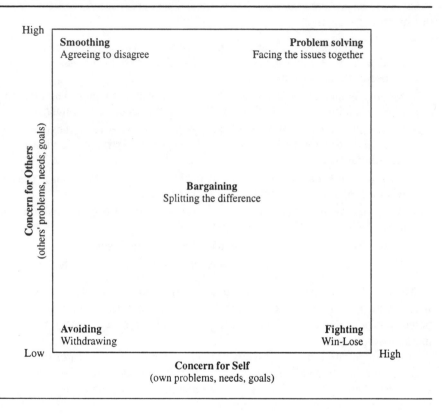

times. The right strategy at the right time is often the key to a successful outcome. While each negotiation is different, and there can be no standard strategy package for every negotiation, we can offer some guidelines for their use.

Fighting

Usually leading to a win-lose outcome ("Do it my way"), this strategy is the one that most often comes to mind, particularly for Americans. Most people, however, attribute this strategy to other people, and suggest that it is not typical of their own approach.

In cross-cultural situations, this strategy might be useful when:

• The task is critical, and no matter how you try, you cannot see how the other side's approach will work.

- You can't possibly adapt to the other side's way of doing things.
- Little time is available to resolve the conflict or complete the task.
- You can afford to fight because the longer-term relationship is not critical.
- You are in a position of power.

Smoothing

Smoothing may be thought of as a lose-win scenario ("I'll adapt to you"), although this may not always be the case. Sometimes it is used as a false front. People will say things like, "I'm really looking out for *your* interests, not mine!" The aim is to smooth things over temporarily, hoping, perhaps, the conflict will dissolve. Such a strategy can be counterproductive if the issue is just put to one side and never addressed, but it can offer a breathing space for reflection. If you change your mind later, however, you may lose substantial credibility.

In cross-cultural situations, this strategy might be useful when:

- The relationship and/or the task is critical.
- The other party can't or won't adapt, but you can.
- The other party has greater power, experience, and/or buying power.

Avoiding

Avoiding is when a party withdraws from the conflict (sometimes called a "strategic withdrawal"). The party is saying, "Let's not deal with the differences."

In cross-cultural situations, this strategy might be useful when:

- The task is not critical.
- The relationship is critical.
- Neither party can adapt.
- Differences are potentially destructive and unmanageable.
- Open and direct communication is not possible.

Bargaining

Bargaining involves recognizing the other party's interests and working toward an equitable bargain. There is often a search for the middle ground. The strategy has merits when the pressure to win or to meet an imminent deadline is not too great. It entails the attitude, "We'll both win some and lose some." However, as Dr. Sashkin points out, "bargaining can degenerate into a game with facades and bluffs, and that can easily lead to distrust . . . At its best, effective bargaining can help the parties build a solid relationship . . . and eventually lead to a problem solving approach."[4]

In cross-cultural situations, this strategy might be useful when:

- The task and/or relationship is critical.
- Both parties are somewhat adaptable.
- There is adequate time and other resources to negotiate trade-offs.

Problem Solving

Problem solving involves a real commitment to working together to formulate new and creative strategies to which all parties can agree. It can demand a significant investment of time and energy. This is the strategy most often associated with positive outcomes.

In cross-cultural situations, this strategy might be useful when:

- Both the task and the relationship are critical.
- Both parties are adaptable.
- Time and other resources are available to explore and discuss issues and synergistically solve problems.
- The corporate culture, strategies, and structures support global teamwork.

Outcome Issues

It is important to be clear about the benefits of reaching an agreement and the possible consequences of not reaching an agreement. Set priorities for desired outcomes (goals and objectives) and those possible outcomes that are unacceptable to you. This provides you with a spectrum of negotiable outcomes (see Figure 5–4).

What is the likelihood you'll need to make some concessions? Unless you have all the power and all the resources, the chances are pretty high. It is important for you to determine your bottom line (least-acceptable outcome) before the negotiation. If you don't, you may find yourself in the heat of a negotiation and losing sight of what is acceptable to you. However, don't become fixated on a certain outcome; give yourself room to maneuver while knowing your limits.

FIGURE 5–4
Spectrum of Negotiable Outcomes

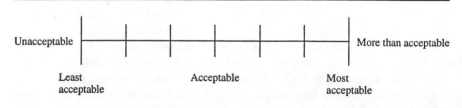

NEGOTIATING AGREEMENTS: WELCOME TO THE NEGOTIATION BOX

Unless an out-and-out fighting, smoothing, or avoiding strategy is adopted, some form of negotiation is going to need to take place. This process aims to foster mutual agreement across all the involved parties with varying degrees of winning and losing and/or the development of new and better approaches. We negotiate across cultural and geographic borders to exchange products and services; transfer technologies and expertise; establish supplier, distributor, and franchise arrangements, set up joint ventures and other cooperative arrangements; and implement mergers and acquisitions. Negotiation is, without a doubt, one of the key skill areas for working effectively across cultures. At the same time, as Frank Acuff points out, Americans have been slow in recognizing this fact:[5]

> In 1987 . . . Japan increased its imports of manufactured goods by 22 percent, while other Asians increased their sales of such goods to Japan almost 60 percent. Overall European sales grew by 27 percent during this period. U.S. sales of manufactured goods grew by an astonishingly low 0.12 percent . . . Part of the problem may lie with trade barriers in Japan, Taiwan, or other parts of the world, but the biggest problem is a U.S. barrier: Americans' own attitudes about where and *how* to do business. [italics ours]

In the previous chapter on communication, we talked about the escalation box. In this chapter we introduce you to the negotiation box (see Figure 5–5).

At the center of the model are the core value orientations of the culture. These are unlikely to be openly addressed during the negotiation, but they can play a significant role in the outcome. Unless the culture is in a deep state of transition, these value orientations are not open to negotiation.

If we take our cultural orientations model, we will be able to see how different orientations may affect negotiation styles (see Table 5–1).

Needs and wants may be expressed in actual stated positions, but more often than not they lie beneath the surface. The psychologist Abraham Maslow identified a hierarchy of needs from physiological, to safety/security, to social, to esteem, and finally to self-actualization. Different cultures may rearrange the order of this hierarchy. For example, many Asian countries will stress social needs over self-actualization. Basic needs are only marginally negotiable. Very often, needs and wants get blended together, and it may take a skilled negotiator to differentiate between the two. Needs can be perceived as "must haves," while wants are "nice-to-haves." If these can be separated, it becomes easier to identify possible solutions within broad, sweeping demands.

Individuals and groups tend to adopt one position on which their interests and needs can be met. They are stated as demands or absolute priorities. Concentrating on positions locks negotiators in the box. You need to focus on the underlying interests and needs, not on the stated position.

The give and take on positions and interests and needs takes place within a context. This refers to the physical setting of the negotiation; the differences in

FIGURE 5–5
The Negotiation Box

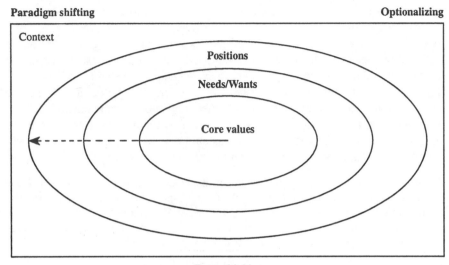

Paradigm shifting   Optionalizing

Context

Positions

Needs/Wants

Core values

Fuzzy thinking

Legend
Negotiability
——— Very unlikely that core values can be negotiated
– – – Interests and needs are somewhat negotiable
◄- - - Likely that a position can be negotiated

Source: ©Training Management Corp. (TMC), *Doing Business Internationally: The Cross-Cultural Challenges,* Seminar and Coursebook (Princeton, NJ, 1992).

such key factors as power, information, and time; and the range of verbal and nonverbal behaviors expressed in the group.

It is often wise to meet in a neutral location with few distractions and interruptions. Neither side should feel placed at a disadvantage in terms of access to information or control over time. If one side is playing the host, it usually has advantages in setting the climate for the discussion. The actual physical arrangements may facilitate cooperation or encourage competition. As Nancy Adler points out, sitting on opposite sides of a boardroom table encourages competitiveness. Alternatively, negotiators may choose to sit at a round table, which encourages cooperation.[6]

The goal should be to develop ground rules, policies, and procedures that help build a climate for negotiation, cooperation, and problem solving. The benefits of reaching an agreement should always be stated clearly, and key differences should be clarified. While it is desirable to open the negotiation to a range of possibilities, it is valuable to contain the conflict and not allow it to spill over into other areas. Universalizing the blame only leads to deterioration of the relationship.

TABLE 5–1
Cultural Orientations and Negotiation Styles

Orientation	Negotiation Impact	Cultural Region
1. Environment		
Control	"We want an implementation schedule before we leave the meeting, along with assigned responsibilities and performance standards."	N. America, W. Europe
Harmony	"We must consult with each other before making such an important decision."	Asia
Constraint	"Such detailed decision making invites disaster. Why tempt fate in such a way? What happens, happens."	Middle East, Latin America, S. Europe, E. Europe
2. Time		
Single focus	"There are a great many issues to discuss, so let's take one at a time and then move on to the next."	N. America, W. Europe
Multifocus	"Let's keep the agenda as open as we can, and allow free and open discussion and see what issues surface along the way."	S. Europe, Latin America, Middle East
Fixed	"Let's begin the meeting at 8:30 AM sharp. We'll spend 15 minutes on introductions, then 30 minutes on the first item on the agenda. After that we should recess for 10 minutes and follow that with an hour dedicated to the second item."	N. America, W. Europe
Fluid	"Let's not rush into a fixed agenda or timetable. Why let an arbitrary schedule dictate how we work together?"	S. Europe, Latin America, Middle East
Past	"Your proposals fly in the face of all of our traditions. How can you expect us to agree to what you say?"	Middle East, parts of Europe and Asia.
Present	"I don't see any quick payback to your proposal. I don't think it'll fly with our shareholders."	N. America
Future	"But where would such a proposal take us in the future? We see no long-term benefits for our company."	Asia (mixed with Past)
3. Action		
Being	"Before we jump into such details, we have planned a social occasion for you that will help us relax and get to know one another."	S. Europe, Latin America
Doing	"We have a great deal to accomplish in this session. These are the primary tasks as we see them."	N. America

TABLE 5–1 *(continued)*

Orientation	Negotiation Impact	Cultural Region
4. Communication		
High Context	"We will now explain in detail the history of the problem, and the results of previous negotiations."	Asia, Latin America, Middle East
Low Context	"I think we all understand the problem here. Why don't we move directly into the key issues to be covered in the negotiation?"	N. America, W. Europe
Direct	"I mean what I say, and I say what I mean. Do we have an agreement or not?"	N. America
Indirect	"It will be difficult." (Meaning, "No. We don't have an agreement.")	Asia
Expressive	"What are you trying to do to me? What you say is absolutely impossible. You insult me by even suggesting such a thing."	S. Europe, Latin America
Instrumental	"No insult intended. I'm just trying to find a way forward so we can get a result."	N. America, W. Europe
Formal	"Let me introduce my esteemed colleagues. On my right is Sir Norman Oakwood, chairman of the board. On my left is the Right Honorable John Smith, MP (Member of Parliament)."	Asia, Latin America, parts of Europe
Informal	"Hi, everyone. Please don't get up. John Doe is on my left. John is director of our western Europe operations, besides being a first-class practical joker."	N. America
5. Space		
Private	"Isn't there somewhere a little more private? Somewhere we won't be disturbed, and can concentrate on the important issues?"	N. America
Public	"This is a very popular restaurant. Here we can relax a little and get to know one another outside of business."	Asia, Latin America
6. Power		
Equality	"Well, let's go around the table and hear everyone's ideas."	N. America, Europe
Hierarchy	"I will tell you how we think. We don't need to spend time on everyone's input."	Middle East, Asia, Latin America
7. Individualism		
Individualistic	"I work alone and make my own decisions."	N. America
Collectivist	"We come to decisions among ourselves. No one is left out of the process."	Asia

TABLE 5–1 *(continued)*

Orientation	Negotiation Impact	Cultural Region
Universalistic	"An agreement is an agreement. It doesn't get changed on a whim."	N. America
Particularistic	"But the situation has changed. You really expect us to stand still while the world moves around us?"	Asia, Latin America, Middle East
8. Competitiveness		
Competitive	"It's everyone for themselves, I'm afraid. That's just the way things are."	N. America
Cooperative	"Why don't we try to work together and reach an understanding that is beneficial to all of us?"	N. Europe
9. Structure		
Order	"Let's make sure that everything is documented and recorded accurately. We don't want any surprises."	N. Europe
Flexibility	"Just give me the key points of the deal; I don't want all the details."	Asia, Middle East
10. Thinking		
Deductive	"Let's begin with the general principles that will guide the rest of the negotiation."	Europe
Inductive	"Let's begin with specific details, such as price, quality, and so on. Then we can think about how all of this hangs together."	N. America
Linear	"I will present my argument in a straight-forward, logical manner."	N. America
Systemic	"The issue is multidimensional and complex. A straight line may be misleading. Let's look at the whole."	Asia

Source: ©Training Management Corp. (TMC), *Doing Business Internationally: The Cross-Cultural Challenges,* Seminar and Coursebook (Princeton, NJ, 1992).

All of the above components of negotiation can lock you in The Negotiation Box: Core values may be nonnegotiable; interests and needs may appear to be questions of survival and also nonnegotiable; the stated positions may appear to be totally incompatible and set in stone; and the disparities in the context—power, information, time, and so on—may seem to leave little room for reaching agreement. There are, however, always other possibilities, new angles, different ways of seeing.

Three techniques for opening up the box are paradigm shifting, optionalizing, and fuzzy thinking. Paradigm shifting is the conscious attempt to flip our way of seeing or thinking onto a new plane. It is a way of challenging our habitual perspectives. Ask yourself if the problem can be redefined. Is there a problem? What if we look at it upside down, back-to-front, inside out, or sideways? Optionalizing is straightforward: The more options that can be identified, the more chances there are for a successful outcome. And fuzzy thinking? This is not undisciplined, imprecise thinking only aimed at making people feel good about themselves. It is based on the principle that nothing is absolute; we mostly live in a world of degrees and shades of gray. In the West, we tend to think in terms of either/or, true/false, yes/no, on/off, all or nothing, or the binary logic of zero and one. Computer scientists and philosophers are now beginning to explore "fuzzy logic." This logic suggests that between extreme positions, of, for example, either/or, is a range of possibilities closed off by traditional thinking. We became used to the idea of "smart bombs" during the Desert Storm conflict. However, much smarter and more adaptable technologies are on their way because of fuzzy logic. Bart Kosko, a leading proponent of the fuzzy idea, discusses technologies that are or can be developed because of this new way of thinking:[7]

> A fuzzy washing machine uses load sensors to measure the size and texture of the wash load and uses a pulsing light sensor to measure the dirt in the wash water. Each second a few fuzzy rules turn these measurements into patterns of water agitation for different lengths of time. Fuzzy vacuum sweepers use infrared sensors to measure dirt density and carpet texture. The data comes in and the fuzzy rules adjust the sweeper's sucking power. Fuzzy TVs measure the relative brightness, contrast, and color in each TV image frame and then "turn the knobs" on these values for each part of each image to give a sharper picture.

Our ability to look into and beyond our traditional true/false, my interest/your interest dichotomies will help make for more productive negotiations based on a vision of expanded opportunities. We should always, therefore, question statements such as, "Well, it's either this or it's that," or "Take it or leave it."

MANAGING THE NEGOTIATION PROCESS

We can also help ourselves from being locked in the negotiation box by managing the negotiation process effectively. As Jeswald W. Salacuse says, "Effective negotiation is not just a matter of following fixed rules and formulas. Every negotiation is special."[8] There are, however, certain generic phases to the negotiation process that every international manager should be familiar with. Our process consists of five subprocesses (see Figure 5–6).

Analyze

Purpose: Prepare a foundation for the negotiation.

- Gather relevant data (see Table 5–2).
- View the issues (and associated conflicts) from both sides.
- Determine your needs and prioritize them.

FIGURE 5–6
The A, B, C, D, E Negotiation Process

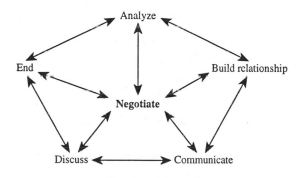

Note: Negotiation is far from a linear process. You may move from A to B and into C and then find you need to return to A before moving back into C. You should always contain elements of B in C, D, and E.

- Establish your bottom-line (least acceptable) position, below which is un-acceptable.
- Decide on the concessions you are willing to make and identify your starting position and fallback positions.
- Consider what the other side is looking for (needs and wants).
- Try to identify what might be their bottom line.
- Develop responses to their possible arguments.
- Don't assume a zero-sum game, that only one side can win or that there is only one possible solution.

Build Relationships

Purpose: Establish trust by demonstrating good faith.

- Greet everyone in an appropriate and respectful manner.
- Use formal titles and honorifics.
- Show respect for the other party's values and customs.
- Determine the rank and authority levels of those in the other party.
- Show appreciation for the time and effort the other party is expending on the negotiation.
- Be positive and stress mutual interests and benefits.
- Practice active listening and observing. Look and listen for meaning.

TABLE 5–2
Some Information-Gathering Suggestions[9]

What do I need to know about the other party?

- What are their levels of authority and decision-making power?
- What are their primary needs and wants?
- What position are they likely to take?
- What is the performance record of their business?
- What are their short-term and long-term strategies?
- What are the major challenges they face?
- What organizational structure do they have in place to support their strategies?`
- How can their corporate culture be characterized?
- What are their primary markets?
- Who are their primary competitors?
- What are their primary growth opportunities?
- What are the sources of their competitive advantage?
- How could they benefit from a relationship with my company?
- What is their history of working with other companies?

What do I need to know about their economic environment?

- What are their monetary and fiscal policies?
- What are the primary sources of business finance?
- What is their level of inflation?
- How does their tax system work?
- What is their interest rate level?
- What are their wage and salary levels?
- What is the currency of the country? Is it easily convertible? What is the exchange rate?
- Do they have membership in any regional economic blocs (European Community, Asian Free Trade Association)?
- What is the level of economic development?
- What role do trade unions play in the country?
- What are the primary economic opportunities for the nation?
- What supplier and distribution systems are in place?
- What restrictions are placed on foreign trade?
- What is the history of the country in relating to foreign corporations?

TABLE 5–2 *(concluded)*

What do I need to know about their political environment?

- What are the major political ideologies?
- What form of government is in place?
- What is the relationship of government to business (local and foreign)?
- How stable is the form of government?
- What are the key elements of their foreign policy?
- What is the nature of political opposition (political parties, terrorist groups)?
- What is the history of social unrest in the country?
- What is the nature, role, and influence of special interest groups?

What do I need to know about their legal environment?

- What is the basis of their legal tradition (Roman law, socialist, Muslim law)?
- How effective is the legal system?
- What is the relationship of law to business?
- What is the law in relation to negotiating or doing business with foreign companies?
- What are the laws in relation to patents, trademarks, brand names, intellectual property, technological innovations, etc.?
- What is the role of lawyers?
- How does the law affect business contracts?

What do I need to know about their national culture?

- What ethnic/cultural groups reside in the country?
- What are their primary cultural orientations to environment, time, action, communication, space, power, individualism, competitiveness, structure, and thinking?
- How do these cultural orientations affect business practices?
- What language(s) is(are) spoken? Is English widely spoken and written?
- What are the key religious, ethical, and philosophical beliefs?
- What the major customs and rituals?
- Who are the country's heroes and heroines?
- What are the major topics of discussion and debate?
- What form does the educational system take?
- What is the nature of cultural change and conflict in the country?
- How does culture affect the status and function of business in the country?

Source: Inspired by Richard Mead, *Cross-Cultural Management Communication* (New York: John Wiley & Sons, 1990), Chapter 9: Preparing for Cross-Cultural Negotiations.

- Keep your interruptions to a minimum. Show respect by allowing the other person to fully express his or her views.
- Demonstrate that you understand what is being said. Put their statements into your own words and feed them back to the other party.
- Be calm, confident, and persistent, without being aggressive.
- Think, and think again, before you speak. Once words are spoken, it is very difficult to retrieve them.
- Check for mutual understanding on a regular basis, particularly when individuals are using a second or third language.

Communicate

Purpose: Clarify issues and identify areas of agreement and disagreement.

- Clarify the agenda.
- Identify the issue(s) as clearly and precisely as possible. Use reasoning and supporting evidence.
- Identify your position (start with high demands).

Note: You may want the other side to begin. This provides you with an opportunity to test your assumptions about their expectations.

- Listen to their definition of the issue(s), reasoning, evidence, and position.
- Ask for clarification of key issues (if needed) and identify missing information.
- Avoid early concessions. Make them late in the process, or not at all.
- Periodically, sum up points of agreement and disagreement.
- Settle easy issues before moving on. Build an agreement pattern as you move through the negotiation. Keep a record of decisions made.
- Remember to communicate respect. Don't cause the other party to lose face and don't be overly direct, aggressive, or moralistic.
- Watch your body language. Be careful about the signals you may be sending—anger, insecurity, doubt, and so on.

Discuss

Purpose: Explore alternative solutions and move toward agreement.

- Whenever possible, adopt a problem-solving mode. Remind the other party of the mutual benefits of reaching agreement.
- Brainstorm options that are low cost/high benefit to both sides. Remember to look beyond either/or thinking.

- Ask open "what if" questions to stimulate ideas and identify paths of most resistance and least resistance.
- Don't make concessions too quickly and only make incremental concessions, not full-blown concessions that take you straight to your least acceptable position.
- Be patient. Don't let impatience lead you into premature agreement. Take breaks. Don't come back with immediate counterproposals. Give yourself time to respond in your own best interests and keep the other side guessing.
- Neutralize tactics used against you. Don't give or take abuse. Keep the discussion on the issue(s), not on the personalities involved.
- Put deadlocks aside temporarily; return to them later after a fuller discussion of issues and options.
- Make statements to the effect, "If we do this . . . will you do the following?" or "If we concede this . . . will you do this?"
- Get the other party in the habit of saying yes; establish a pattern of agreement.
- Listen for potential offers and follow up on them.
- Continue to sum up agreements and disagreements as you proceed.
- Identify the solution that most closely matches the needs and wants of all parties.

End

Purpose: Seek closure of the negotiation.
Note: Don't always expect to reach an agreement at the first meeting. Remember, many cultures want to build a relationship with you before transacting business. Think in terms of consultative selling (long-term commitment and relationship) rather than transactional selling (short-term, little commitment).

- Don't settle for any agreement just for the sake of settling. If in doubt, don't. Think of the impact on other interested parties, for example, shareholders and customers.
- Make the agreement as specific as you can without offending the other party. Pay attention to the language, agreed dates, responsibilities, procedures, and so on, while putting some trust in the spirit of the agreement.
- Stop negotiating when an agreement has been reached. Overnegotiating may lead to agreement failure.
- If a final agreement is not possible, aim for an agreement in principle.
- Don't close the door on a future relationship.
- Stay positive and respectful.
- Thank the other party for their participation and say that you look forward to a long and prosperous relationship.

Two basic modes for moving through this process are pushing and pulling.[10] The push mode involves the negotiator in pressing forward to his or her desired outcome by taking the lead, challenging, highlighting disagreements, attacking weak points, and being judgmental and evaluative. The pushing mode is the primary mode of American negotiators.

The pull mode, dominant in many other parts of the world, relies more on active listening, looking for similarities and areas of common ground, appreciating and building on ideas presented by the other side (as well as your own), mutual problem solving, and slowly moving toward agreement. Rossman makes the interesting point that many American women are more comfortable with the pull mode than are the men:[11]

> In a decision-making or negotiating situation, many women seek everyone's opinion and try to build consensus. When women do this at business meetings in the United States, male executives sometimes become impatient and frustrated at this seeming failure to "get to the point." But this is the negotiating style that succeeds in the Far East, Middle East, Latin America, and some European countries . . . Women see themselves as "'bridges"; men consider themselves "vises" forcing the sides together.

This difference in style may provide many American women with a competitive advantage in negotiating overseas.

HANDLING PERSUASION TACTICS

Throughout the negotiation process, you will consciously, or unconsciously, use persuasion tactics. Tactics are part of any negotiation. They are what each side does to try to *persuade* the other side during the negotiation process. It is always important to remember that a negotiation is not simply an intellectual debate of issues. It is a deliberate attempt to persuade the other party to give you what you want at the least cost to yourself. Common tactics encountered in cross-cultural negotiations include the following.

Personal Attacks

Personal attacks may be the result of genuine personality clash, a means to intimidate and bring the negotiations to an abrupt close, or a tactic to bully you into greater concessions. It is usually best to let the other party vent his or her feelings, and then try to refocus the discussion on the problem at hand. Make it clear, however, that you do not intend to be a victim of bullying and insults. You are willing to discuss the problem at hand, but only in a manner that conveys mutual respect. You can ask questions to gain more specific information, such as, "Have I done something to cause you offense?" In a cross-cultural situation, this is always a possibility. Try to identify the cause of the offense and then practice damage control. Be prepared to end the session, if necessary, or to bring in a third party. You may also want to consider changing the physical location of the negotiation or the room set-up or conducting the negotiation in a more formal manner.

Ultimatums

Ultimatums are inflammatory in nature (e.g., "Take it or leave it") and are used when a party wants the negotiation to end because, perhaps, the party is at their bottom-line position. They can also be used when a stronger party wants to pressure a weaker one into accepting a less than desirable agreement. You may want to test the ultimatum by asking probing questions or by ignoring it and moving on. Given the circumstances, you may also make it clear that you do not respond to threats of any kind and that if the other party wants to continue to talk they should do so without any more ultimatums. Persistence is often the key to cross-cultural negotiations. As Calvin Coolidge is reputed to have said:[12]

> Nothing in the world can take the place of persistence. Talent will not; nothing is more common than unsuccessful men of talent. Genius will not . . . the world is full of educated derelicts. The slogan "Press on" has solved and always will solve the problems of the human race.

Crunch Time

The other party may say, "You've got to do better than that." Obviously this is vague, and you need to find out in specific terms how you are expected to do better. But don't get trapped into just discussing the demands of the other side. Reiterate how your position is fair. If necessary, make small concessions, but make the other party work for these; don't give them away. Whenever possible, obtain concessions from the other side first.

Good Cop/Bad Cop

In the good cop/bad cop tactic, one negotiator takes a very aggressive position and makes a large demand. Later, another negotiator offers a more reasonable (although still undesirable) demand. Given the shock of the first demand, you may be more willing to accept the second demand. Always prepare for the possibility of the "bad cop" and arm yourself against the tempting seduction of the "good cop." You may also want to consider using your own "bad cop" as a foil for the other party's.

Threats

The other party may threaten to walk out as a sign that they are very dissatisfied with the negotiations. If they have made up their minds, there is little you can do. You can suggest that they leave someone behind, or that they get back to you when they have had a chance to rethink. You may also try to refocus the discussion on a small, uncontroversial item, just to get the meeting back on track.

Nibbling

An agreement is about to be reached, and suddenly the other party wants something else thrown into the pot. This may often happen toward the end of a negotiation when agreement seems very close at hand, and you just want to close the discussion. You don't have to accept the nibble. Say, "I'm afraid that won't be possible," and see what happens. If the whole deal falls through, it probably wasn't very stable in the first place. You might also say, "OK, you can have that, but I will have to withdraw one of my earlier concessions."

Playing Dumb

It is possible to delay decision making and gain more time by pretending not to understand or saying that the presentation of the issues was unclear when it really wasn't. Prepare for this, and make your presentations as clear as possible. Also, never take the other side's understanding for granted. Have them restate your key points in their own words.

Bluff

One of the most damaging negotiation tactics, the bluff, is a claim that cannot be substantiated or an action that cannot be followed through. When revealed as a bluff, it causes the responsible party to lose all credibility. And without credibility, a negotiator has little to work with. One common bluff is the "phantom competitor" (that company that is just waiting to take your place if the negotiation fails). Ask questions about the competitor. Probe. Don't accept a superficial but intimidating statement at face value.

Information Dump

In an information dump, the other party loads you with so much information, you cannot possibly digest it all in a reasonable amount of time. Either they are trying to answer your concerns even before they are raised, or they are trying to hide key issues in a mass of material. You can only judge this on a case-by-case basis. It helps if you are patient enough to develop a relationship with the other party, rather than rushing into an agreement.

It is always important to try to identify the tactic used against you and to respond appropriately. We have identified appropriate responses to the tactics listed above. In general, your options are to use the same tactic back, ask probing questions to diffuse the tactic, or acknowledge the tactic (without accepting it) and refocus on another issue.

NEGOTIATION GUIDELINES

We all make mistakes in negotiating, but some mistakes are more common than others, and hence more avoidable. To avoid the most common mistakes made by American managers in conducting international negotiations, we suggest the following guidelines:

- Negotiate in good faith. Be genuine and honest.
- Learn as much about the other side as you can: primary cultural orientations; business, social, economic, political, and religious concerns, and so on. Knowledge is not only power; it is the pathway to understanding and the precursor of wisdom.
- Prepare well; anticipate as many issues as you can. Be especially prepared to deal with technical questions. Know your spectrum of negotiable outcomes.
- Spend time building rapport. Be modest but confident.
- Expect ambiguity; don't rush in to attempt straightening it out. You will be perceived as aggressive and pushy, and even untrustworthy.
- Respect status and power differences without giving your own power away. Don't try to jump over levels to reach the "real" decision makers.
- Remember to persuade rather than debate.
- Don't make early concessions; be firm, and look for, and make, compromises only if the negotiation is locked in the negotiation box and can't move. Be resistant without being threatening. Timing is critical.
- Expect negotiations to take time. Be patient. Don't keep pressing to move on or to close.
- Soften your directness. Don't cause the other side to lose face.
- Be flexible in your thinking. Be able to switch from inductive to deductive and from linear to systemic. Be creative and intuitive, and demonstrate your intellect.
- Watch your language. Stay away from confusing jargon, idioms, and colloquialisms.
- Listen to feedback very closely. Ask questions to clarify, when necessary. But don't interrogate.
- Slow down. Don't react too quickly, and don't lock yourself into arbitrary deadlines.

- Take time to renew your physical and mental resources.
- Be positive, enthusiastic, and warm.

NEGOTIATION AND JOINT VENTURES

One of the most challenging cross-cultural negotiations in the global market-place today is the joint venture (JV). Companies enter into JVs for many reasons, including access to new technologies, skills, knowledge, markets, capital, distribution channels, and R&D, or the creation of new opportunities for cost-effectiveness. The JV can take many forms, ranging from highly specific contractual arrangements to the formation of a jointly owned business entity[13] (see Figure 5–7).

Specific contractual arrangements refer to very limited arrangements, such as licensing agreements. The commitment of time and resources in the project is small, and although culture is a factor in the success of the arrangement, its significance is relatively small.

There is a mid-range of JVs we call mid-alliances. Christophe Dupont gives such examples as the sharing of R&D expenditure, joint product design/promotion, and arrangements for sharing information and technical data. The time and commitment needed to make these arrangements successful is greater than those for specific contractual arrangements, and the importance of culture is amplified.

The most time- and resource-intensive arrangement is that of a jointly owned business. From initial meetings exploring mutual interests to a final agreement to setting up an operational venture, years can elapse. The level of complexity that needs to be managed in joint ownership is much higher

FIGURE 5–7
Joint Venture Types, Culture, and Complexity

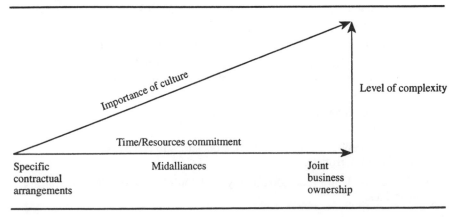

than in other forms of JV. As a consequence, the potential impact of cultural differences in management styles and techniques, business philosophies and values, operational methodologies, risk assessment, and so on is amplified even further.

The complexity and prolonged nature of joint ownership negotiations makes them vulnerable to exhaustion and analysis paralysis. Such dangers point to the need for strategies that focus heavily on relationship building, conflict management, priority setting, and big-picture thinking. Without the latter, the negotiation may lose sight of the business context that gives it meaning.

To succeed, the emphasis must be on melding differential strengths to create mutual benefits over time. The time factor is very important: Economic conditions change, the alliance partners evolve and shift business priorities, and governments may create fundamentally different conditions for working together. Negotiations, therefore, need to be sensitive to the changes occurring in the wider environment.

Ideally, different companies bring different strengths to the table. Currently, as Joel Bleeke and David Ernst point out, the following trade-offs are paramount:[14]

- Asian countries bring cash and access to their markets while looking for manufacturing, R&D, or technological skills.
- American companies look to exchange skills for cash.
- European companies offer access to an expanding market in exchange for cash and skills, or offer cash and skills for access to markets in eastern Europe.

In a JV negotiation, therefore, it is very important to understand the following:

- What are the expectations of each side?
- What will each side contribute to the venture?
- What are the potential benefits for each side?
- What are the key challenges to be overcome in forging a successful alliance?
- How will each side measure the success and failure of the partnership?
- What role are governments likely to play (if any)?
- How will a partner/competitor relationship be arranged?
- What must each side do to be sensitive to the values and business ways of the other side?

While many considerations in the negotiations can be reduced to economic pluses and minuses, many others will be rooted in cultural orientations. In terms of measuring success, for example, U.S. companies are likely to focus on quick

profits. Japanese companies, on the other hand, may focus on strategic positioning, market share, or learning, postponing profits for several years.[15]

DOING THE RIGHT THING

One of the most commonly asked questions in international training seminars is,
"What is the right (ethical) thing to do?" There are, of course, no easy answers.
Business, like the rest of life, is messy. Contradictions, paradoxes, and ambigui-
ties abound. One solution seems to raise other problems; there are multiple viewpoints on what we consider to be a single issue. There are also many different
schools of ethical thought, and no formulas exist for deriving clear-cut ethical solutions. It is not unusual for large U.S. hospitals to have a medical ethicist on
staff; as business becomes increasingly global and cross-cultural, we may find
corporations beginning to hire individuals who can guide them through the
labyrinth of ethical questions, for example:

- Should I be making a payment to service this contract?
- Should I invest in a country that practices discriminatory policies against
  segments of its population?
- Should I install safety standards in a foreign plant that would be unacceptable in my home country?
- Should I adopt inadequate environmental practices in a foreign country
  where regulations are few and far between?
- To what extent should we adopt the poverty-level wages of the country in
  which we are going to build our plant?

Such issues can arise in negotiations, and it is best to have some guidelines to
help you through. One guideline is to consider fundamental rights. Thomas Donaldson in *The Ethics of International Business* has drawn up a list of 10 fundamental international rights:[16]

1. The right to freedom of physical movement.
2. The right to ownership of property.
3. The right to freedom from torture.
4. The right to a fair trial.
5. The right to nondiscriminating treatment (freedom from discrimination
   on the basis of such characteristics as race or sex).
6. The right to physical security.
7. The right to freedom of speech and association.
8. The right to minimal education.

9. The right to political participation.

10. The right to subsistence.

Donaldson also develops what he calls an ethical algorithm.[17] He begins with the question, "Is the practice permissible for the multinational company when it is morally and/or legally permitted in the host country, but not in the home country?" From here, he identifies two types of conflict:

1. The host country's moral reasoning is related to its economic development. For example, a Latin American country has a lower minimum wage than that in the United States because of its lower level of economic development.

   In such a case, Donaldson suggests the following formula: "The practice is permissible if and only if the members of the home country would, under conditions of economic development relatively similar to those of the host country, regard the practice as permissible."

2. The host country's moral reasoning is independent of its economic development. For example, hiring is done on the basis of family or clan loyalty rather than merit. In this case, the decision is based on cultural orientation rather than economics.

   Here, Donaldson argues, the multinational must avoid ethnocentrism ("My way is the only way") while also rejecting the relativistic ("You have your way, I have mine") that ignores wider ethical standards. His answer is to pose two questions. The practice is permissible if the answer to *both* questions is no.

   - Is it possible to conduct business successfully in the host country without undertaking the practice?
   - Is the practice a clear violation of a fundamental international right?

Assume for a moment that in Country X a company wants to open a plant. In Country X, it is strict government policy that women be paid only 50 percent of a man's salary for the same work. In Donaldson's algorithm, this situation fails the ethics test. The answer to the first question is no, but the answer to the second is yes (on the basis of discrimination).

Another approach is to apply a set of standard questions to the issue. Although they are not directed at cross-cultural situations as such, the following questions developed by Lax and Sebenious are useful for decision making:[18]

1. Are you following rules that are understood and accepted? (In poker, for example, everyone understands that bluffing is part of the game.)

2. Are you comfortable discussing and defending your action? Would you want your colleagues and friends to be aware of it? Your spouse, children, or parents? Would you be comfortable if it were on the front page of a major newspaper?

3. Would you want someone to do it to you? To a member of your family?

4. What if everyone acted that way? Would the resulting society be desirable? If you were designing an organization, would you want people to act that way? Would you teach your children to do it?

5. Are there alternatives that rest on firmer ethical ground?

It is also important to understand that a legal framework exists in the United States for conducting business abroad. The Foreign Corrupt Practices Act (FCPA), which has been in effect since late 1977, has two major components: anti-bribery, and record keeping and internal control.

Anti-Bribery

Under the FCPA, it is a crime for a bribe to be made to a foreign official, a foreign political party, party officials, or candidates for political office for the purpose of obtaining or retaining business or for directing business to another person. It is also a crime if the bribe is paid directly to a third-party agent, consultant, or intermediary with the purpose of being passed on to one of the above.

The penalties for violating the FCPA are severe. Companies that commit an offense can be fined up to $2 million. Individuals may be fined up to $100,000 and imprisoned for up to five years. Individual fines cannot be paid by the company. There is no threshold amount to trigger the statute. Any payment qualifies if it is made with a corrupt purpose.

Not all payments are considered bribes, so it is important for you to be able to distinguish between those that are acceptable and those that are unacceptable.

Payments for *routine* governmental action by a foreign official, political party, or party official are allowed. Such payments are known as "facilitating," "expediting," or "grease" payments. The Act specifies what type of action is considered routine:

- Dispensing permits, licenses, and other official documents needed to do business in a foreign country.
- Processing visas, work orders, and other governmental papers.
- Providing police protection and mail service, and scheduling inspections related to contract performance or transporting goods.
- Providing utilities (phone, power, and water), loading and unloading cargo, and protecting perishables from deterioration.

Any decision made or encouraged by a foreign official with respect to whether or on what terms new businesses will be awarded or business will be continued with a particular party is definitely not routine governmental action.

Record Keeping and Internal Control

Every Securities Exchange Commission (SEC) reporting company must make and keep books, records, and accounts that accurately and fairly reflect both the transactions and resulting dispositions of the company's assets.

- Quantitative and qualitative aspects of transactions must be recorded.
- The parent company is responsible for the books and records of subsidiaries.
- Every SEC reporting company must devise and maintain a system of internal accounting controls that meets four objectives:

    1. All transactions are executed in accordance with authorizations.
    2. The method of recording transactions will facilitate the preparation of financial statements according to generally accepted accounting principles (GAAP).
    3. Access to corporate assets will be safeguarded by management.
    4. Recorded and existing assets will be compared at reasonable intervals and discrepancies resolved.

While only the anti-bribery provisions of the Act specify that violations are punishable as crimes, failure to observe the accounting requirements may also lead to criminal prosecution.

The Act, at least on the surface, is relatively clear. However, if you have doubts about the legality of a practice, seek legal advice. Some tough questions include:

- When does a facilitating payment become a bribe?
- Who is or isn't—a foreign government official?
- What if—without my knowledge—an agent of mine violates the Act?

The FCPA provides a legal framework for negotiating and conducting business. It provides *minimum* guidelines for decision making and action. Above and beyond the FCPA are the ethical standards of the company and the individual employee. Many companies have instituted a code of business conduct that stipulates appropriate behaviors for conducting business at home and abroad. Such codes include:

- Guidelines for business conduct toward each other, customers, suppliers, distributors, competitors, joint venture partners, agents, consultants, and so on.
- Guidelines for situations that could cause conflict of interest.
- Guidelines in relation to responsibilities for protecting company assets, including physical, financial, and informational resources.

- Guidelines for relevant legislation and regulatory codes.
- Guidelines on how to apply the code, seek help, report violations, and so on.

Along with the shared values of a company, such codes provide individuals and teams with a common set of standards. Although such codes cannot delineate every situation, particularly in the global environment, they outline principles that can guide the analysis and evaluation of new situations as they arise. When a negotiator or negotiation team has clearly defined, deeply held principles, it becomes much easier to negotiate persuasively, in good faith, and with integrity.

SUMMARY INSIGHTS

Negotiation is a critical international business skill. The potential for conflict is increased in a global business environment in which cultural differences—not just economic interests—play a key role. Conflict is neither positive nor negative; how it is handled, however, may produce results that facilitate learning and trust or lead to destroyed relationships and lost opportunities. The direct, confrontational American style of handling conflict is not shared with many other cultures. The Japanese and the British, for example, tend to avoid open conflict, seeking to handle it indirectly.

Choosing an appropriate strategy for handling conflict—smoothing, problem solving, bargaining, avoiding, and fighting—will depend on a range of situational factors, including the criticality of the task, the adaptability of both sides, the time available, the criticality of the relationship, the possibility of open and direct communication, and the extent to which the corporate culture supports collaborative problem solving and conflict management.

The negotiation process consists of five subprocesses (A, B, C, D, E): analysis, building relationships, communicating, discussing, and ending. Analysis prepares the ground for the negotiation by establishing objectives and limits. Building relationships establishes trust by demonstrating good faith. Communicating clarifies the issues and identifies areas of agreement and disagreement. Discussing explores alternative solutions and moves the negotiation toward agreement. Ending seeks closure, while recognizing that many cross-cultural negotiations take time and a commitment to building a long-term relationship.

Each negotiation may become trapped in the negotiation box. Techniques for getting out of the box include paradigm shifting, optimalizing, and fuzzy thinking. Each technique challenges us to look beyond our traditional true/false, my interest/your interest dichotomies and to expand our vision of possibilities.

Avoiding mistakes in cross-cultural negotiations can be enhanced by following a set of guidelines, including negotiating in good faith, learning the primary cultural orientations of the other party, preparing well, spending time to build relationships, working with ambiguity, slowing down, and making sure the other party doesn't lose face.

It is also important to conduct negotiation within the appropriate ethical and legal frameworks. The Foreign Corrupt Practices Act provides the legal context for American businesses operating overseas. Guiding principles can also be derived from company value statements and codes of conduct. Such principles should guide the negotiator in determining "What is the right thing to do?"

DISCUSSION QUESTIONS

- Have you ever been involved in a cross-cultural conflict? What happened? What did you do to manage the conflict? Do you think another strategy would have been more effective?

- Have you ever been involved in a cross-cultural negotiation? What was the outcome? What worked and what didn't work?

- What is the most difficult phase of the negotiation process for you? How can you make this phase easier to handle?

- Which negotiation tactics do you tend to overuse or underuse?

- Which negotiation tactics do you find are most often used against you?

- Which of our negotiation guidelines do you think will be most difficult for you to follow? Why? What problems are you likely to encounter if you don't follow the guideline?

NOTES

1. Louis E. Boone, *Quotable Business* (New York: Random House, 1992), p 305.

2. Jerry Harvey, *The Abilene Paradox* (Lexington, MA: Lexington Books, 1988), p 15.

3. Reproduced from *Managing Conflict Constructively* © 1989 by Dr. Marshall Sashkin with the permission of Organization Design & Development, Inc., King of Prussia, PA.

4. Ibid.

5. Frank L. Acuff, *How to Negotiate Anything with Anyone Anywhere Around the World* (New York: Amacom, 1993), p 14.

6. Nancy J. Adler, *International Dimensions of Organizational Behavior,* 2nd. ed. (Boston, MA: PWS-Kent, 1991), p 190.

7. Bart Kosko, *Fuzzy Thinking: The New Science of Fuzzy Logic* (New York: Hyperion, 1993), p 39.

8. Jaswald W. Salacuse, *Making Global Deals: Negotiating in the International Marketplace* (London: Century Business, 1992), p 3.

9. Richard Mead, *Cross-Cultural Management Communication* (New York: John Wiley & Sons, 1990).

10. Marlene L. Rossman, *The International Businesswomen of the 1990s: A Guide to Success in the Global Marketplace* (New York: Praeger, 1990), pp 41–43.

11. Ibid., p 41.

12. Boone, *Quotable Business*, p 51.

13. Christophe Dupont, "International Business Negotiations," *International Negotiation: Analysis, Approaches, Issues*, ed. Victor A. Kramenyuk (San Francisco: Jossey-Bass, 1991), p 338.

14. Joel Bleeke and David Ernst, "Sleeping with the Enemy," *Harvard International Review*, Summer 1993, pp 12–13.

15. Ibid., p 64.

16. Adapted from *The Ethics of International Business* by Thomas Donaldson. Copyright © 1989 by Oxford University Press, Inc. Reprinted by permission.

17. Ibid., pp 101–06.

18. *The Manager as Negotiator: Bargaining for Cooperation and Competitive Gain* by David A. Lax and James K. Sebenius. Copyright © 1986 by David A. Lax and James K. Sebenius. Reprinted with permission of The Free Press, an imprint of Simon & Schuster.

Chapter Six

Success in Global Management

The ability to learn faster than your competitors is the only sustainable source of competitive advantage.

Arie De Geus, *Royal Dutch/Shell*

Global managers are made, not born.

Percy Barnevik, *Asea Brown Boveri*

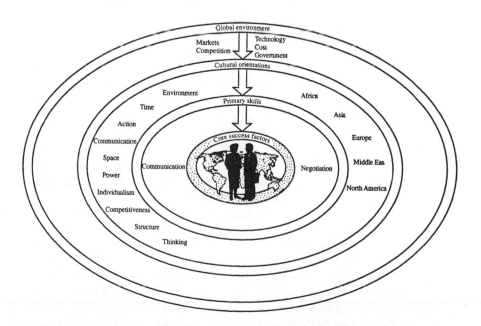

INTRODUCTION

Janus, the ancient Roman god of gates and doorways, is depicted with two faces looking in opposite directions. Today, successful businesses view the 1990s as the gateway to the twenty-first century, an era of unprecedented global competition and often contradictory trends: simultaneous globalization and fragmentation in various markets. In retrospect, the acceleration of change during the 1980s was extensive, and business managers have drawn valuable lessons about the pace of change and the increasingly global nature of the business environment—whether in Toronto, Tokyo, or Turin. To confront the situation, management—like Janus—will need to manage with a keen eye on the present and future as well as the past.

GOING GLOBAL—THREE KEY INFLUENCES

While the nature of marketplace changes has not been cataclysmic, their impact will be greater than previously experienced as global interdependence rises. As Kenichi Ohmae observed in "Managing in a Borderless World," the primary rule is one of equidistance, to see and to think globally.[1] Let's test Ohmae's observation by answering the following question: What do American steelmakers, German auto manufacturers, French chemical producers, Japanese electronics firms, Australian beer and wine growers, Indian software designers, Mexican telephone manufacturers, and Brazilian fruit producers all have in common? All have the same idea in mind: competition—to find flexible ways to link up with their counterparts and clients in markets *worldwide*.

Globalism, the word is everywhere. Yet not everyone is a major international or multinational company striving to become a global corporation. Nevertheless the scope of interchange between different nationalities is growing. Characteristic of this trend are efforts by both economic powerhouses in more mature industry sectors such as Siemens, Toyota, Motorola, Exxon, and GM pursuing economic goals *in one world market* and small firms targeting a single objective in a focused export market. The bottom line is that resources and markets are global, and the resulting demands on companies, both large and small, to produce and manufacture, conduct research, raise capital, buy supplies, and market and distribute products and services requires being wherever the organization can do the job best. That can mean North America, Western and Eastern Europe, Latin America, and the Pacific Rim countries as well as other countries worldwide.

It used to be said that the sun never sets on the British Empire. As a metaphor, the observation works fine; however, the sun as a measure is outmoded these days. A sunup, sundown kind of business mentality is a thing of the past. Competition in business today is global, no matter where it occurs and for virtually any marketplace on a 24-hour basis. One result of this virtual marketplace, estimates the U.S. Department of Commerce, is that 80 percent of all U.S. goods and services are open to foreign competition. Clearly, the distinction between domestic and international companies—and their executives and managers—is becoming obsolete—business is being conducted around the clock and markets are broadly more diverse geographically and culturally.

To succeed, global competence in management ranks is critical—to ignore the ability to manage globally is to neglect the true nature of contemporary competition. For many, the management of global business activities means stepping into the unknown. Companies compete in the

"global village"	(borderless marketplace)
	where business is managed by a cadre of
'globalites"	(global managers)
	whose
"global brains"	(strategic awareness)
	and
"global perspective"	(international vision)
	enable them to implement business plans and sell to their customers on a
"global basis"	(thinking globally and acting locally)
	thereby effectively managing the
"globalization"	(international expansion)
	of their company.

"Global" and "globalization" have become amorphous and cumbersome terms—business colloquialisms—describing what is actually an array of ideas, concepts, and trends that have dramatically stormed the environment in which companies operate. Although some argue these expressions represent nothing more than jargon, an important number of executives argue that while the words may be common buzzwords, the concepts behind them of broad, international competition for marketplace advantage are serious concerns.

There is little doubt that globalization has risen to the top of many corporate agendas. Going global for many is a matter of survival, and it means radically changing the way their company works. These expressions describe the economic and demographic realities in the growth of world trading blocs that are forcing companies to carefully analyze the trends, forces, issues/needs, obstacles and consequences of markets to develop global strategies. As shown in Figure 6–1, the issues and needs influencing this environment stress the synergies required between businesses and the cultural considerations essential to compete in the multifaceted marketplace of the 1990s; for example:

Issue	*Need*
Global vision	Need for management across national boundaries
Multinational partnerships	Need for intercultural communication competence
Leverage innovations in multiple locations	Equidistant cultural perspectives

FIGURE 6–1
Context Map for Global Business Environment[2]

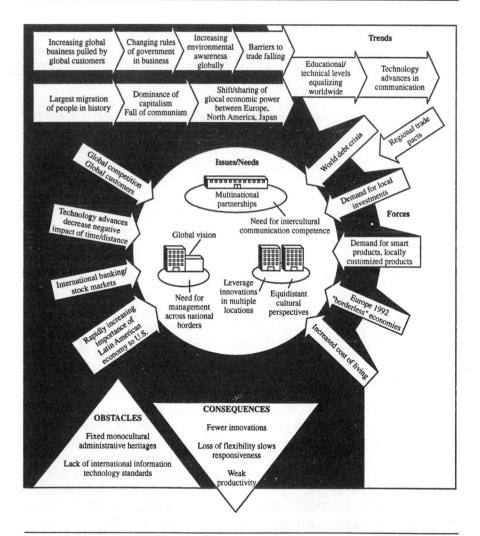

Source: Adapted from Robert Johansen, "Managing Globally," in Gregory Schmid, ed., *1993 Ten-Year Forecast* (Menlo Park, CA: Institute for the Future, 1993).

Increasingly critical to a company's success in the global marketplace is the development of global leaders and managers who are capable of traveling, working, communicating, and negotiating in this borderless world. Corporate development of global managers is viewed as critical to gaining and sustaining access to markets worldwide. When devising strategies to develop global managers, firms must take into consideration several influences which have significant impact on development policies: 1) dynamics of a global workforce, 2) business reengineering, and 3) organizational issues.

Influence # 1: The Dynamics of a Global Workforce

For the remainder of the decade, the demographic and economic growth rates of countries worldwide will accelerate the movement of human resources. Key factors in this movement require increased attention and assimilation into corporate strategy and planning. It is clear that direct foreign investment aimed at expanding into relatively affluent markets where an oversupply of well-educated and highly trained labor exists is a dominant strategic approach. In turn, markets will experience substantial relocations of people across national boundaries, as developing countries educate more people than they can productively employ, and industrialized countries seek talent for aging and slow-growing economies. A critical factor inherent in this expansion of markets is the dramatic growth and location of the global workforce. The workforce is undergoing a long-term structural change with population rates of growth setting the stage for the most significant economic differences that exist in the marketplace.

Talent is a universal phenomenon and the market for talent is a global one. For example, the developing regions of the world have a projected annual labor force growth rate of 2.1 percent. Some countries, such as Mexico, the Philippines, and Pakistan, are experiencing growth from 2.5 percent to 3.0 percent. The industrialized world (the United States, Japan, Germany, United Kingdom, and France) is experiencing a flatter growth rate of less than 1 percent.[3] In light of such transition, we face the requirement of developing competitive strategies stressing and incorporating the increased cultural diversity and capability of this workforce. Subsequent parcelling out via outsourcing of increasingly sophisticated work to faraway nations with highly capable labor forces is key to market penetration. A further determinant in the marketplace environment is the liberalization of protectionist immigration policies throughout the world—Japan, most western and eastern European countries, as well as the United States and Canada. The resultant movement of labor from and between Western and developing countries such as within Asia or eastern Europe has critical consequences for the industrialized world. It is true, nevertheless, that, like people, work will flow to the places best equipped to perform it most economically and efficiently.

As William B. Johnston points out in "Global Work Force 2000: The New World Labor Market," the globalization of labor is an inevitable corollary to the globalization of product, financial, service, and information markets. Although the United States has often been referred to as a true melting pot of cultures, based on its fundamental values and the liberal immigration policy fostered during the first half of the twentieth century, it is only in the 1990s that America has realized the importance of its diverse and culturally rich populations.

We now appreciate that this diversity impacts globally, be we American, Japanese, or Brazilian, for whom the "give and take" of business is still crucial at the *personal, face-to-face* level. Even in light of rapid advances in technology and communication, multicultural interaction is an essential element for success in the global marketplace. The resulting implications concerning understanding, communicating, and negotiating effectively across cultures are dramatic.[4] The rules of doing business often prove elusive, skewed as they are by cultural differences.

In the examples of international joint ventures which follow, we can begin an assessment of the impact of culture on doing business based on some of the concepts we have examined in this book. For example,

- General Electric bought Tungsram, a Hungarian light bulb maker, in 1990, to take advantage of a recognized brand name, an established pan-European distribution network, and highly skilled electrical design engineers who worked at comparatively low wages. The Tungsram capability for making advanced lighting fixtures supports GE markets in Japan, Europe, and the United States.
  Impact of Culture: What issues does the Hungarian versus American work ethic raise for the operation of the venture? To what extent does a low salary base and high rate of moonlighting in Hungary have dramatic influence on worker productivity?

- Metropolitan Life Insurance established operations in Ireland to analyze medical insurance claims and new policies for American operations requiring extensive knowledge of medicine, the American medical system, and the insurance business. Not only did Met Life tap into a well-educated, highly qualified workforce, the company was able to benefit from a high work ethic, lower operating costs, and tax incentives provided by the Irish Development Authority.
  Impact of Culture: How did the Americans build the team environment while handling the high relationship-building/hierarchy requirements of the Irish, which pose constraints to the operational environment?

- Texas Instruments, Motorola, and IBM have set up software programming offices in southern India to hire local research and development talent unavailable in the United States and Europe at 50 percent cost efficiencies in wages employing Indian managerial and technical talent. The overall cost efficiencies of India are clearly apparent as the complexity of design and software work increases.
  Impact of Culture: In a research environment, what problems are posed by the indirectness of manner of Indian personnel and the need for collective hierarchy in work and task delegation?

- Daniel Industries, a Texas gas pipeline instrumentation company, bought Messtechnik Babelsberg in 1991, a former East German measuring-instrument firm, whose skilled and trained engineers enabled Daniel to enter the European market at a cost of land, labor, and buildings about half as much as in the former West Germany.
  Impact of Culture: What significant impact did the introduction of English language standards, especially the language of basic Western business concepts and terminology, have on the new venture?[5]

Hungary, Ireland, India, and the former East Germany are each examples of cultural "allies and islands" to which American companies and their managers are exposed along with the accompanying culturally diverse people interactions resulting from new market penetration. We need to think carefully about understanding the work values and practices as well as the communication and negotiation challenges arising from each of these country involvements for their American and partner management staff.

Thousands of executives and managers are called upon to help achieve the global, as opposed to national or regional, business visions of their companies—to participate in global task forces, to travel and work in different nations, to manage in the world of "borderless organizations"—in short, to exhibit a global mindset and demonstrate skills and abilities when often only force of personality is present. Too often companies send their managers abroad with little more than a "wing and a prayer." The lack of preparation often leads to aborted assignments, lost opportunities, and wasted resources.

Influence # 2: Business Reengineering

To survive in this new marketplace, globalizing companies must ask themselves to define, from their own corporate perspective, the range of issues and corporate pressures they are encountering. In turn, they must consider innovative and aggressive approaches to cope with an increasingly competitive environment on a national and international scale. More importantly, they frequently find themselves reassessing their organizational structures in an effort to evaluate how they can regroup their people and resources in new and effective ways.

As Michael Hammer and James Champy point out in their thought-provoking new study, *Reengineering the Corporation,* the theory of *business reengineering* addresses the urgent need for a new business model to meet the pressures of the changing marketplace in order to achieve real business-unit impact: competition, reduced workforce, flatter organizations, less bureaucracy, greater spans of control, decision making lower in the organization, and high team/task force orientation globally, among numerous others. In their words, the problems faced by American industry today are urgent, and only those "companies that act with dispatch . . . will be able to compete successfully in a world in which the only predictable constant has become rapid and relentless change."[6]

Research has shown that success in reeingineering projects is heightened when the redesign penetrates the core of a business and fundamentally changes a well-defined set of crucial organizational elements. These elements or "depth levers," as described in a recent study conducted by McKinsey & Company, include roles and responsibilities, measurements and incentives, organizational structure, information technology, shared values, and skills.

Faced with accelerating marketplace change, senior management must invest time and energy to lead their organizations through periods of radical change "by combining a tenacious pursuit of performance objectives with a flair for building consensus at all organizational levels."[7] Management can then successfully craft policy and market responses that combine business acumen with cultural awareness by:

- Creating and implementing complex business strategies and practices for increased profitability and market share.

- Meeting the needs and expectations of global and local customers and coping with decreasing degrees of strategic freedom.

- Identifying and evaluating opportunities from a global, cross-functional perspective.

- Building global networks and increasing the flow of value-added resources.

- Working across organizational, cultural, and geographic boundaries to optimize results.

- Leading multicultural teams to maximize innovation and project success.

- Managing change, complexity, and adaptability to build and sustain competitive advantage while integrating totally new technologies into the process.

- Protecting and nurturing invisible assets: intellectual property, commitment of people, brands, multicultural workforce.

- Facilitating the complex interface between public and private policy as well as relationships with host governments.

- Maximizing and transferring organizational/personal learning to increase productivity.[8]

In a globalizing company, these factors, although not patently predictable, involve management teams, which are often highly multicultural and geographically dispersed, in a complex decision-making process. Reengineering project teams—to be successful—require the best people regardless of their national origin; nothing can limit business expansion more than a shortage of leaders and managers who are unprepared to handle all the nuances of such a business environment.

Even with sufficient breadth and depth, a reengineering project may fail unless management clearly keeps the lines of communication open in order to defuse any political resistance. In a redesign effort, which could easily involve joint international pilots of the new design, such as in Tokyo, Frankfurt-Paris, or Buenos Aires-Mexico City, effective communication clearly involves sensitivity to and understanding of cultures. The cross-cultural ramifications of any such project pose an immense human resource challenge, a convincing reason that cultural know-how is crucial to successful reengineering in a globalizing company.

Influence # 3: Organizational Issues

In addressing successful globalization, three principal organizational factors affect the initiative: strategy/structure, corporate culture, and human resources. Success in global markets often means dramatic change across the whole corporation from the most senior management all the way down to the production line. Proper alignment of these factors, therefore, increases the probability of effective globalization of an organization. Competing in global markets means surviving in an ever-changing market and world economy and taking advantage of any opportunity to benefit from technology and culture.

Factor # 1—strategy and structure. Strategy/structure defines the organization from the perspective of degrees of centralization versus decentralization in conjunction with the "geographical-functional-business-product structure"—all of which enables the company to achieve maximum competitiveness and the capability to respond effectively on a global basis.[9]

The strategic management process of globalizing firms has long-term implications, requiring a balanced choice of strategy decisions involving numerous variables: values and problem-solving methods of owners, managers, and employees; corporate decision-making systems; formal selection procedures; reward systems; compliance with organizational requirements; regulation and control processes; accurate communication; responsiveness to change; risk assessment and risk taking; business expansion from a geographic perspective; product designation and strategy vis-à-vis markets; entry strategies; financial sourcing; appropriateness of strategic alliances; distinct/universal market determinants, and human resource deployment and retention, to name just a few considerations.

A definite key to successful management of this process is to have and develop global managers who are capable of making decisions in the evolving global business environment.

Factor # 2—corporate culture. Developing the corporate culture is viewed as one of the key strategic approaches by which a company can remain competitive and survive on a domestic and worldwide basis. It is the glue that holds the corporate community together, containing the values, norms of behavior, systems, policies, and procedures by which the organization adapts globally. From a practical viewpoint, top management in many companies worldwide have given attention to the role that is played by organizational culture, that is, "the way things are done," in globalization.

As companies expand internationally, there is a need to fit the corporate culture with the various national cultures of their overseas operations to obtain the maximum benefit from their global opportunities ("think globally, act locally"). Building a global corporate culture requires top management's dedication to communicating the vision and values of the company, thereby promoting an international spirit and direction. Once successfully developed, a global corporate culture transforms the company and its management into an organization where there is little, if any, single-country bias.

At a meeting of the Top Management Forum, organized by the Management Centre Europe of the American Management Association/International, in June of 1992, a group of 150 senior executives from Europe and North America debated the issue of developing the corporate culture required to survive today's globalization process.

The consensus opinion of conference attendees clearly outlined the ideal characteristics of a successful global corporate culture. In defining an appropriate model, numerous speakers contrasted the traditional, doctrinaire, and bureaucratic organization with the "nimbleness" required to manage the changes in corporate structure and activities to be successful in today's global business arena. The ideal global corporation, according to the conference's senior executives, must possess five key attributes, which are:

- Be lead by the top management team which has a mission/vision statement driven by a fundamental understanding of meeting competitive requirements of the world's markets. In short, management must ensure the company's survival in its transition to going global.

- Be able to manage change in terms of both the external and internal factors governing globalization.

- Have effective global managers who encompass a strong commitment to training, have the encouragement of local country development plans, and insightful market research in the identification of local and global products and services.

- Be decentralized to allow local business units the autonomy to produce products that meet local culture needs *and* centralized, at the corporate core, to enable the company to coordinate work around the globe and capitalize on synergies and economies of scale.

- Be fast-acting to keep close watch on local market conditions and adjust research, development, production as necessary and, at the same time, be multicultural and multilingual to capitalize on a synergistic mix of outsourcing and internal production.[10]

It is important to note how both corporate culture and strategy/structure, which fit within one's organizational objectives, are affected by the relationship with national cultures, management values, and practices. Table 6–1 provides an overview of these interactions wherein organizational effectiveness relies heavily on corporate/national cultural relationships.

Factor # 3—human resources. The human resources of a company, in particular its global managers, represent the essential element to manage the competitive process on a worldwide basis. At the core of any globalization effort, a company's global managers must possess the mindset to operate in a worldwide context and the capability to manage a complex, uncertain, ever-changing environment. In this regard, a globalizing organization must carry out the implementation of its business strategy by linking operational strategy with managing and effectively utilizing culturally diverse human resources.

TABLE 6–1
Model of Cultural Assumptions/Organizational Structure[11]

Structure	Assumption	Features
Multidomestic (ethnocentric)	Diversity has no impact.	• Organization a collection of discrete subunits that think and act independently. • Recognizes cultural differences yet unable to control. • Each national unit seen as independent and autonomous. • Random interaction with parts.
International (polycentric)	Diversity causes only problems.	• Diversity seen as source of conflict, inconvenience, and inefficiency. • Homogeneity seen as natural, desirable, good. • Headquarters' culture applies universally. • One way to manage only.
Multinational (regiocentric)	Diversity can either lead to benefits or cause problems.	• Diversity seen as basic, indispensable, and irreducible. • Homogeneity seen as a source of competition and conflict. • Cultural interaction remains at level of balanced and stable coexistence. • Only external pressures force new interaction(s).
Global/ Transnational (geocentric)	Diversity can simultaneously cause problems and lead to benefits.	• Diversity generates new patterns of mutually beneficial relations. • Constantly create new, improved, mutually beneficial ways of interacting. • Heterogeneity essential and indispensable.

Source: Adapted from Lisa Advent Hoecklin, *Managing Cultural Differences for Competitive Advantage,* Report No. P656 (London: Economist Intelligence Unit, 1993) , pp. 29–53.

In order to provide value to the business, human resources practices should focus on the development of specific competencies for securing the competitive advantage in a global environment. The key elements in the equation are still people *and* culture. The real challenges of human resources management, in cooperation with line management, is thus to provide a system for the development, support, and enhancement of the organizational and individual competencies required in the process of globalization. They should provide:

- *Partnership for organization development*   Establish the HRD function as a major partner with line management to link strategic business goals and objectives to develop competent and efficient management staff.

- *Leadership in training and development*   Create a cadre of leaders with the mindsets, skills, and competencies needed to manage on a global basis. Provide a broad variety of training and development opportunities for managers.

- *Direction in career development*   Align individual career planning and organizational career management processes to achieve an optimal match of individual and organizational needs and effectiveness.[12]

The role of human resources professionals is to provide the development and learning systems that will enable global organizations to grow and succeed in the 1990s and beyond. Managers are being increasingly affected by the complex, uncertain, and challenging aspects of international business whether they live in the United States or travel globally in their jobs. With the exception of a few companies, the development of global managers has not received the reflection and commitment required to create a systematic process; yet, it is imperative for a company's globalization effort to succeed that it develop a cadre of managers who possess the requisite mindset, competencies, and skills to operate successfully in a global environment.

The changes occurring in the human resources paradigm have critical implications for a company's success in managing the global development process and linking it effectively to strategic business issues. Fundamentally, the human resources paradigm is changing from an administration-centered one to a strategy-centered approach as shown in the following comparison.

Administration-centered	*Strategy-centered*
• Maintain personnel records	• Align HR initiatives with greatest business opportunities
• Pay salaries	
• Administer benefits	• Support the changing role of managers
• Recruit people	• Create opportunities for action learning
• Arrange company parties	• Develop knowledge-based partnerships
• Design and deliver training programs	• Support empowerment and accountability
	• Facilitate knowledge creation and transfer
• Administer layoff programs	• Support teamworking and networking
	• Put right people in right place doing the right things to implement strategies and sustain competitive advantage
	• Blend insiders and outsiders to make strategies work
	• Develop key competencies to world-class levels
	• Build competitive culture of responsiveness, personal and organizational learning, and continuous improvement
	• Develop systems and processes to identify and develop global leaders at multiple organizational levels

As pointed out by Rhinesmith in his study *A Manager's Guide to Globalization,* the leadership challenge is clear:[13]

> Almost every study of global corporations has concluded that without an integrated and forceful human resource function, the talent and mindsets necessary to manage these new complex organizational forms will not be developed and the organizations will fail.

THE COMPETITIVE ADVANTAGE— THE GLOBAL MANAGER

As companies move toward becoming global organizations, managements' ranks and their conduct of business have become increasingly multicultura.. Throughout this global expansion process, companies continuously encounter work situations that contain dynamic cultural factors, the manner in which people live and work. Elaborating effective solutions to daily global tasks and activities, influenced by the nuances of culture, pose hard challenges that—in addition to the requirements of professional and technical expertise—confront ever the nos skilled manager:

- Does yes actually mean yes or something entirely different?
- How do I build an effective multicultural team when our department s travel budget is minimal and we meet infrequently?
- How do we achieve the goals and objectives set for our global task forc. when time and the decision-making process are viewed differentl' by team members?
- How can we comply with our director's request to arrange a conference call when participants are in three different time zones with no commor business hours between them?
- Why did the extensive and multiple contract meetings—preparation, pre sentation, renegotiation—with the prospective Malaysian partner fai 'vher a contract appeared a foregone conclusion?
- What does the hesitation expressed by our Saudi partners towara (ur fe male legal partner joining the negotiations in Riyadh actually mean?[14]

These questions form the tip of the iceberg, causing confusion that is otter difficult to cope with for managers whose perspective of the strategic company vision, although compelling, is often quite daunting in its implementation. Effective integration of activities across business and national boundaries demands that today's managers be able to function in a diverse multicultural environment Referring to the Old Testament, Geert Hofstede comments, "Today's interna tional business and public organizations often resemble the Babel Construction Corporation."[15]

Profiling the Global Manager

As a result, many organizations face the question, What is the new breed of manager required to be successful in today's international organizations? What is the profile of a successful global manager? Is such a person one who is sensitive to and adept at managing cultural diversity, and who functions effectively in different cultural environments? As companies achieve global or transnational forms of business, the interaction between corporate and national cultures becomes increasingly more important. Adaptiveness to cultural differences thus becomes a major factor in successfully managing the global marketplace.

What is clear is that no one can operate as if it is "business as usual." Andre Laurent of the Institut Européan d'Administration des Affairs (INSEAD) writes:[16]

> In order to build, maintain, and develop their corporate identity, multinational organizations need to strive for consistency in their ways of managing people on a worldwide basis. Yet, and in order to be effective locally, they also need to adapt those ways to the specific cultural requirements of different societies. While the global nature of the business may call for increased consistency, the variety of cultural environments mav be calling for differentiation.

The objective of developing a corps of seasoned global managers has emerged as a key strategic concept for companies positioning themselves to remain highly competitive well into the next century. When we look at how companies have determined what characteristics they want in their international managers, it becomes evident that there is often more than one kind of global manager and that more people in organizations than previously imagined have an international dimension to their work.

Although there does not exist a universal description for a "global manager," some argue that global management supports a network of global manager types as opposed to one single global manager model. For example, Christopher Bartlett and Sumanra Ghoshal of Harvard distinguish between four types of global managers, business, country, functional, and corporate, who have emerged as a result of the dynamic character of today's marketplace (see Table 6–2).[17]

The challenges of being an effective global manager clearly require a blend of multidimensional skills, abilities, and knowledge. The process of developing global managers (see Figures 6–2, 6–3) is influenced by several key factors, which are:

- Personal (early socialization, early responsibilities, and personal qualities).
- Professional (management education and training, including experiential, on-the-job training and overseas assignments, and technical competence).
- Organizational (depth and extent of the corporate culture and commitment to global business processes to sustain individual growth and leadership qualities).[18]

TABLE 6–2
Types of Global Managers

Type	Description

Business manager
   Strategist
   Architect
   Coordinator
	Responsible for furthering the company's global scale of effi-ciency and competitiveness. Requires perspective to recognize opportunities and risks across national and functional boundaries and the ability to coordinate activities and link capabilities across those barriers.

Country manager
   Sensor
   Builder
   Contributor
	Responsible for sensitivity and responsiveness to the local mar-ket; also for satisfying host government's requirements and de-fending company's market position against local and external competitors.

Functional manager
   Scanner
   Cross-Pollinator
   Champion
	Responsible for worldwide learning. Required to create and spread innovations and transfer specialized knowledge while also connecting scarce resources and capabilities across borders. They serve as linchpins, connecting areas of specialization through informal networks.

Corporate manager
   Leader
   Talent Scout
   Developer
	Responsible for integrating the many levels of responsibility. They lead in the broadest sense while also identifying and devel-oping business, country, and functional managers and balancing the negotiations among the three.

As the acceleration of global change and competition transforms corporations, multicultural competence is an essential level enabling managers of global or transnational firms to compete successfully in the global market. Without multi-cultural competence, managers in globalizing companies will be unable to achieve their goals and objectives at the pace and efficiency required to remain competitive. Multicultural competence is also critical to companies that are al-ready well along in the process of global development.

DEVELOPING A BROADER PERSPECTIVE

Corporations operating in the international environment and their management must acquire a new mindset toward the conduct of business as an essential for survival in the global marketplace of the 1990s. The fundamental corporate chal-lenge is to develop *and* transform the collective and individual mindset in the management ranks by broadening the manager's view of the world and business. In order to differentiate between "traditional" and "global" mindsets, a brief defi-nition is helpful.

FIGURE 6–2
Model of Spheres of Influence on the Development of a Global Manager[19]

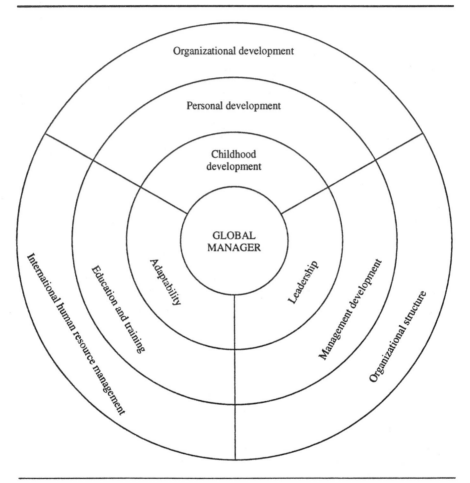

Source: Adapted with permission from Spyros G. Makridakis and Associates, *Single Market Europe: Opportunities and Challenges for Business* (San Francisco, CA: Jossey-Bass, 1991).

- *A traditional mindset,* a mental inclination, tendency, or habit. A fixed state of mind. "Differing ways that the subject at hand is perceived, understood, and reasoned about."[20]

- *A global mindset,* to constantly scan and interpret the world from a broad perspective, looking for unexpected trends and opportunities. The capacity to envision the future direction in an increasingly complex environment.

Differences in the way of thinking between a "traditional" and "global mindset" are important considerations in determining the criteria by which an effective global manager is developed and contributes to the organiza-

FIGURE 6–3
Factors Contributing to the Development of the Global Manager[21]

Personality Development		Professional Development		Organizational Development
Adaptability factors		Training and education		Organizational structure
• Cultural diversity in family. • Early international experience. • Bilingualism. • Multiple roots.	P e r s o n a l i t y	• Analytical skills. • Professional skills. • Study in other cultures. • Interpersonal skills. • Languages.	O r g a n i z a t i o n a l	• Geocentric/regiocentric. • Use of third country nationals. • Flat/lateral relationships. • Multicultural.
Leadership factors Management	s c r e e n	Management development	s c r e e n	International human resource
• Self-confidence. • Responsibility. • Curiosity. • Imagination. • Communication skills. • "Core values". • Career goals and expectations.		• Early responsibility. • Variety of tasks. • Early international experience.		• Career path responsibility. • Re-entry management. • Selection criteria. • Communication. • Mentoring. • Cultural complexity factor.
		Personal development • Supportive spouse. • Adaptable spouse. • "Moveable" children. • Variety of interests.		

Source: Adapted with permission from Spyros G. Makridakis and Associates, *Single Market Europe: Opportunities and Challenges for Business* (San Francisco, CA: Jossey-Bass, 1991).

tion. Distinguishing between the traditional and global viewpoints is shown in Table 6–3.

In a global business environment, a mindset is a filter through which we look at the world. It guides how we think we should behave and provides explanations for why things are the way they are. People with global mindsets tend to manage well a common set of critical characteristics, as shown in Table 6–4. Let's look further at the characteristics associated with each of the mindset components shown in Table 6–4.

Knowledge

A global manager's technical, business, and industry knowledge is the most fundamental quality that allows him or her to successfully manage the competitive

TABLE 6–3
Traditional versus Global Mindsets[22]

Traditional Manager Mindset	Global Manager Mindset
Perspective	
• Narrow	• Broad
• Functional	• Cross-functional
• Specialized	• Cross-cultural
Organizational Life	
• Forces to be prioritized	• Contradictions to be balanced
• Eliminate conflict	• Conflict as opportunity
Dealing with Unexpected	
• Trust hierarchical structures	• Trust networked processes
Working Style	
• Personal self-awareness	• Cultural self-awareness
• Individual mastery	• Teamwork
Change	
• Avoid surprises	• Create change
• Change as threat	• Change as opportunity
Learning	
• Master specific knowledge/skills	• Lifelong learning

Source: ©Training Management Corporation (TMC), *The Effective Global Manager,* Seminar and Coursebook (Princeton, NJ, 1993).

process, both domestic and foreign. This knowledge must be broad as well as deep and must have a well-developed international dimension that includes constant scanning of information and competitive and market conditions on a global basis.

Conceptualization/Analysis

Global managers must have a highly developed conceptual capacity to deal with the complexity of global organizations. Managers need to be both analytic and holistic in their thinking. Holistic thinking entails a "systems view" of the world and the organization, whereas, analytical thinking breaks complicated issues into parts that can be managed and made actionable by others.

Flexibility

This characteristic allows global managers to meet the demands of the organization and to adjust to global and local demands through coordination and allocation of the organization's resources. The manager must be able to work with

TABLE 6–4
The Global Mindset[23]

People with global mindsets tend to:

- DRIVE for the broader, bigger picture (knowledge).
- BALANCE contradictory demands and needs (analysis).
- TRUST networked processes rather than hierarchical structures to deal with the unexpected (flexibility).
- VALUE multicultural teamwork and diversity for accomplishing personal, professional, and organizational objectives (sensitivity).
- FLOW with change as an opportunity (judgment).
- EXPAND knowledge and skills on an ongoing basis (reflection).

Source: ©Training Management Corporation (TMC), *The Effective Global Manager,* Seminar and Coursebook (Princeton, NJ, 1993).

decision-making and problem-solving processes, rather than policies and procedures, to achieve results.

Sensitivity

Global managers must be able to conduct the majority of their creative and operational work in multicultural teams. Learning to be cross-culturally sensitive takes time. It requires self-confidence as well as a predisposition to recognize others' views and a willingness to question personal assumptions, values, and beliefs about the world and the way it operates.

Judgment

Global managers frequently have to make many decisions with a lack of information, and they may have doubts about the degree to which they have the expertise to make proper judgments. The interpretation of ethical dilemmas from a cross-cultural perspective is just one of the many challenges of judgment that these managers face.

Reflection

Lifelong learning and education drive most successful global managers because they recognize they can never know enough to deal with the world around them. Reflection provides the perspective necessary for dealing with the next round of challenges.[24]

LINKING CHARACTERISTICS
TO COMPETENCIES

Based on the characteristics outlined above, we can extend the developmental frame of reference to competencies. Essential to the new vision of the global manager is a set of competencies that provide the invaluable foundation upon which the successful individual builds his/her ability(ies) to function in a rapidly evolving global environment. The transition from mindset to competencies through the filter of personal characteristics is shown in Figure 6–4.

According to Rhinesmith, the six competencies reflective of a successful global manager are:

- Managing competitiveness, in which managers constantly scan their environment for changes in market, competitive, and supplier conditions, as well as socioeconomic and political trends that may affect the organization and its strategic intent.

- Managing complexity, which involves the skills to manage trade-offs of many competing interests, as well as the inherent contradictions and conflicts that exist in all global organizations.

- Managing adaptability, which entails developing a global corporate culture with the values, beliefs, systems, and norms of behavior that allow it to be responsive to constant change and to deal with ambiguity.

FIGURE 6–4
From Mindsets to Competencies[25]

Mindset	Personal characteristics	Competency
• Drive for big picture	Knowledge	Managing competitiveness
• Balance contradictory demands and needs	Analysis	Managing complexity
• Trust networked processes rather than hierarchical structures	Flexibility	Managing adaptability
• Value multicultural teamwork and diversity	Sensitivity	Managing teams
• Flow with change	Judgment	Managing uncertainty
• Expanding knowledge and skills	Reflection	Managing learning

Source: ©Training Management Corporation (TMC) *The Effective Global Manager,* Seminar and Coursebook (Princeton, NJ, 1993).

- Managing teams within a multicultural environment, which requires cultural sensitivity and managerial skills to lead, understand, manage, and supervise people from a wide range of cultures in a broad range of situations.

- Managing uncertainty of one's environment in a way that provides for continuous improvement, while providing structure and taking advantage of opportunities that arise from lack of structure.

- Managing learning, which requires managers to not only learn about themselves on a continuing basis, but also to train and develop others and facilitate constant organizational learning so that the organization can be responsive and adaptive to global change and challenge.[26]

These components and characteristics of today's global mindset are in sharp contrast to the "traditional" mindsets of managers in domestic U.S. organizations prevalent during the 1980s and before, attitudes that are now inappropriate for a global business environment. The relationships and challenges between domestic and global mindsets, personal characteristics, and competencies of an effective global manager are identified in Tables 6–5 and 6–6.

PROFILING THE CRITICAL SUCCESS FACTORS

The move to become a global player—whether it is a proactive decision or one imposed by competitive dynamics—has far-reaching implications for an organization and its management team. The basis on which a company "goes global"

TABLE 6–5
Relationships among Domestic and Global Mindsets,
Personal Characteristics, and Competencies[27]

Domestic Mindset	Global Mindset	Personal Characteristics	Competency
Functional expertise	Bigger, broader picture	Knowledge	Managing competition
Prioritization	Balance of contradictions	Conceptualization	Managing complexity
Structure	Process	Flexibility	Managing adaptability
Individual responsibility	Diverse teamwork and play	Sensitivity	Managing teams
No surprises	Change as opportunity	Judgment	Managing uncertainty
Trained against surprises	Openness to surprises	Reflection	Managing learning

TABLE 6-6
Challenges Emerging from Mindsets and Competencies[28]

Mindsets	Competencies	Management Challenges (Examples)	
		Organizational	*Individual*
1. DRIVE for a broader, bigger picture.	Managing competitiveness	• Translate global mission, vision, and corporate success factors into business unit objectives. • Connect the right information to the right people at the right time to maximize competitive advantage.	• Developing systems thinking. • Conducting environmental scanning to identify global opportunities.
2. BALANCE contradictory demands and needs.	Managing complexity	• Maximize communication flow within organizational matrix. • Facilitate global and local responsiveness. • Balance conflicting interests of multiple stakeholders.	• Building mind matrixing. • Handling contradictions. • Managing complex relationships.
3. TRUST networked processes rather than hierarchical structures to deal with the unexpected.	Managing adaptability	• Implement global strategy and structure. • Establish feedback mechanisms to optimize process adaptability and responsiveness. • Communicate accountability.	• Creating networks across organizational boundaries. • Maximizing influence without formal authority.
4. VALUE multicultural teamwork and diversity for accomplishing personal, professional, and organizational objectives.	Managing teams	• Maximize cultural learning to build added-value teamwork. • Promote constructive conflict to generate best results. • Build collaboration and open communication.	• Developing cultural self-awareness. • Building global teams. • Applying cross-cultural conflict management and negotiation skills.
5. FLOW with change as an opportunity.	Managing uncertainty	• Support and encourage the change process. • Promote creativity and innovation in the business unit. • Maintain cohesion and high performance.	• Making decisions under uncertain circumstances. • Managing and motivating others without clear guidelines.
6. EXPAND knowledge and skills on an ongoing basis.	Managing learning	• Implement strategies for creating a learning organization. • Promote the transfer of learning across the organization. • Support global learning within and between units.	• Recognizing learning opportunities. • Sharing critical learning with others.

Source: ©Training Management Corporation (TMC), *The Effective Global Manager*, Seminar and Coursebook (Princeton, NJ, 1993).

requires a deliberate evaluation of what kind of manager or managers it needs to make the organization work globally. The successful companies are likely to be determined more by their ability to build effective management capability and skills rather than by an exceptional strategic vision. Success will be measured across the scope and breadth of its managerial ranks, which carry out the organization's strategic objectives.

In recent surveys conducted by top international management consulting firms involving European, American, and Japanese companies, researchers have compiled a number of attributes of the successful global manager:

- Strategic awareness is characteristic of those managers who can operate across different national boundaries and those who travel mentally by understanding the international implications of their work. Based on these abilities managers can develop a global view of their own perspective. General Electric calls it "global brains," the capacity to comprehend world trends as they affect business, competitors, and standards of competition worldwide.

- Adaptability to new situations is characteristic of those managers who are fundamentally flexible enough to be able to "constantly reframe their fields of reference" versus an affinity to view things, people, and cultures from an ethnocentric (inherent superiority of one's own group and culture) viewpoint. An adaptable person rejects stereotypes; realizes valuable new skills of impact and influence through the experience of culture shock; is capable of retreating to a neutral activity, such as a hobby, reading, and so on; and constantly seeks explanations about what is going on in the business and personal work interactions.

- Sensitivity to different cultures, often termed intercultural competence, is characteristic of those individuals who possess an understanding of their own cultural roots; avoid promoting stereotypes about other nationalities and cultures, and understand the variations in business practice and management style characteristic of people's behavior in different cultures.

- Ability to work in international teams is being capable of responding to the complexity of prevailing conditions demanding joint approaches to problem-solving and a collegial style of leadership. Teams possess a high potential for creativity, yet require the ability to manage the differences in values and behavior of team members from different cultural backgrounds.

- Language skills, acquisition of a foreign language(s) is emphasized by many organizations as important to facilitate a free flow of communication throughout a global organization, which must cope with a multitude of languages, despite English being the *lingua franca* of international business.

It is significant that four of the top five characteristics surveyed are "soft" management skills as opposed to "hard" or technical functional skills. Overall, 10 of 13 critical success factors identified by researchers encompass management versus technical/functional skills and abilities. The complete listing of key characteristics is shown in Table 6–7.

The effective global manager represents a unique breed, possessing qualities that make him or her, first and foremost, an *integrator*. As technically qualified managers who can transcend divisional or nationalistic concerns to understand and mediate conflicts and problems inherent in global competition, they possess both national/local focus and a decidedly multinational reach and understanding. Being open-minded, they are able to confront different points of view and seize on opportunities in global business characterized by different goals and objectives as the result of multiple product lines, countries, and cultures.[29]

With these requirements in mind, a broad profile of the set of core and secondary skills essential to an effective global manager has been developed as shown in Table 6–8 along with their managerial implications.

It is a corporation's commitment to the development of global management talent, which includes a mix of local and third-country nationals, that many executives acknowledge today as one of the most effective and least costly measures to adopt in view of essential productivity and global competitiveness.

DEVELOPING GLOBAL MANAGERS

The development of managers to acquire broad-based international experience, skills, and competencies is crucial to company survival in globalization.

TABLE 6–7
Critical Success Factors for the International Manager[30]
(% respondents who ranked a characteristic as among the five most important)

Strategic awareness	71
Adaptability to new situations	67
Sensitivity to new cultures	60
Ability to work in international teams	56
Language skills	46
Understanding international marketing	46
Relationship skills	40
International negotiation skills	38
Self-reliance	27
High task-orientation	19
Open, nonjudgmental personality	19
Understanding international finance	13
Awareness of own cultural background	2

TABLE 6–8
Manager Profile[31]

Core Skills	Managerial Implications
Multidimensional perspective	Extensive multiproduct, multi-industry, multi-functional, multicompany, multicountry, and multi-environmental experience.
Proficiency in line management	Track record in successfully operating a strategic business business unit(s) and/or a series of major overseas projects.
Prudent decision-making skills	Competence and proven track record in making the right strategic decisions.
Resourcefulness	Skillful in getting himself or herself known and accepted in the host country's political hierarchy.
Cultural adaptability	Quick and easy adaptability into the foreign culture—an individual with as much cultural mix, diversity, and experience as possible.
Cultural sensitivity	Effective people skills in dealing with a variety of cultures, races, nationalities, genders, religions. Also sensitive to cultural difference.
Ability as a team builder	Adept in bringing a culturally diverse working group together to accomplish the major mission and objective of the organization.
Physical fitness and mental maturity	Endurance for the rigorous demands of an overseas assignment.
Secondary Skills	*Managerial Implications.*
Computer literacy	Comfortable exchanging strategic information electronically.
Prudent negotiating skills	Proven track record in coordinating successful strategic business negotiations in multicultural environment.
Ability as a change agent	Proven track record in successfully initiating and implementing strategic organizational changes.
Visionary skills	Quick to recognize and respond to strategic business opportunities and potential political and economic upheavals in host country.
Effective delegatory skills	Proven track record in participative management style and ability to delegate.

Executives of successful global companies are convinced that global managers can be developed to acquire the necessary skills and experience to be effective international managers in the 21st Century. In fact, essential to overall strategy is the linkage of strategic intent and business planning with aggressive management and development of a company's international human resources.

Training and development activities that are unrelated to a company's strategic goals and objectives are likely to be ineffective.

As emphasized in *World-Class Training,* Bren White underscores the challenge represented by training—a critical "value-producing learning process" if implemented in a consistent and innovative manner to sustain change at a strategic level. Among the essential characteristics in managing change through training are:

1. A strong and all-pervasive focus rather than a national, regional, or local one.
2. Training that is flexible and self-adapting.
3. A focused and integrated learning process.
4. Many disciplines under an organizational development framework.
5. A philosophy that encourages learning in many forms.
6. Customer-focused training.
7. Training that is continuously employed to achieve competitive advantage.
8. Training that is of strategic value to the organization.
9. Training administrative processes, courses, seminars, and forums that directly contribute to the successful implementation of business strategies for targeted markets.
10. Training that fully captures the imagination of all potential customers.[32]

A number of methods support the development of global managers to expand awareness, add knowledge, or develop new skills. It is important to remember that a fully integrated approach to developing global managers must also target opportunities and experiences that apply to issues such as:

- Global sourcing.
- Assessment and selection.
- Multicultural team-building.
- Staff exchanges, rotational assignments, and network development.
- Expatriate assignments, local national positions, transfers, and re-entry.
- Repatriation.
- Career pathing.
- On-the-job training and mentoring.
- Performance management.[33]

Let's briefly look at five developmental areas that form a crucial component of an integrated international human resources policy: cross-cultural awareness training, effective communication and language development, country specific training, host country workforce training, and business management programs.

Cross-cultural awareness training targets the critical notion of working and socializing with people from different cultural backgrounds. The emphasis in cross-cultural training is on building an understanding of how culture affects work relationships, interpersonal behaviors, culture shock and stress, business practices and behavior, the influence of differences across culture impacting teamwork and productivity.

Effective communication and language development accentuates the dynamics in communication among cultures and language development.

Business success overseas frequently depends on effective communication in the host country language; yet, the importance of language skills varies by country. For example, a degree of fluency in French or Spanish would be essential if a global manager was being assigned to France or Mexico. In the situation where the manager is not on a long-term assignment, he or she should try to learn a set of basic phrases and expressions in the host language. Their use in casual conversation is a meaningful emphasis on the manager's interest in the host culture. Language development is recommended prior to an individual's arrival in a country and the content of the training should be designed on a case-by-case basis.

Country specific training is aimed often at expatriates going on assignment overseas, who need to increase their knowledge and understanding of a host country culture and cultural adaptation issues for trailing dependents. Training in this field may involve any of the following:

- Predeparture orientation
- Family adjustment to an overseas assignment
- Doing business internationally
- Culture-specific training
- International briefings
- Regional/country business briefings
- Working with (specific nationality)
- Repatriation training

Host country workforce (LN, TCN) training for nationals who will be working with American expatriates (either overseas or on headquarters assignments). Neglect of this element attests to past ethnocentric beliefs that the expatriate alone is the key determinant of success in an overseas assignment.

Training for the host-country national involves information about the expatriate culture, targeting areas of concern for potential conflict in order to identify and effectively deal with issues when they occur, such as:

- What kinds of behavior the workers can expect.
- Why the expatriate manager may behave in an unpredictable, unconventional, and often unacceptable way from the host-country culture point of view.
- How to cope effectively with cultural differences.

Management programs are an important element in training for global expertise. They include executive education, MBA degree programs, university general management and functional programs, and internal corporate programs. An increasing number of companies are developing global managers through advanced management courses at major business schools, which now play an important role in the internationalization process. Courses at schools such as INSEAD, London Business School, Institute for International Management Development, Wharton, and Harvard provide managers with the opportunity to acquire the latest in global management skills and techniques while benefitting from the cross-fertilization and interaction with senior managers of other companies. These schools have made fundamental changes in partnering with business to provide programming that addresses the crucial need to link the process of strategic thinking to action and implementation. In view of the need for the global manager to be a lifelong learner, business schools are also providing the global managers an important capability—learning how to learn.

While the allocation of funds for management programs for the development of global managers is relatively limited when compared to annual human resource development budget allocations, the demand and urgency of investment in this area will increase dramatically by the year 2000.

MANAGEMENT DEVELOPMENT INITIATIVES— CORPORATE CASE STUDIES

Learning in a global organization occurs at all levels of the organization in both a global and local context. The approach and process of global learning represent strategic investments around the world to achieve a competitive advantage in the most effective and profitable manner. The level and importance of corporate initiatives dedicated to management and organization development can be illustrated by the training or "synergy centers" established by General Electric, Nippon Electric Corporation, Rhone-Poulenc Rorer, Motorola, Asea Brown Boveri, and Singapore International Airlines. It is important to remember that there is no standard approach, in terms of structure or style, to ensure global learning and management development. Each organization must create a learning environment unique to its own people, mission, vision, history, and culture.

Now, let's briefly examine how these companies leverage their learning worldwide.

GENERAL ELECTRIC (United States)

General Electric is a diversified company involved in financial services, electronics, electrical equipment (aircraft engines, medical systems, lighting, power systems), aerospace, and communications and services. GE's 1992 sales totaled approximately $62.2 billion.

GE has long maintained a leadership role in development through its world-renowned Management Development Center in Crotonville-on-the-Hudson, New York. The primary objective of the center is to leverage GE's global competitiveness as an instrument of cultural change, by improving business acumen, leadership abilities, and organizational effectiveness.

The center's programming is centered on a five-stage development sequence, from entry- to officer-level workshops, using three innovative organizational development techniques to foster global learning throughout the company: work-out sessions, best practices, and process mapping, aimed at fostering employee involvement.

- Work-out—multiday sessions, involving groups of 40 to 100 people, led by a senior management leader, who identifies an issue or problem to be solved. Broken into teams, often led by an outside facilitator, the group identifies solutions and prepares proposals for reporting back to the leadership and group. Proposals are then debated, a Yes or No is given on the spot, or a team is created to resolve the issue by a certain date. Work-out empowers employees to be involved in the decision-making process.

- Best practices—studies of companies who exhibit exemplary, best management ideas and practices on a global basis not just on a functional level. This research provides General Electric with an empirical basis for changing management practices to emphasize the how versus the what in accomplishing tasks.

- Process mapping—definition of a full and detailed outline of a business process to address a specific issue, job, or project, involving both internal and external resources essential to completion of the task.

The focus is on action learning or dealing with real business issues and planning.

A typical example of this action learning approach is the business manager course, a four-week action learning experience, the core of which is creating five- to seven-person teams that spend over a week in the field, both domestically and globally, consulting and working on real, unresolved GE strategic problems.[34]

NIPPON ELECTRIC CORPORATION (NEC) (Japan)

Nippon is a global leader in computers and industrial electronic systems, home electronics, and communications equipment. Sales for NEC and its consolidated subsidiaries (76 total) for the fiscal year 1992 amounted to $28.3 billion.

NEC's approach to global management development is reflective of a broader Japanese outlook, linking business success to education, which is viewed as part of a lifelong process of learning. This means that learning is a major factor in organizational and company culture development, emphasizing the uniqueness of the Japanese experience. Secondly, a critical issue is harmonizing NEC's impressive organizational capabilities and practices with its non-Japanese employees around the world. Underlying this issue is a fundamental communications problem involving the need to overcome culture and language issues juxtaposed with the "loss" of the Japanese uniqueness through mixing with other nationalities. NEC's approach to global development in this context is unique and future-oriented in comparison with other major Japanese corporations.

To address global development needs, the firm established the NEC Institute of Management in 1983—a strategically concentrated system of management education services committed to education (management and professional skills), internationalization training (cross-cultural adaptability management), intercompany education, lifelong learning, and effective communication throughout the total NEC organization.

The NEC education/vision is predicated on meeting three key objectives: companywide internationalization, strengthening of international operations, and strengthening of overseas affiliates. The focus of NEC's global education is training on:

- International management—senior and middle management programs.
- International business—traditional functional courses and seminars.
- Area studies including predeparture orientations for overseas country assignments, repatriation courses, and language training where a major emphasis is on corporate capability in English.

RHONE-POULENC RORER (France)

Rhone-Poulenc is the eighth largest chemical company in the world, structured around four major business units: basic and specialty chemicals, health products, fibers, and agrochemicals. The company attained a 1992 sales figure of about $15.8 billion.

A firm advocate of decentralization, Rhone-Poulenc created the International Human Resources Committee, which emphasizes national management decision making for human resources and management development. In 1987, breaking with tradition, the Committee created a new policy encouraging international careers and developing "citizens of the world." Key to Rhone-Poulenc's desire to be a global, not simply French, company is seen in the Young International Managers Program, which is aimed at developing a cadre of young, international managers who are flexible, culturally open, willing to change work habits/methods with the intention of facilitating relationships between head office and various national units unimpeded by national and cultural barriers.[35]

MOTOROLA (United States)

Motorola is a major electronics and electrical equipment company with approximately $13.3 billion in sales in 1992.

Motorola has a long-standing tradition of training. It firmly believes that its employees are a key strategic resource and has an ambitious education and training strategy for its employees worldwide. Motorola underscores the fact that a skilled and educated workforce is a key competitive advantage.

To emphasize its commitment, Motorola created Motorola University in 1989 with a $60 million education budget to build an educational system that stresses that education is a "strenuous, universal, unending human activity that neither business nor society can live without." The training focuses on the needs of the organization at all levels from the production worker to the CEO and assures continuous training of employees and fosters the building of partnerships and dialogues with external educational institutions.

Training and development at the University focuses on general management skills and functional business unit specializations, such as communications, semiconductors, automotive electronics, government electronics, and information systems. The ultimate objective is to build a learning organization that is responsive to the cultural differences of its employees, customers, and resources worldwide leading to the growth of knowledge and skills globally for all of Motorola.

The Global Design and Delivery System of the University is an essential component of achieving the overall training and development objectives. It consists of a multistep approach which entails a needs analysis, pilot testing, cultural adjustments and translations, if appropriate, and final approval by the global client. The importance of accommodating local country needs, requirements, and learning habits is an underlying factor in the success of the University on a worldwide basis.

Overall, the Motorola approach to learning is based on a global strategy that addresses technology management, empowerment, globalization, cultural sensitivity, and networking and alliances in an integrated process.

ASEA BROWN BOVERI (Switzerland)

ABB is a diversified company whose major business segments include power plants, power transmission, metallurgy, process automation, mass transit rail systems, environmental control, and reinsurance and leasing. ABB's sales totalled an estimated $32 billion in 1993.

ABB functions as a matrix organization divided into eight major business groups. The eight groups are built around business areas (65), plants and companies (1,300), and individual profit centers (5,000), within 150 countries. Its unique business structure is successfully based on the ABB strategy of learning and knowledge transfer. For example, the 65 business area chiefs meet quarterly to design global strategies and foster information exchange.

Specialized business areas, such as hydroelectric plants on electric metering, develop special technical expertise, which results in their being designated as centers of excellence. The centers of excellence have the responsibility to share and transfer expertise throughout the ABB companies of the business structure. A continuous sharing of learning occurs when business area staff travel, confer with country specific managers, and reinforce the transfer of expertise.

From a formal training perspective, the majority of ABB companies have their own technical training functions in support of their respective products and services, which are highly successful due to the company operating environment and a systematic operational approach. Training centers exist throughout ABB at the global level through global training centers which support the eight main businesses by developing standard courses, which are distributed for use in local country training centers. The relationship of the training centers is informal with local centers having full autonomy under country specific management operation.

Asea Brown Boveri is considered a model for the global corporation of the future—an efficient organizational structure; dedicated to "instant" transfer of skills, knowledge, and information; committed to ongoing training and development; and determined to maximize teams and network techniques to support a systematic approach to the transfer of expertise and learning as an undisputable competitive advantage.

SINGAPORE INTERNATIONAL AIRLINES
(Singapore)

SIA is a leader in airlines services, aircraft engine overhauling services, simulator training, airport terminal services, tours, property development, aviation, and general insurance.

Indicative of SIA's leadership role in global development programming was the creation of the Management Development Center in 1987. SIA spends $80–120 million per year on employee training, which includes job specific training from cabin crew to flight operations to maintenance staff; commercial and engineering training; general people management and performance appraisal related courses; and senior staff through executive training programs.

The main objective of the MDC is to develop managers who can succeed in the business environment of the future. The Center's management development curriculum is divided into three categories: management development (basic to strategic), management skills (problem-solving, decision-making, delegating), and self-development programs, such as computer, area studies, business practices, to name a few electives. At a senior management level, programming is based on core, complementary, optional and specialized training. For example, a new manager would participate in a one-week company orientation program, followed by a two-week basic management course, then a one-week airline industry seminar. As managers advance in the organization, they would be scheduled to participate in an array of programs such as the Middle Management Program, the Senior Management Program, Managing International Business Program, and so on.

SIA believes that management development ensures competitiveness in the international marketplace. The Management Development Center targets the development of managers for today's global workforce while preparing them to meet the challenges of the 21st century.[36]

SUMMARY INSIGHTS

Current thinking about the characteristics and competencies of an effective global manager, especially the aspects of working across cultures, is rich and diverse, although sometimes difficult to access conveniently. This book has addressed essential cross-cultural issues with the intent of raising the reader's awareness concerning the impact of culture on the conduct of business in the global marketplace. The global manager profile provides an overview of the critical success factors for managers who conduct business activities on an international basis. It is very important to acknowledge that to successfully raise awareness about culture involves continuous learning, and entails organizational and individual responsibility.

To ensure success, the organization clearly has a role in methodically developing its global managers. Senior management working closely with human resource development professionals as partners in the strategic plan design and implementation process is essential to maintaining the competitive global advantage.

Among the initiatives management can take to underscore the subtle, yet critical, impact of culture on global management practices are the following:

- Communicate broadly the global vision, strategy, and challenges of the company; demonstrate commitment to being a global organization.
- Identify the cultural competencies, issues and, opportunities facing managers in their company.

- Establish training and development of *global* managers using a variety of methods (formal/informal training, international assignments, task force initiatives, etc.).
- Select managers for specific assignments and task forces who demonstrate aptitude, interest, and capability for working effectively across cultures.
- Encourage and support employees to learn more about cross-cultural issues on a continuous basis.
- Leverage culturally diverse managers and teams to achieve maximum synergy and contribution to the achievement of corporate strategic goals and objectives.
- Assemble an information library about the countries/regions where the company does business and make the information readily available.
- Maintain an understanding of and differentiate between your own culture and foreign national cultures.

Beyond the corporate commitment, a number of personal and social factors contribute to being a successful global manager. Personal background exerts an exceptionally strong impact on formulation of successful global managers.[37] On an individual level, the characteristics of successful global managers can be summarized as follows:

- Patient but persistent.
- Willing to fail and learn from failures.
- Possessing a good sense of humor.
- Strongly imaginative.
- Emotionally stable.
- Curious—socially and intellectually.
- Perceptually acute.
- Capable of listening well.
- Intuitive about communications, especially the silent language of culture (nonverbal).
- Comfortable with uncertainty.[38]

A global perspective is mandatory today. Intensified global competition, organizational upheaval, high-tech communications networks, and economic instability require the global manager to make critical decisions within short time frames. Managing internationally in the 1990s requires a broad background and experience within the global marketplace. Key to success is a heightened level of cultural knowledge, skills, and sensitivity, which contribute to developing a competitive edge, translating in turn to market share and revenue enhancement. Cultural empowerment is the *sine qua non* for the successful manager and global company of the year 2000 and beyond.

DISCUSSION QUESTIONS

Review the following checklists and discuss the questions with your colleagues.

CHECKLIST

PROFILING GLOBAL COMMITMENT AND AWARENESS[39]

Try your company out against these indicators of corporate commitment and awareness of the requirements of creating a world-class organization.

1. Is top management continuously stressing its desire to become a global competitor?
2. Are corporate values in tune with each of the country cultures and business environments in which you operate?
3. Are there increasing numbers of task forces with executives from around the globe?
4. Does the board of directors have members from different nations?
5. Does the board of directors meet only in the headquarters city?
6. Does the company host many international events, meetings, and conferences?
7. Do top executives travel regularly to international affiliates?
8. Are training dollars invested in language training and cultural orientation for wide groups of employees or only for those going abroad?
9. How aware are managers of cultural diversity and of the effects of stereotypical thinking on the way they manage and communicate?
10. How much do managers know about global competitors and what it will take to outperform them?
11. How much senior executive time and attention is devoted to the international aspects of staffing?

Profiling international awareness is essential to the task of creating competency for managers involved globally. Discuss this comparative chart with your colleagues to evaluate your/their level of global competence.

GLOBALLY COMPETENT MANAGERS[40]

Transnational Skills	Globally Competent Managers	Traditional International Managers
Global perspective	Understand worldwide business environment from a global perspective.	Focus on a single foreign country, on managing relationships between headquarters and that country.
Local responsiveness	Learn about many cultures.	Become an expert in one culture.
Synergistic learning	Work with and learn from people from many cultures simultaneously.	Work with and coach people in each foreign culture separately and/or sequentially.
	Create a culturally synergistic organizational environment.	Integrate foreigners into the headquarters' national organizational culture.
Transition and adaptation	Adapt to living in foreign cultures.	Adapt to living in foreign cultures.
Cross-cultural interaction	Use cross-cultural interaction skills on a daily basis throughout one's career.	Use cross-cultural interaction skills primarily on foreign assignments.
Collaboration	Interact with foreign colleagues as equals.	Interact within clearly defined hierarchies of structural and cultural dominance.
Foreign Experience	Transpatriation for career and organization development.	Expatriation or inpatriation primarily to get the job done.

NOTES

1. Kenichi Ohmae, *The Borderless World: Power and Strategy in the Interlinked Economy* (New York: McKinsey & Company, 1990), pp 17–31.

2. Fisher Grosel, ed. *1993 Ten-Year Forecast* (Menlo Park, CA: Institute for the Future, 1993).

3. Reprinted by permission of *Harvard Business Review*. An excerpt from Global Work Force 2000: The New World Labor Market by William B. Johnson March–April 1991. Copyright © 1991 by the President and Fellows of Harvard College; all rights reserved.

4. Johnson, "Global Work Force 2000."

5. "The New Global Work Force," *Fortune*, August 27, 1993.

6. Michael Hammer and James Champy, *Reengineering the Corporation: A Manifesto for Business Revolution* (New York: Harper Business, 1993), p 6.

7. Gene Hall, Jim Rosenthal, and Judy Wade, "How to Make Reengineering Really Work," *Harvard Business Review*, November–December 1993, pp 119–131.

8. Michael Moynihan, *Developing Effective Global Managers for the 1990s* (New York: Business International, 1991), pp 2–5; Robert Moran and William G. Stripp, *International Negotiation* (Houston: Gulf Publishing, 1991).

9. Stephen Rhinesmith, *A Manager's Guide to Globalization: Six Keys to Success in a Changing World* (Homewood, IL: Business One Irwin, 1993), pp 13–14.

10. Joshua Greenbaum, "View from the Top: Survival Tactics for the Global Business Arena," *Management Review,* October 1992, pp 49–53.

11. Lisa Advent Hoecklin, *Managing Cultural Differences for Competitive Advantage,* Report No. P656 (London: Economist Intelligence Unit, 1993), pp 29–53.

12. Michael J. Marquardt and Dean W. Engel, *Global Human Resource Development* (Englewood Cliffs, NJ: Prentice-Hall, 1993), pp 7–8.

13. Rhinesmith, *Manager's Guide,* p 168.

14. Grosel, *1993 Ten-Year Forecast,* pp 127–128.

15. G. Hofstede, "Cultural Dimensions in People Management: The Socialization Perspective," in *Globalizing Management, Creating and Leading the Competitive Organization* (New York: John Wiley, 1992), pp 139–158.

16. A. Laurent, "The Cross-Cultural Puzzle of International Human Resource Management," *Human Resource Management* 25 (1986), pp 91–102.

17. Reprinted by permission of *Harvard Business Review.* An excerpt from What is a Global Manager by Christopher A. Bartlett and Sumantra Ghoshal, September–October 1992. Copyright © 1992 by the President and Fellows of Harvard College; all rights reserved.

18. Manfred Kets de Vries and Christine Mead, "Identifying Management Talent for a Pan-European Environment," in Spyros G. Makridakis and Associates, *Single Market Europe: Opportunities and Challenges for Business* (San Francisco: Jossey-Boss, 1991), pp 215–35.

19. Makridakis, *Single Market Europe* (San Francisco: Jossey-Bass, Publishers, 1992) p 232.

20. Glen Fisher, *Mindsets: The Role of Culture and Perception in International Relations* (New York: John Wiley, 1988).

21. Makridakis, *Single Market Europe,* p 233.

22. Training Management Corporation, *Effective Global Manager,* Seminar and Workbook, 1993.

23. Training Management Corporation, *Effective Global Manager.*

24. Rhinesmith, *Manager's Guide,* pp 28–31.

25. Training Management Corporation, *Effective Global Manager.*

26. Rhinesmith, *Manager's Guide,* pp 32–33.

27. Reprinted from *Training & Development (Journal).* Copyright © October 1992, the American Society for Training and Development. Reprinted with permission. All rights reserved.

28. Training Management Corporation, *Effective Global Manager.*

29. Lawrence Hebriniak, "Implementing Global Strategies," *European Management Journal* no. 10, 4, (December 1992), pp 392–403.

30. David Weeks, *Recruiting and Selecting International Managers,* Report # 998 (The Conference Board, 1992, p 12.

31. Reprinted with the permission of *HR Magazine* published by the Society for Human Resource Management, Alexandria, VA.

32. Bren D. White, *World-Class Training; How to Outdistance the Global Competition* (Dallas: Odenwald Press, 1992), pp 17–27.

33. Rhinesmith, *Global Mindsets,* pp 169–170; Gregory Chowanec and Charles N. Newstrom, "The Strategic Management of International Human Resources," *Business Quarterly,* Autumn, 1991, pp 65–70.

34. Michael Marquardt and Agnus Reynolds, *The Global Learning Organization: Gaining Competitive Advantage through Continuous Learning* (New York: Irwin Professional Publishing, 1994), pp 189–96.

35 Kevin Barham and Marion Devine, *The Quest for the International Manager: A Survey of Global Human Resources Strategies* (London: The Economist Group, 1992), pp H7–55, 97–105.

36. Marquardt and Reynolds, The Global Learning Organization, pp 144–49, 213–20, 247–59.

37. Makridakis, *Single Market Europe,* pp 231–34.

38. Peter Dowling and Randall S. Schuler, *International Dimensions of Human Resource Management* (Boston: PWS-Kent Publishing Company, 1990), p. 14.

39. Ibid., pp 15–18.

40. Nancy J. Adler, and Susan Bartholomew, "Managing Globally Competent People," *Academy of Management Executive,* 1992.

Epilogue

The world is getting smaller, international business is becoming more important, and managers worldwide are becoming more sophisticated. It is only as we recognize the extent to which we are culture bound that we can go beyond the limitations of our own necessarily narrow perspectives. . . . To the extent that organizations recognize individual cultural differences, they allow us to contribute based on our uniqueness.[1]

Nancy Adler

It is uncontestable that a significant, often subtle, characteristic of doing business internationally is the nature of culture and its impact on the conduct of business in a global and/or diverse work environment. Our emphasis on and exploration of culture (attributes, "allies and islands," communication, negotiation, critical success factors) is tempered by the fact that we are not advocating that everyone become a "global manager" or that people "go native" and give up their nationalities. Far from it. We have made a concerted effort to nurture an understanding of the relationship between culture and business.

Our intent is to raise the level of sensitivity and awareness among *all* individuals who work in the global arena. It is critical to understand and respect how interpersonal relationships are affected by culture, how management practices differ based on cultural factors, how work gets done in various cultures, how culture masks opportunities and obstacles, how we can develop stronger analytical skills for dealing with issues and problems affected by culture, and how we must manage cultural differences to create a global perspective.

This book is meant to encourage the exploration of culture's impact on business practices. National and organizational boundaries are less a limitation than in the past—the excitement and challenge of working effectively across these boundaries is a key to business success. We hope that this guide to cross-cultural success fosters expansion of your knowledge beyond your own national boundaries, understanding of your personal cultural attributes, and encouragement of further exploration and application.

While the book's theme is focused on culture, our thinking throughout has been conditioned by the realization that we, as Percy Barnevik of Asea Brown Boveri says, *"have to acknowledge cultural differences without becoming paralyzed by them."*[2]

With this in mind, it is our premise that cultural awareness is an important organizational/management skill for companies to develop in their people. A resulting increase in business acumen, derived from the ability to work effectively across cultures and national boundaries, contains the real key to future growth.

NOTES

1. *International Dimensions of Organizational Behavior* (Boston, MA: Kent Publishing, 1986).
2. "The Logic of Global Business: An Interview with ABB's Percey Barnevik," *Harvard Business Review,* March–April 1991.

Appendix:
Useful Resource List

Africa Economic Digest, 15 Gromer Street, London WC1H9LS, England
   Weekly periodical.
African Business, PO Box 261, Great Queen Street, London WC2B 5BN, England
   Monthly publication.
Asia Week, Vicwood Plaza, 30th Floor, 199 Des Voeux Road Central, Hong
Kong or 2323 Randolph Avenue, Avenel, NJ
Asian Wall Street Journal, 200 Liberty Street, New York, NY
(212–416–2242)
   Weekly periodical.
Background Notes (updated periodically), U.S. State Department, Public Affairs
(202–647–2518)
   International news: political, economic, and cultural, with statistics on a
   country-by-country basis.
Bibliography of International, Intercultural Literature, American Society for
Training and Development, 1630 Duke Street, Box 1443, Alexandria, VA
(703–683–8100)
   Annotated bibliography of books and articles that relate to international/inter-
   cultural training.
Business America: The Magazine of International Trade
(biweekly), U.S. Department of Commerce (202–482–3251)
   Information on global human resource issues.
Business Information Center, Seagate Associates Inc., West 115 Century Road,
Paramus, NJ (201–262–5200)
   International trade and economics.
Business Information Service for the Newly Independent States
(BISNIS), U.S. Department of Commerce, International Trade Administration,
Room H-7413, 14th Street and Constitution Avenue, NW, Washington, DC
(202–482–4655)
   "One-stop shopping" information service for U.S. firms interested in doing
   business in the newly independent states of the former Soviet Union.
Business International Publications, 215 Park Avenue South, New York, NY
(212–460–0600)

Source: Training Management Corporation, *Doing Business Internationally: The Cross-Cultural Challenges,* Princeton Training Press, (Princeton, NJ 1992).

Publications on doing business in Latin America, Europe, Eastern Europe, Middle East, Africa, and Asia as well as on international currencies, investing, licensing, trading, and financing.

Business Japan, Nihon Kogyo Shimbun, Sankei Building, 7-2, 1-chome, Ohtemachi, Chiyoda-Ku, Tokyo, Japan or 150 East 52nd Street, 34th Floor, New York, NY
Monthly periodical.

Canadian Business, 70 The Esplanade, Toronto, ON MSE 1R2, Canada
Monthly periodical.

Canadian Consulate, 1251 Avenue of the Americas, 16th Floor, New York, NY (212–768–2400)
Comprehensive information services and publications pertaining to doing business in Canada.

Caribbean and Central American Databook, Caribbean/Central American Action, 1211 Connecticut Avenue, NW, Suite 510, Washington, DC (202–466–7464)
Current facts on the 35 countries of the Caribbean basin.

The Christian Science Monitor (daily), The Christian Science Publishing Society, Boston (617–450–2000)
International news.

Coopers & Lybrand Country Guides, Coopers & Lybrand (International) Publications, 1251 Avenue of the Americas, New York, NY (212–536–3157)
Guides for businesspeople and investors for key countries worldwide.

Countries Encyclopedia (PC and MAC), Bureau Development, 141 New Road, Parsippany, NJ (800–828–4761)
667.5 MB database containing information on more than 190 countries and territories, for IBM and Macintosh computers.

Country Market Information Sources, International Trade Administration, U.S. Department of Commerce, Washington, DC
Country desk officers on hand to provide trade, commercial policy, promotional, economic, and marketing information (call the Department of Commerce at 202–482–3022 to obtain specific country desk numbers).

Craighead Publications Inc., PO Box 149, Darien, CT (203–655–1007)
Country reports.

Culturgrams, Brigham Young University, Kennedy Center Publications, Provo, UT (800–528–6279)
Culture capsules for countries throughout the world.

Eastern Europe Business Information Center, U.S. Department of Commerce, Room H-7412, Washington, DC (202–482–2645)
Fax delivery service and publications on country and industry facts, telecommunication markets, financing, export, opportunities, and so on.

East European Investment Magazine, 119 Fifth Avenue, 8th Floor, New York, NY (212–388–1500)
Definitive magazine on investment activity in Russia, the other ten CIS countries, the Baltics, and Eastern Europe.

Economic Bulletin Board, 202–377–1986.
On-line trade leads, time-sensitive market information, and the latest statistical releases from a variety of federal agencies.

The Economist (weekly), The Economist Newspaper Ltd., London or 111 West 57th Street, NY (071–839–7000 in London and 212–541–5730 in NYC)
International, political, and economic news.

The Economist Intelligence Unit: How-to Guides for International Managers, Business International Corp., New York, NY (212–460–0600)
Reports on business strategies from leading international companies.

Europe, Delegation of the European Communities, 2100 M Street NW, Suite 700, Washington, DC (202–862–9500)
Monthly periodical on European Community countries.

The Europa World Yearbook (annual), Europa Publishing Co. Ltd., London
Country-by-country news, issues, and statistics summaries.

Export Programs: A Business Directory of U.S. Government Resources, Trade Information Center, International Trade Administration, U.S. Department of Commerce, Washington, DC (1–800–USA–TRADE)
"One-stop" information center for U.S. companies seeking information on export counseling, market information and trade leads, overseas and domestic trade activities, and financing and technical assistance.

Facts on File, 460 Park Avenue South, New York, NY (212–683–2244)
Weekly summaries of international and national news.

Far Eastern Economic Review, Review Publishing Co., Ltd., GPO Box 160, Hong Kong or New York Office: 420 Lexington Avenue, New York, NY (Hong Kong: 852–832–8338; US: 212–808–6615)
Far Eastern Economic Review weekly magazine, annual Asia Yearbook, All-Asia Travel Guide and Japan in Asia (book).

Foreign Affairs (quarterly), Council on Foreign Relations, New York, NY (212–734–0400)
International news and issues commentary.

Foreign Broadcast Information Service Reports (daily by region), National Technical Information Service, Springfield, VA (703–487–4600)
International news: translations of newspaper articles from around the world.

Foreign Policy (quarterly), Carnegie Endowment for International Peace, Washington, DC (202–862–7900)
International news and issues commentary.

Global Finance, 55 John Street, 7th Floor, New York, NY (212–766–5868)
International business and finance trends and market strategies.

Harvard Business Review, Graduate School of Business Administration, Harvard University, Boston, MA (617–495–6192)

Inteligencia Competitiva, 2305 Old Orchard Drive, Marietta, GA (404–973–0457)
Information, marketing assistance and business research on Mexico.

Intercultural Press: Current Intercultural Resources, Yarmouth, ME (207–846–5168)
Listing of cross-cultural books, videos, and other materials.

Latin America/Caribbean Business Bulletin, Latin America/Caribbean Business Development Center, U.S. Department of Commerce, International Trade Administration, Washington, DC (202–482–0841)

Region briefs, references, events, and business opportunities.

Latin America Monitor, Business Monitor International, 56–60 St. John Street, London EC1M 4DT (071–608–3646)

Regional reports plus six annual reports on key Latin American developing economies.

Middle East Economic Digest, 21 John Street, London WC1N 2BP, England

Weekly periodical.

The National Trade Databank, U.S. Department of Commerce, Office of Business Analysis, HCHB Room 4885, Washington, DC (202–482–1986)

A "one-stop" source of international trade data, updated monthly and released on CD-ROM.

The New York Times (daily), New York, NY (212–556–1234)

International and national news.

Third World Week, North-South News Service, Hanover NH

Third world international news.

World Economic Development Congress: Directory of World Markets, c/o Bay Colony Corporate Center, 1000 Winter Street, Suite 3700, Waltham, MA (617–487–7900)

Historical and forecast information on the largest nations in the world today

World Factbook, Central Intelligence Agency, Superintendent of Documents, U.S. Government Printing Office Washington, DC (202–783–3228 or 703–351–2053)

International geographic, government, economic, population, communications, and defense statistics and facts.

World Media Handbook 1992–1994, United Nations Publications, Sales Section Room DC2-0853, Department 929, New York, NY (800–342–4220)

Listing of newspapers, magazines, new agencies, broadcasting organizations and journalists' associations for more than 150 countries worldwide.

World Press (monthly), The Stanley Foundation, Muscatine, IA (319–264–1500)

Selection of stories from newspapers and periodicals from around the world.

Worldwide Government Report, Belmont Publications, NW, Washington, DC (800–332–3535)

Biweekly report of events affecting government structures and personnel around the world.

W-2 Publications, 202 The Commons, Suite 401, Ithaca, NY (607–277–0934)

Monthly market reports for Europe and Asia Pacific as well as telephone research assistance.

Glossary

attribution Attributing a cause (true or false) to a behavior that is outside of our normal expectations, for example that unwillingness to make prolonged eye contact is *caused* by that person having something to hide.

business reengineering Creating a new business model (strategy and structure) to meet the pressures of the changing marketplace in order to achieve real business-unit impact.

collective learning mindset A shared mindset in an organization that seeks to promote continuous learning aimed at identifying opportunities for creating and delivering added value to stakeholders.

co-option Technique used in transnational organizations to facilitate consensus across the organization. To optimize decision making, each individual needs to understand, share, and internalize the company's purpose, values, and key strategies.

configuration of values The set of value orientations (e.g., fixed time, private space) that when considered as a whole define the cultural characteristics of a specific society or region.

cultural allies Cultures that share similar characteristics because of historical connections, such as Australia, the United States, Great Britain.

cultural competence The ability to adapt successfully across a wide range of cultures.

cultural frame An individual's perceptual window/mental framework (based on cultural value orientations) through which he or she defines self, others, and the world.

cultural islands Specific cultures that tend to be unique; for example, Japan.

culture The fundamental values, beliefs, attitudes, and patterns of thinking that are embedded in a society's or region's view of how the world works and of how individuals and groups can and should operate in that world.

domestic enterprise A company that produces, markets, and sells its products and services only to its home market.

escalation box The potential for culturally different individuals to become trapped in a cycle of escalating conflict. To get out of the "box," the participants need to slow down, reflect on their cultural differences, and work toward mutual understanding and the establishment of common ground.

ethonocentricity A belief in the inherent superiority and naturalness of one's own culture.

export company A successful national business that markets and sells its products and services in foreign countries, but operates primarily from its sense of domestic competitiveness and advantage. It works through export agents or foreign distributors.

fuzzy thinking Moving beyond either/or, yes/no, on/off, all/nothing thinking to explore a wider range of possibilities. It promotes expansive thinking and questions any attempt to arbitrarily impose limits on available opportunities.

global brains Strategic awareness.

global company A global company shares resources on a global basis to access the most profitable/highest volume markets with the highest-quality products at the lowest cost.

globalites Global managers.

global mindset Scanning and interpreting the world from a broad perspective and looking for unexpected trends and opportunities in the global marketplace. The capacity to envision the future direction in an increasingly complex environment.

global village Borderless marketplace.

glocal A company, strategy, and so on that are simultaneously global and local.

glubricant Term used to identify information technology tools because they provide the structural glue to integrate the organization and the lubricant to keep the flow of business on target.

informated organization Organization in which all levels have immediate access to key information for control and decision making. Reliance on expert systems and databases.

isomorphic attribution Looking at unexpected behavior from the viewpoint of the person exhibiting that behavior.

international company An export company operating through an international division.

mindset A relatively stable set of attitudes, viewpoints, and so on based on experience that predisposes an individual to perceive and act in consistent ways.

multinational company A company whose national/regional operations tend to act independently of one another.

negotiation box The potential for negotiators to become trapped in working with stated positions rather than focusing on fundamental needs and wants. To get out of the "box," the participants need to be able to generate multiple options, move beyond either/or thinking, and challenge their paradigms.

niche markets Newly created original markets.

noise makers Causes of interference in the cross-cultural communication process; for example, style and stereotypes.

optionalizing The ability to generate alternatives through such techniques as brainstorming.

paradigm A model or example. A set of implicit or explicit rules for how something works or should be done.

paradigm shifting Breaking out of established ways of doing or seeing; challenging existing perspectives.

stakeholders Those individuals and groups who have a "stake" in the success of the business, such as shareholders, suppliers, and customers.

synergy The creative output of a whole that is greater than the sum of the individual contributions.

transnational company Characterized by an integration of resources and responsibilities across all business units regardless of national boundaries, while being anchored to a strong corporate identity.

value cluster See configuration of values.

value orientation A cultural preference for certain outcomes over others; for example, for individual autonomy over collectivism.

Abbreviations

Abbreviation	Explanation
AT&T	American Telephone and Telegraph
BP Oil	British Petroleum
BT	British Telecom
CEO	Chief Executive Officer
DMNC	Diversified Multinational Corporation
EEC	European Economic Community
FCPA	Foreign Corrupt Practices Act
GAPP	Generally Accepted Accounting Principles
GATT	General Agreement on Tariffs and Trade
GDP	Gross Domestic Product
GE	General Electric Co.
GM	General Motors
GNP	Gross National Product
HCN's	Host Country Nationals
HQ	Headquarters
HR	Human Resources
HRD	Human Resources Department
HRIS	Human Resources Information System
HRM	Human Resource Management
ICI	Imperial Chemical Company
IHRD	International Human Resources Department
IMD	Institute for Management Development
INSEAD	Institut Européen d'Administration des Affairs
JV	Joint Venture
LBS	London Business School
MBA	Master of Business Administration
MCI	Microwave Communications Inc.
MNC	Multinational Corporation
MTV	Music Television
NAFTA	North American Free Trade Agreement
OECD	Organization of Economic Cooperation & Development
P&G	Procter & Gamble
PERT diagrams	Project Evaluation and Review Technique
PLO	Palestine Liberation Organization
RCA	Radio Corporation of America
R&D	Research and Development
SEC	Securities Exchange Commission
U.K.	United Kingdom
U.S.	United States

Index

Other books of interest to you . . .

A MANAGER'S GUIDE TO GLOBALIZATION
Six Keys to Success in a Changing World
Stephen H. Rhinesmith

Co-published with the American Society for Training and Development.
Helps you develop a corporate culture that allows your organization to adapt to
an increasingly challenging international market.
1-55623-904-1   240 pages

GLOBAL TRAINING
How to Design a Program for the Multinational Corporation
Sylvia B. Odenwald

Co-published with the American Society for Training and Development.
Any company searching for ways to research, develop, and implement an international training program will find the answers along with how-to tips that make
the application of the ideas presented as easy as possible.
1-55623-986-6   240 pages

MANAGING GLOBALLY
A Complete Guide to Competing Worldwide
Carl A. Nelson

A results-oriented book that pioneers strategic management, a process that holds
the key to organizational success and survival in the new economic age. This
how-to workbook includes practical checklists, flow charts, and matrices, making it possible for you to develop a global strategy through a step-by-step
process.
0-7863-0121-X   350 pages

Training Management Corporation

To obtain information on the *Doing Business Internationally: The Guide to Cross-Cultural Success* seminar, or other seminars and publications, please contact Danielle Walker, Training Management Corporation (TMC) at (609) 497–1290 or return the business reply card included with this book